CRACK CAPITALISM

John Holloway

Instituto de Ciencias Sociales y Humanidades
Benemérita Universidad Autónoma de Puebla

www.plutobooks.com

First published 2010 by Pluto Press
345 Archway Road, London N6 5AA

www.plutobooks.com

Distributed in the United States of America exclusively by
Palgrave Macmillan, a division of St. Martin's Press LLC,
175 Fifth Avenue, New York, NY 10010

British Library Cataloguing in Publication Data
A catalogue record for this book is available from the British Library

ISBN   978 0 7453 3009 9   Hardback
ISBN   978 0 7453 3008 2   Paperback

Library of Congress Cataloging in Publication Data applied for

This book is printed on paper suitable for recycling and made from fully
managed and sustained forest sources. Logging, pulping and manufacturing
processes are expected to conform to the environmental standards of the
country of origin.

10   9   8   7   6   5   4   3

Designed and produced for Pluto Press by
Chase Publishing Services Ltd, 33 Livonia Road, Sidmouth, EX10 9JB, England
Typeset from disk by Stanford DTP Services, Northampton, England
Simultaneously printed digitally by CPI Antony Rowe, Chippenham, UK and
Edwards Bros in the United States of America

Contents

Part IV
The Dual Character of Labour

Part V
Abstract Labour: The Great Enclosure

Part I
Break

1
Break. We want to break.
We want to create a different world.
Now. Nothing more common, nothing
more obvious. Nothing more simple.
Nothing more difficult.

Break. We want to break. We want to break the world as it is. A world of injustice, of war, of violence, of discrimination, of Gaza and Guantanamo. A world of billionaires and a billion people who live and die in hunger. A world in which humanity is annihilating itself, massacring non-human forms of life, destroying the conditions of its own existence. A world ruled by money, ruled by capital. A world of frustration, of wasted potential.

We want to create a different world. We protest, of course we protest. We protest against the war, we protest against the growing use of torture in the world, we protest against the turning of all life into a commodity to be bought and sold, we protest against the inhuman treatment of migrants, we protest against the destruction of the world in the interests of profit.

We protest and we do more. We do and we must. If we only protest, we allow the powerful to set the agenda. If all we do is oppose what they are trying to do, then we simply follow in their footsteps. *Breaking* means that we do more than that, that we seize the initiative, that we set the agenda. We negate, but out of our negation grows a creation, an other-doing, an activity that is not determined by money, an activity that is not shaped by the rules of power. Often the alternative doing grows out of necessity: the functioning of the capitalist market does not allow us to survive and we need to find other ways to live, forms of solidarity and cooperation. Often too it comes from choice: we refuse to submit our lives to the rule of money, we dedicate ourselves to what we consider necessary or desirable. Either way, we live the world we want to create.

Now. There is an urgency in all this. Enough! *¡Ya basta!* We have had enough of living in, and creating, a world of exploitation, violence and starvation. And now there is a new urgency, the urgency of time itself. It has become clear that we humans are destroying the natural conditions of our own existence, and it seems unlikely that a society in which the determining force is the pursuit of profit can reverse this trend. The temporal dimensions of radical and revolutionary thought have changed. We place a skull on our desks, like the monks of old, not to glorify death, but to focus on the impending danger and intensify the struggle for life. It no longer makes sense to speak of patience as a revolutionary virtue or to talk of the 'future revolution'. What future? We need revolution now, here and now. So absurd, so necessary. So obvious.

Nothing more common, nothing more obvious. There is nothing special about being an anti-capitalist revolutionary. This is the story of many, many people, of millions, perhaps billions.

It is the story of the composer in London who expresses his anger and his dream of a better society through the music he composes. It is the story of the gardener in Cholula who creates a garden to struggle against the destruction of nature. Of the car worker in Birmingham who goes in the evenings to his garden allotment so that he has some activity that has meaning and pleasure for him. Of the indigenous peasants in Oventic, Chiapas, who create an autonomous space of self-government and defend it every day against the paramilitaries who harass them. Of the university professor in Athens who creates a seminar outside the university framework for the promotion of critical thought. Of the book publisher in Barcelona who centres his activity on publishing books against capitalism. Of the friends in Porto Alegre who form a choir, just because they enjoy singing. Of the teachers in Puebla who confront police oppression to fight for a different type of school, a different type of education. Of the theatre director in Vienna who decides she will use her skills to open a different world to those who see her plays. Of the call centre worker in Sydney who fills all his vacant moments thinking of how to fight for a better society.

4

Of the people of Cochabamba who come together and fight a battle against the government and the army so that water should not be privatised but subject to their own control. Of the nurse in Seoul who does everything possible to help her patients. Of the workers in Neuquén who occupy the factory and make it theirs. Of the student in New York who decides that university is a time for questioning the world. Of the community worker in Dalkeith who looks for cracks in the framework of rules that constrain him so that he can open another world. Of the young man in Mexico City, who, incensed by the brutality of capitalism, goes to the jungle to organise armed struggle to change the world. Of the retired teacher in Berlin who devotes her life to the struggle against capitalist globalisation. Of the government worker in Nairobi who gives all her free time to the struggle against AIDS. Of the university teacher in Leeds who uses the space that still exists in some universities to set up a course on activism and social change. Of the old man living in an ugly block of flats on the outskirts of Beirut who cultivates plants on his windowsill as a revolt against the concrete that surrounds him. Of the young woman in Ljubljana, the young man in Florence, who, like so many others throughout the world, throw their lives into inventing new forms of struggle for a better world. Of the peasant in Huejotzingo who refuses to allow his small orchard to be annexed to a massive park of unsold cars. Of the group of homeless friends in Rome who occupy a vacant house and refuse to pay rent. Of the enthusiast in Buenos Aires who devotes all his great energies to opening new perspectives for a different world. Of the girl in Tokyo who says she will not go to work today and goes to sit in the park with her book, this book or some other. Of the young man in France who devotes himself to building dry toilets as a contribution to radically altering the relation between humans and nature. Of the telephone engineer in Jalapa who leaves his job to spend more time with his children. Of the woman in Edinburgh who, in everything she does, expresses her rage through the creation of a world of love and mutual support.

This is the story of ordinary people, some of whom I know, some of whom I have heard of, some of whom I have invented. Ordinary people: rebels, revolutionaries perhaps. 'We are quite ordinary women and men, children and old people, that is, rebels, non-conformists, misfits, dreamers', say the Zapatistas in their most profound and difficult challenge of all.[1]

The 'ordinary people' in our list are very different from one another. It may seem strange to place the car worker who goes to his allotment in the evening next to the young man who goes to the jungle to devote his life to organising armed struggle against capitalism. And yet there is a continuity. What both have in common is that they share in a movement of refusal-and-other-creation: they are rebels, not victims; subjects, not objects. In the case of the car worker, it is individual and just evenings and weekends; in the case of the young man in the jungle, it is a very perilous commitment to a life of rebellion. Very different and yet with a line of affinity that it would be very wrong to overlook.

Nothing more simple. The sixteenth-century French theorist La Boétie expressed the simplicity of revolution with great clarity in his *Discourse on Voluntary Servitude* (1546/2002: 139–40):

> You sow your crops in order that he [the lord] may ravage them, you install and furnish your homes to give him goods to pillage; you rear your daughters that he may gratify his lust; you bring up your children in order that he may confer upon them the greatest privilege he knows – to be led into his battles, to be delivered to butchery, to be made the servants of his greed and the instruments of his vengeance; you yield your bodies unto hard labour in order that he may indulge in his delights and wallow in his filthy pleasures; you weaken yourselves in order to make him the stronger and the mightier to hold you in check. From all these indignities, such as the very beasts of the field would not endure, you can deliver yourselves if you try, not by taking action, but merely by willing to be free. Resolve to serve no more, and you are at once freed. I do not ask that you place hands upon the tyrant to topple him over, but simply that you support him no longer; then you will behold him, like a great Colossus whose pedestal has been pulled away, fall of his own weight and break in pieces.

Everything that the tyrant has comes from us and from his exploitation of us: we have only to stop working for him and he will cease to be a tyrant because the material basis of his tyranny will have disappeared. We make the tyrant; in order to be free, we must stop making the tyrant. The key to our

6

emancipation, the key to becoming fully human is simple: refuse, disobey. *Resolve to serve no more, and you are at once freed.*

Nothing more difficult, however. We can refuse to perform the work that creates the tyrant. We can devote ourselves to a different type of activity. Instead of yielding our 'bodies unto hard labour in order that he may indulge in his delights and wallow in his filthy pleasures', we can do something that *we* consider important or desirable. Nothing more common, nothing more obvious. And yet, we know that it is not so simple. If we do not devote our lives to the labour that creates capital, we face poverty, even starvation, and often physical repression. Just down the road from where I write, the people of Oaxaca asserted their control over the city during a period of five months, against a corrupt and brutal governor. Finally, their peaceful rebellion was repressed with violence and many were tortured, sexually abused, threatened with being thrown from helicopters, their fingers broken, some simply disappeared. For me, Oaxaca is just down the road. But for you, gentle reader, it is not much farther, and there are many other 'just down the roads' where atrocities are being committed in your name. Abu Ghraib, Guantanamo – and there are many, many more to choose from.

Often it seems hopeless. So many failed revolutions. So many exciting experiments in anti-capitalism that have ended in frustration and recrimination. It has been said that 'today it is easier to imagine the end of the world than the end of capitalism' (Turbulence 2008: 3). We have reached a stage where it is easier to think of the total annihilation of humanity than to imagine a change in the organisation of a manifestly unjust and destructive society. What can we do?

2
Our method is the method of the crack.

The image that keeps coming to my mind is a nightmarish one inspired by Edgar Allen Poe.[1] We are all in a room with four walls, a floor, a ceiling and no windows or door. The room is furnished and some of us are sitting comfortably, others most definitely are not. The walls are advancing inwards gradually, sometimes slower, sometimes faster, making us all more uncomfortable, advancing all the time, threatening to crush us all to death.

There are discussions within the room, but they are mostly about how to arrange the furniture. People do not seem to see the walls advancing. From time to time there are elections about how to place the furniture. These elections are not unimportant: they make some people more comfortable, others less so; they may even affect the speed at which the walls are moving, but they do nothing to stop their relentless advance.

As the walls grow closer, people react in different ways. Some refuse absolutely to see the advance of the walls, shutting themselves tightly into a world of Disney and defending with determination the chairs on which they are sitting. Some see and denounce the movement of the walls, build a party with a radical programme and look forward to a day in the future when there will be no walls. Others (and among these I include myself) run to the walls and try desperately to find cracks, or faults beneath the surface, or to create cracks by banging the walls. This looking for (and creation of) cracks is a practical-theoretical activity, a throwing ourselves against the walls but also a standing back to try and see cracks or faults in the surface. The two activities are complementary: theory makes little sense unless it is understood as part of the desperate effort to find a way out, to create cracks that defy the apparently unstoppable advance of capital, of the walls that are pushing us to our destruction.

We are mad, of course. From the point of view of those who defend their armchairs and discuss the arrangement of the furniture in the run-up to the next election, we are undoubtedly mad, we who run about seeing cracks that are invisible to the eyes of those who sit in the armchairs (or which appear to them, if at all, as changes in the pattern of the wallpaper, to which they give the name of 'new social movements'). The worst of it is that they may be right: perhaps we are mad, perhaps there is no way out, perhaps the cracks we see exist only in our fantasy. The old revolutionary certainty can no longer stand. There is absolutely no guarantee of a happy ending.

The opening of cracks is the opening of a world that presents itself as closed. It is the opening of categories that on the surface negate the power of human doing, in order to discover at their core the doing that they deny and incarcerate.[2] In Marx's terms, it is critique *ad hominem*, the attempt to break through the appearances of a world of things and uncontrollable forces and to understand the world in terms of the power of human doing.[3] The method of the crack is dialectical, not in the sense of presenting a neat flow of thesis, antithesis and synthesis, but in the sense of a negative dialectics, a dialectic of misfitting.[4] Quite simply, we think the world from our misfitting.

The method of the crack is the method of crisis: we wish to understand the wall not from its solidity but from its cracks; we wish to understand capitalism not as domination, but from the perspective of its crisis, its contradictions, its weaknesses, and we want to understand how we ourselves are those contradictions. This is crisis theory, critical theory. Critical/crisis theory is the theory of our own misfitting. Humanity (in all its senses) jars increasingly with capitalism. It becomes harder and harder to fit as capital demands more and more. Ever more people simply do not fit in to the system, or, if we do manage to squeeze ourselves on to capital's ever-tightening Procrustean bed, we do so at the cost of leaving fragments of ourselves behind, to haunt. That is the basis of our cracks and of the growing importance of a dialectic of misfitting.

We want to understand the force of our misfitting, we want to know how banging our head against the wall over and over again will bring the wall crumbling down.

3
It is time to learn the new language of a new struggle.

There is a great anguish in all of this. It is the anguish of *'what can we do?'* We see and feel the injustices of capitalism all around us: the people sleeping in the streets even in the richest cities,[1] the millions who live on the brink of starvation until then they die of it. We see the effects of our social system on the natural world: the colossal accumulation of rubbish, the global warming for which there may be no remedy. We see the powerful on the television and want to scream at them. And all the time: what can we do, what can we do, what can we do?[2]

This book is the daughter of another. *Change the World without taking Power* (Holloway 2002/2005) argued that the need for radical social change (revolution) is more pressing and more obvious than ever, but we do not know how to bring it about. We know, from experience and from reflection, that we cannot do it by taking state power. But then how? The echo comes back over and over again: but then how, then how, how, how, how? In one meeting after another: 'Yes, we do not want to get involved in the smug, false, destructive world of state politics, but then how, what do we do? We created a great experiment in Oaxaca where the people took control of the city for five months, but then we were brutally repressed, so now how, where do we go?' Now, with the manifest crisis of capitalism, the question comes more and more urgent: but then how? what do we do?

The daughter is quite independent of the mother: there is no need to have read *Change the World* in order to understand the argument here. Yet the concern is the same: how can we think of changing the world radically when it seems to be so impossible? What can we do?

This book offers a simple answer: *crack capitalism*. Break it in as many ways as we can and try to expand and multiply the cracks and promote their confluence.

The answer is not the invention of this book. Rather, this book, like all books, is part of a historical moment, part of the flow of struggle. The answer it offers reflects a movement that is underway already. In this world in which radical change seems so unthinkable, there are already a million experiments in radical change, in doing things in a quite different way. This is not new: experimental projections towards a different world are probably as old as capitalism itself. But there has been a surge in recent years, a growing perception that we cannot wait for the great revolution, that we have to start to create something different here and now. These experiments are possibly the embryos of a new world, the interstitial movements from which a new society could grow.

The argument, then, is that the only possible way of conceiving revolution is as an interstitial process. It is often argued that the transition from capitalism to a post-capitalist society, unlike that from feudalism to capitalism, cannot be an interstitial movement. This view has been restated very recently by Hillel Ticktin: 'The move from capitalism to socialism is qualitatively different from that of feudalism to capitalism, in that socialism cannot come into being in the interstices of capitalism. The new society can only come into being when the world capitalist system is overthrown.'[3] The argument here is that, on the contrary, the revolutionary replacement of one system by another is both impossible and undesirable. The only way to think of changing the world radically is as a multiplicity of interstitial movements running from the particular.

It is in the interstices that the 'ordinary people' who are the heroes of this book are to be found. The objections to the ordinariness of our people come thick and fast: the car worker who goes to the allotment, the girl who reads her book in the park, the friends who come together to form a choir, the engineer who gives up his work to look after his children – how can they possibly be considered as the protagonists of an anti-capitalist revolution? And yet the answer is simple once we think of revolutionary change as being necessarily interstitial:

who brought about the social transformation from feudalism to capitalism? Was it Danton and Robespierre, or was it the thousands of unsung and possibly boring burghers who simply started to produce in a different way and to live their lives according to different criteria and different values? In other words, social change is not produced by activists, however important activism may (or may not) be in the process. Social change is rather the outcome of the barely visible transformation of the daily activities of millions of people.[4] We must look beyond activism, then, to the millions and millions of refusals and other-doings, the millions and millions of cracks that constitute the material base of possible radical change.

But we must be clear that the answer offered by the book – *crack capitalism* - may be an answer-no-answer. Perhaps it is like a hologram that seems so solid that you want to reach out and touch it and you stretch out your hand and it is not there. Can we really crack capitalism? What does it mean? Is capitalism really a hard surface that we can crack, or is it just a slimy sludge that, when we try to crack it, just oozes back into place, as nasty and complete as ever?

Or again, is there perhaps something that our tired eyes do not see? Could it be that our attempted cracks are creating something beautiful that is emerging from the depths of the slime? Something that our eyes have difficulty in seeing, our ears in hearing? Something that speaks with a voice that we do not understand?

If both mother and daughter stutter and mumble incoherently, perhaps it is because they are straining to see, to hear, to speak a new language of an emerging constellation of struggle. There are times when patterns of conflict change, outward signs of underlying structural faults, manifestations of crisis. The problem is that each significant shift in pattern brings problems of understanding, because our minds are used to the old pattern. But if we apply the old concepts, there is a danger that, whatever our intentions, however militant our commitment to communism (or whatever), our thinking becomes an obstacle to the new forms of struggle. Our task is to learn the new language of struggle and, by learning, to participate in its formation. Possibly what has already been said in these opening pages is a faltering step in the learning and formation of this language: that is my highest ambition, that is the wager of this book.

The learning of a new language is a hesitant process, an asking-we-walk, an attempt to create open question-concepts rather than to lay down a paradigm for the understanding of the present stage of capitalism.[5] This book is arranged in theses, each one being a question framed as a challenge, a provocation. These theses can be seen as a series of dares, in which I challenge you, gentle reader, to follow me to the next point in the argument. At times I feel the book is a train journey in which I do my best to push readers off at each stop: if all the steps in the argument are accepted, then perhaps I shall not have pushed hard enough.

In all this there is an anxiety, a doubt, a danger: when we strain to see something we barely see, to hear something we can scarcely discern, it may be that we are sharpening our eyes and our ears, or it may be simply that we are fantasising, that that which we can scarcely see and hear really does not exist, that it is simply the product of our wishful thinking. Perhaps, but we need to act, to do something, to break the terror of our headlong rush towards destruction. Asking we walk, but walking, not standing still, is how we develop our questions. Better to step out in what may be the wrong direction and to go creating the path, rather than stay and pore over a map that does not exist. So let us hold our fears and doubts in one hand and look at the source of hope, the million attempts to break with the logic of destruction.

Part II
Cracks: The Anti-Politics of Dignity

4

The cracks begin with a No, from which there grows a dignity, a negation-and-creation.

Imagine a sheet of ice covering a dark lake of possibility. We scream 'NO' so loud that the ice begins to crack. What is it that is uncovered? What is that dark liquid that (sometimes, not always) slowly or quickly bubbles up through the crack? We shall call it dignity. The crack in the ice moves, unpredictable, sometimes racing, sometimes slowing, sometimes widening, sometimes narrowing, sometimes freezing over again and disappearing, sometimes reappearing. All around the lake there are people doing the same thing as we are, screaming 'NO' as loud as they can, creating cracks that move just as cracks in ice do, unpredictably, spreading, racing to join up with other cracks, some being frozen over again. The stronger the flow of dignity within them, the greater the force of the cracks.

Serve no more, La Boétie tells us, and we shall at once be free. The break begins with refusal, with No. No, we shall not tend your sheep, plough your fields, make your car, do your examinations. The truth of the relation of power is revealed: the powerful depend on the powerless. The lord depends on his serfs, the capitalist depends on the workers who create his capital.

But the real force of the *serve no more* comes when we do something else instead. Serve no more, and then what? If we just fold our arms and do nothing at all, we soon face the problem of starvation. The *serve no more*, if it does not lead to an other-doing, an alternative activity, can easily become converted into a negotiation of the terms of servitude. The workers who say 'no' and cross their arms, or go on strike, are implicitly saying 'no, we shall not carry out this command', or 'we shall not carry on working under these conditions.' This does not exclude the continuation of servitude (of the relationship of employment) under other conditions. The 'serve no more' becomes a step in the negotiation of new conditions of servitude.

It is a different matter when the negation becomes a negation-and-creation.[1] This is a more serious challenge. The workers say 'no' and they take over the factory. They declare that they do not need a boss and begin to call for a world without bosses.[2]

Think of the sad story of Mr Peel, who, Marx tells us

> ... took with him to Swan River, West Australia, means of subsistence and of production to the amount of 50,000 pounds. Mr. Peel had the foresight to bring with him, besides, 3,000 persons of the working-class, men, women and children. Once arrived at his destination, 'Mr. Peel was left without a servant to make his bed or fetch him water from the river.' Unhappy Mr. Peel who provided for everything except the export of English modes of production to Swan River. (1867/1965: 766; 1867/1990: 933)

What happened was that land was still freely available in Swan River, so that the 3,000 persons of the working class went off and cultivated their own land. One can imagine the scene as the unhappy Mr. Peel's initial anger, when the workers refused to carry out his orders, turned to despair when he saw them going off to develop an alternative life free of masters. The availability of land made it possible for them to convert their refusal into a decisive rupture and to develop an activity quite different from that planned for them by Mr. Peel.

Think of the exciting story of the teachers in Puebla.[3] When the government announced in 2008 the creation of a new scheme to improve the quality of education by imposing greater individualism, stronger competition between students, stricter measurement of the output of teachers, and so on, the teachers said 'No, we will not accept it.' When the government refused to listen, the dissident teachers moved beyond mere refusal and, in consultation with thousands of students and parents, elaborated their own proposal for improving the quality of education by promoting greater cooperation between students, more emphasis on critical thinking, preparation for cooperative work not directly subordinate to capital, and began to explore ways of implementing their scheme in opposition to the state guidelines, by taking control of the schools.[4] Here too the initial refusal begins to open towards something else, towards an educational activity that not only resists but breaks with the logic of capital.

In both of these cases, the No is backed by an other-doing. This is the dignity that can fill the cracks created by the refusal. The original No is then not a closure, but an opening to a different activity, the threshold of a counter-world with a different logic and a different language.[5] The No opens to a time-space in which we try to live as subjects rather than objects. These are times or spaces in which we assert our capacity to decide for ourselves what we should do – whether it be chatting with our friends, playing with our children, cultivating the land in a different way, developing and implementing projects for a critical education. These are times or spaces in which we take control of our own lives, assume the responsibility of our own humanity.

Dignity is the unfolding of the power of No. Our refusal confronts us with the opportunity, necessity and responsibility of developing our own capacities. The women and men who left Mr. Peel in the lurch were confronted with the opportunity and necessity of developing abilities suppressed by their previous condition of servitude. The teachers who reject the state textbooks are forced to develop another education. The assumption of responsibility for our own lives is in itself a break with the logic of domination. This does not mean that everything will turn out to be perfect. The dignity is a breaking, a negating, a moving, an exploring. We must be careful not to convert it into a positive concept that might give it a deadening fixity. The women and men who deserted Mr. Peel may well have turned into small landholders who defended their property against all newcomers. The teachers who take their schools to create a critical education may possibly reproduce authoritarian practices as bad as those which they are rejecting. It is the moving that is important, the moving against-and-beyond: the negating and creating of those who abandoned Mr. Peel, more than the new spaces that they created; the taking of the schools by the teachers, more than the schools that they have taken. It is the assuming of our own responsibility that is important, though the results may well be contradictory.[6]

Dignity, the movement of negating-and-creating, of taking control of our own lives, is not a simple matter: it is, we said, a dark liquid bubbling up from a lake of possibility. To give a positive solidity to what can only be a moving of refusing and creating and exploring can easily lead to disillusion. A pro-Zapatista collective, or a social centre, or a group of *piqueteros* ends in conflict and disarray and we conclude that it was all an illusion, instead of seeing that such dignities are inevitably contradictory and experimental. The cracks are always questions, not answers.

It is important not to romanticise the cracks, or give them a positive force that they do not possess. And yet, this is where we start: from the cracks, the fissures, the rents, the spaces of rebellious negation-and-creation. We start from the particular, not from the totality. We start from the world of misfitting, from the multiplicity of particular rebellions, dignities, cracks, not from the great unified Struggle that simply does not exist, nor from the system of domination. We start from being angry and lost and trying to create something else, because that is where we live, that is where we are. Perhaps it is a strange place to start, but we are looking for a strange thing. We are looking for hope in a dark night.[7] We are trying to theorise hope-against-hope. This is surely the only subject matter of theory that is left.

5

A crack is the perfectly ordinary creation of a space or moment in which we assert a different type of doing.

'No, in this space, in this moment, we are not going to do what capitalist society expects of us. We are going to do whatever we consider necessary or desirable.' We take the moment or space into our own hands and try to make it a place of self-determination, refusing to let money (or any other alien force) determine what we do.

This is surely what all the 'ordinary people' mentioned at the beginning of the book have in common: the refusal to let the logic of money shape their activity, the determination to take a space or moment into their own hands and shape their lives according to their own decisions.[1] In some cases, this is direct and un-theorised: the friends who form a choir because they like to sing, the nurse who really tries to help her patients, the car worker who spends as much time as possible on his allotment. In other cases, it is part of an understanding that the rule of money is the centre of a whole system of social organisation, a system of domination that we call capitalism: in that case, the refusal to let money determine our activity is part of a conscious rejection of capitalism and understood as part of the struggle against capitalism: the theatre director in Vienna, the people of Cochabamba who fought against the privatisation of water, the peasants in Chiapas who struggle to change their communities, and so on. It is not that there is any clear division between those who are 'class conscious' and those who are not: there is rather a constantly shifting spectrum of awareness of the resonances and implications of what they are doing, an awareness that may be only indirectly connected to the impact of the actions themselves. The car worker who goes to the allotment in the evening may well have read *Capital* and be meditating on the evils of capitalism and the urgent necessity of a radical change in the relation between humans and other forms of life as he waters his plants, while the woman who clashes with the army to prevent the privatisation of water may be thinking simply of how to feed her family rather than of the global struggle against the commodification of basic necessities. There is a dynamic in all of this. The point about cracks is that they run, and they may move fast and unpredictably. That is why it does not help to make sharp distinctions. The car worker is watering his plants on the allotment today, but he may be out on the streets fighting Monsanto tomorrow. The woman who fights for water today may start reflecting tomorrow on the way in which capitalism is destroying the world. The movement of the cracks is a movement of experience, very often a learning-in-struggle,[2] although it would be wrong to think of the movement as unidirectional: it also happens that people get tired and the crack freezes over again.

All of these people reject, in one way or another, the determination of their activity by money and oppose to that logic another concept of doing, an other-doing, which they seek to determine themselves, individually or collectively. They try to do what they themselves consider desirable or necessary. Of course this is not pure self-determination, because what we consider desirable or necessary is affected by the society in which we live and because we do not control the environment in which we act, but it is a drive *towards* social self-determination, it is a push not only against but also beyond the determination of our lives by capital.

The crack does not stand on its own. Very often it is an excess, an overflowing from a more limited struggle. The teachers in Puebla fight against the neo-liberal restructuring of education that the government seeks to impose; when the government refuses to accept their proposal, they draw up their own alternative plan for improving the educational system.[3] A factory closure is announced and workers start to negotiate the terms of redundancy; when they do not get what they want, they decide to occupy the factory and run it as a cooperative, and then they start to call for a world without bosses. Students protest against the introduction of fees, and, when there is no response, they take their desks and chairs out on to the streets and begin to implement a different sort of education. In each of these cases, the cracks, the spaces or moments in which we reject external authority and assert that 'here and now we rule', are outgrowths of more limited struggles. We come up against the limits of the system, and the anger that is inherent in any conflict drives us beyond those limits to assert a different logic, a logic (or perhaps anti-logic) of self-determination. The logic of demands gives way to the simple assertion of our own rule.

The cracks are not always a direct spill-over from more limited struggles. Sometimes they arise from a conscious decision of a group of people to reject the constraints of capitalism. It may be a group of students who decide that they do not want to subject their lives to the requirements of capital and will find a way of living against and beyond the system in so far as they can; or various groups coming together to found a social centre, both as a centre for anti-capitalist activity and as a space for developing other social relations; or a group of friends who decide that the best way to stop the destruction of nature is to live on the land and produce their own food bio-intensively. Often such activities are part-time:[4] the people in the social centre, say, devote as much time as possible to anti-capitalist struggle, but they also take jobs at least occasionally in order to survive; or the friends who decide to live by cultivating their own food create their ideal community using the pensions they have already earned by working. There is no purity here, but there is a common rejection of the cohesive logic of capitalism, and an attempt to create something else.

The cracks may result, then, from a conscious opting-out, but they may also result from a forced expulsion from capitalist social relations. More and more people are being pushed out of employment or finding that they have no way of becoming employed, or, if at all, then only on a very casual and precarious basis. They are obliged to make their lives in other ways. The state systems of unemployment benefits and social assistance (where they exist) are designed to extend the discipline of employment even to the unemployed, to make sure that the unemployed really function as an industrial reserve army. But most of the unemployed in the world fall outside these systems and have to find a way of surviving on the basis of some combination of occasional employment, petty trading or services (selling chewing gum or cleaning car windscreens at traffic lights, for example), and of developing forms of solidarity among family members, friends or neighbours. The power of money and of the commodity remains enormous in such cases, yet the forms of social solidarity often generate ways of living and organising that run counter to the logic of capital. If a large part of the world's population survives on less than a dollar a day, it is usually because they have constructed forms of mutual solidarity and support that generally do not exist in the more 'advanced' parts of the world.[5] In many parts of the world, the construction of alternative social relations is simply a necessity: capitalist employment is irrelevant and the capitalist state does not function even as police or constructor of roads. For the state and for capital, these are no-go areas, not necessarily because of any political revolt, but simply because the police are afraid to go in. Simple survival requires that people come together and take over the running of their neighbourhood or town, and in the process radical relations of solidarity are often constructed. An important example of this is El Alto, the indigenous city that grew up on the outskirts of La Paz in Bolivia and became the centre of the movements of rebellion in recent years. Raúl Zibechi argues that these slums, which have spread with great rapidity as a result of the neo-liberal destruction of agriculture, have created cracks in capitalist domination and in state control, and that these cracks have been at the centre of the outbreaks of revolt in Latin America in the last twenty years.[6]

Are we to say, then, that any construction of other forms of organisation outside the mainstream of capitalist social relations should be seen as a crack in capitalist domination? Not if we think of a crack as a space or moment of negation-and-creation, of refusal and other doing. Being unemployed or living in a slum in Mumbai does not necessarily involve any refusal of capitalism. It is rather that the relations of mutual support that are created in such situations can easily become the material basis for a sort of flip-over, a real *détournement* in which victims suddenly emerge as rebels, and the structures of suffering are suddenly transformed into anticipations of a better world. This has happened, for example, with the *piquetero* movement, the movement of the unemployed workers in Argentina, where some groups (such as the MTD de Solano)[7] moved radically from demanding employment to saying that they did not want to be employed, that they did not want to be exploited, that they wanted to devote their lives to meaningful activity chosen by them. A similar shift can be seen on a smaller scale with the German *Glückliche Arbeitslose* (happy unemployed) movement.[8] The example already mentioned of El Alto is another important case: the structures of mutual support developed to deal with grinding poverty and government neglect (not remnants of rural communities but developed to meet the demands of city life)[9] were turned around to become the basis of one of the most important movements of rebellion in recent years. Something similar has happened with the black, the gay and the indigenous movements: that which was previously seen as a mark of shame suddenly becomes turned around into a badge of pride. In all of these cases, there is an exclusion from the mainstream which is reversed when those who are excluded declare that they do not want to be included, that they prefer to go their own way. Exclusion becomes refusal, and the patterns of alternative social relations constructed to deal with the exclusion become real cracks, powerful spaces of refusal-and-creation. The world is turned upside down.

Certainly there are differences between the cracks created by a conscious opting out (such as a group of friends who decide to form a social centre) and those that arise from the turning around of an exclusion (as in the case of the *piquetero* groups). However, the differences should not be exaggerated. It is often difficult to distinguish choice from necessity: a decision by computer programmers not to work for the arms industry but to devote their time to the creation of software to be shared freely may well be a response to what they experience as an existential necessity. What is important is not to draw dividing lines but to see the lines of continuity. The enormously successful anti-poll tax campaign in Britain in the early 1990s was built around the slogan 'can't pay, won't pay', indicating the unity of those who could not pay the tax and those who chose not to pay a tax they considered unjust. In the same way, we should perhaps think of these refusals of capitalism as a fast-moving kaleidoscope of insubordination in which it makes little sense to establish clear distinctions.

The central issue is the counterposing of a distinctly different logic here and now to the logic of capitalism. There is nothing unusual in this: it is part of everyday life. It is the anti-logic of what we think of as humanity, of decency, of dignity; even in the most harmless-looking examples, there is always an underlying insubordination or non-subordination. Dignity will not wait: the crack is a here-and-now insubordination, not a project for the future. It is not 'after the revolution, our lives will not be subordinated to capital', but 'here and now, we refuse to subordinate our activity to the rule of capital: we can and will and are doing something else.' There is a shift in the temporality of rebellion. In all sorts of ways, the urgency of the situation of humanity imprints itself on the way that people struggle. The old notion of planning for the future revolution sounds hollow when we know that there may be only a very limited future. Communism (or whatever we choose to call it)[10] becomes an immediate necessity, not a future stage of development.

6
Cracks break dimensions, break dimensionality.

Perhaps the most obvious way of thinking of cracks is in spatial terms: 'Here in the Lacandon Jungle (or in Oaxaca, or in El Alto, or in this Social Centre, or in this occupied factory, or in this autonomous municipality) we shall not accept the rule of capital or the state, we shall determine our own activity.'

It is sometimes argued that territoriality is crucial to the development of the new movements of rebellion in the last twenty years or so. Thus Zibechi:

> Establishing a territorial base is the path taken by the Sem Terra [the landless peasants of Brazil], through the creation of an infinite number of little self-governed islands; by the indigenous of Ecuador who expanded their communities to reconstruct their ancestral 'ethnic territories' and by the Indians in Chiapas who colonised the Lacandon Jungle ... This strategy, which originated in a rural context, began to establish itself among the fringes of the urban unemployed: the excluded created settlements on the edges of the big cities by taking and occupying land. In the whole continent, several million hectares have been recovered and conquered by the poor, causing a crisis of the instituted territorialities and re-modelling the physical spaces of resistance. From their territories, the new actors develop long-term projects, central to which are the capacity to produce and reproduce life ... . (2008: 25)

The latter point is crucial, because it provides a material base for the movement towards autonomy (ibid.: 135).

There is no doubt that the creation of a territorial base for developing different social relations, whether this base be the Lacandon Jungle, the settlements of the landless peasants in Brazil, or a social centre in Milan, can give a particular strength to movements of negation-and-creation. There is, however, a problem in giving exclusive emphasis to territoriality simply because it may have the effect of excluding the many, many people who are ardent rebels but who do not have any strong links with a territory that is on the brink of rebellion. Rebelliousness then can easily become diverted into solidarity: since Munich or Edinburgh or New York or wherever I happen to live is not about to declare itself an autonomous, anti-capitalist city, I shall go and give my support to those territories where exciting things are happening, I shall go and spend three months in a Zapatista community. This may well be a real help to the Zapatistas and may help to construct an international movement, but it evades the central question of how we assume, wherever we live, the responsibility of breaking with capital here and now.

There is no reason, however, why we should think of cracks only in terms of spatial ruptures. The struggle to de-commodify a certain type of activity and subject it to popular control can be thought of in similar terms: here too there is a struggle to remove an area of activity from the workings of capitalism and organise it along different lines. Thus, for example, the Coordinadora de Defensa del Agua y de la Vida (Coordinator of the Defence of Water and Life) which fought to stop the privatisation of water in Cochabamba claimed that they had opened 'a crack in the neoliberal model ruling in Latin America and the world'[1] (Ceceña 2004: 19). There are important struggles going on all over the world to remove areas such as water, natural resources, education, health care, communication, software[2] and music from the workings of capitalism. All of these can be seen as attempts to create no-go areas, to cut off an area and put up signs all around it saying 'capital, keep out!'[3] These struggles arise in many forms: as popular revolts against the privatisation of water (as in Cochabamba), as student strikes against the introduction of fees or the privatisation of universities (as in Greece, Mexico City, Buenos Aires), as the organisation of alternative radio stations which seek to establish a different type of communication (crucial in the uprising in Oaxaca, but of growing importance all over the world), as the creation of schools as centres for learning dignity and rebellion (by the MST in Brazil or the Zapatistas in Chiapas), as the installation of people's kitchens (*ollas populares*) in the streets of Buenos Aires, as the simple assumption by millions and millions of people every day that the laws of intellectual property should not be taken seriously (the downloading of music, videos and software, or the copying of books, for example).

Sometimes it is the simple No! that is most evident in such struggles, but there is often (or perhaps always) an other-doing implicit in the No. When the people of Atenco rose up against the building of a new airport for Mexico City on their land (and won), they were implicitly saying 'we refuse to accept the logic of money, we shall continue to do what we know and like, cultivating our land.' The same is true of the No-TAV struggles in Northern Italy: the emphasis is the No to the high-speed train, but implicit in that is the defence of an other-doing, living with a different rhythm. But sometimes the other-doing is very much to the fore, as in alternative schools, where the rebels say very clearly that they are creating another type of education to replace the authoritarian or alien education provided by the state.

This sort of activity- or resource-related crack is sometimes seen in terms of the defence or creation of 'commons' or a 'common'. Capitalism, ever since its beginning, has been a movement of enclosure, a movement of converting that which is enjoyed in common into private property. The most obvious example from early capitalism is the enclosure of the land, but any form of private property involves an enclosure, an appropriation, a separating of something from common enjoyment or use. The neo-liberal phase of capitalism has seen an acceleration of this process of enclosure and has engendered a huge number of struggles to defend or extend that which is held in common. Dyer-Witheford suggests that it is helpful to think of three types of commons other than land: 'today commons also names the possibility of collective, rather than private ownership in other domains: an ecological commons (of water, atmosphere, fisheries and forests); a social commons (of public provisions for welfare, health, education and so on); a networked commons (of access to the means of communication)' (2007: 28). The commons can be seen as the embryonic form of a new society: 'If the cell form of capitalism is the commodity, the cellular form of a society beyond capital is the common' (ibid.). These common areas, at least to the extent that there is genuine social control and not just state ownership, can be seen as so many cracks in the domination of capital, so many no-go areas where the writ of capital does not run, gashes in the weave of domination. Or rather: if capital is a movement of enclosing, the commons are a disjointed common-ing, a moving in the opposite direction, a refusing of enclosure, at least in particular areas.

A third dimension for thinking about cracks is that of time. This is a crucial dimension of struggle. For those of us who live in the cities, it is often very difficult to think of cracks in spatial terms, at least in the short term. To declare our city or our locality an autonomous zone is for many of us a far-off dream. In many city spaces, there does not exist the sense of community that would make that realistic in the short term. Certainly there are plenty of spatial cracks in the cities: social centres, squats, community gardens, publicly enjoyed spaces, but often our communities are formed on a temporal basis.[4] We come together and share a project of some sort, in an event, a meeting, a series of meetings; or we go down into the streets in a moment of celebration or anger. Later, perhaps, we disperse and go our different ways, but while we are together, our project, celebration or rage may create an otherness, a different way of doing or relating. The *argentinazo* of 19/20 December 2001 in the cities of Argentina was not just a spatial crack, it was also a temporal crack, a moment of rage and celebration when people descended to the streets with their pots and pans to declare that they had had enough, that all the politicians should go (*¡que se vayan todos!*) and that there must be a radical change.[5] A social energy was released, different ways of relating were created. This was a temporal crack in the patterns of domination. The same could be said of any other uprising or explosion of popular discontent – the great world event that we usually refer to as '1968', for example. Often such explosions are seen as failures because they do not lead to permanent change, but this is wrong: they have a validity of their own, independent of their long-term consequences. Like a flash of lightning, they illuminate a different world, a world created perhaps for a few short hours, but the impression which remains on our brain and in our senses is that of an image of the world we can (and did) create. The world that does not yet exist displays itself as a world that exists not-yet.[6]

Carnival, at least in the medieval world, can be seen as such a temporal crack in the patterns of domination, a time in which the normal relations of hierarchy are not just reversed but abolished. This is not just a letting-off of steam that is functional for the reproduction of domination, but something much deeper. Tischler, quoting Bakhtin, says the carnival 'was the triumph of a sort of transitional liberation' which supposed 'the provisional abolition of hierarchical relations, privileges, rules, taboos. It was opposed to all perpetuation, all perfection and regulation, pointed to a future still incomplete' (Tischler 2008a: 22). A crack, then: a moment in which relations of domination were broken and other relations created. This is a time too in which laughter breaks through the seriousness of the business of domination and submission, not individual laughter but a collective laughter that opens towards another world: 'the laughter of carnival is the vehicle of a concrete humanisation, in the real and simultaneously utopian time of the carnival; it is the language of life that does not allow the separation of subject and object, and throws off abstraction as a tool of power and submission' (ibid.: 24).[7] This idea of 'laughter as a revolutionary principle' (ibid.: 17) is taken up by many recent struggles, such as the 'J-18 Carnival against Capital' in London and the Clandestine Insurgent Rebel Clown Army which has played an important part in recent protests in Europe.[8] Cafassi speaks of the uprising in Argentina as an explosion of 'joyous rage' (2002: 79). Rebellion has never been far from carnival, but this has become more explicit in recent years: 'Since the 1960s, uprisings have become more explicitly carnivalesque, perhaps in part because revolt now is not just against the enclosure of the economic and physical commons, but the cultural and social commons' (Solnit 2005: 17).

Disasters, strangely perhaps, provide another example of cracks. Disasters (such as earthquakes, hurricanes, tsunamis, wars and so on) can bring not just human suffering but also a breakdown of social relations and the sudden emergence of quite different relations between people, relations of support and solidarity. Rebecca Solnit quotes one of the people who suffered the effects of Hurricane Juan in Halifax, Nova Scotia: 'A lot of the boundaries of alienation, the routines of our daily life, media, property were lifted, and there was a sense of relief about that' (2005: 1). She comments:

> Disasters suspend ordinary time and with it our ordinary roles and fates. Limits fall away. The storyline crashes. We wake up to other possibilities of what we might do, who we might speak to, where our lives might be going, even who we might be (and the intimations of mortality often intensify the pleasures of being alive). Everyday anxieties and desires no longer matter ... There is something exhilarating about the possibilities, for the joy of these occasions is as much what may come as what is, an unrecognized pleasure in uncertainty. The aftermath of disaster is often peculiarly hopeful. (2005: 5)

All our expectations about time and how things work are suddenly torn apart, the state is often hopelessly incompetent (or just a corrupt obstacle) and people help one another, developing alternative forms of social organisation to deal with the situation of suffering. The world is turned upside down just as surely as it is in a carnival: not just the physical but the social world as well.[9] That is why natural disasters often pose a threat to governments: through and beyond the suffering, they open a window onto the possibility of another world and lay bare the miseries of the existing one. Solnit, building on Henri Lefebvre's account of the Paris Commune, points to the close relation between disasters, carnivals and uprisings:

> Henri Lefebvre writes of the Paris Commune of 1871, 'A fundamental spontaneity ... sets aside secular layers of sediment: the State, bureaucracy, institutions, dead culture. It transforms itself in one leap into a community, a communion in whose midst work, joy, pleasure, the achievement of needs—and first of all social needs, and the need for sociability—will never be separated.' ... Layers of sediment are set aside. A dam cracks, a flood rushes forth carrying all along: disaster and revolution serve as each other's metaphors. (Solnit 2005: 8)[10]

The notion of a temporal crack in domination is something akin to the idea of the 'temporary autonomous zone' or

TAZ, coined by Hakim Bey (1985). His argument is that we cannot wait for a future revolution,[11] that indeed the idea of a future revolution has become the enemy of emancipation. We can however create now 'free enclaves' or 'temporary autonomous zones, moments of "uprising"': 'an uprising is like a "peak experience" as opposed to the standard of "ordinary" consciousness and experience … such moments of intensity give shape and meaning to the entirety of a life' (ibid.). Such uprisings are temporary and do not even seek permanence: 'The TAZ is like an uprising which does not engage directly with the State, a guerrilla operation which liberates an area (of land, of time, of imagination) and then dissolves itself to re-form elsewhere/ elsewhen, *before* the State can crush it' (ibid.). The pursuit of autonomy involves a nomadic moving between or creating of these transient zones of freedom and intensity of experience. The link between these zones is provided by the Web, 'the alternate horizontal open structure of info-exchange, the non-hierarchic network' (ibid.) The examples Bey offers cover a wide spectrum:

> The dinner party is already 'the seed of the new society taking shape within the shell of the old' (IWW Preamble). The sixties-style 'tribal gathering', the forest conclave of eco-saboteurs, the idyllic Beltane of the neo-pagans, anarchist conferences, gay faery circles … Harlem rent parties of the twenties, nightclubs, banquets, old-time libertarian picnics – we should realize that all these are already 'liberated zones' of a sort, or at least potential TAZs. (ibid.)

The notion of the TAZ is sometimes linked to the rave movement of the 1980s and 1990s (Gibson 1997, for example), but, for those of us more peaceably inclined, presumably it could be applied to a day in the park or a quiet afternoon reading a good book or chatting to friends, not to mention a theatre performance or a concert.[12]

Perhaps we can even go a step further and, following a suggestion by Horkheimer, say that just doing something for its own sake can be seen as an anti-capitalist crack, simply because it breaks the instrumental chain of reasoning typical of capitalism, whereby everything has to be justified as a means to an end:

> Less and less is anything done for its own sake. A hike that takes a man out of the city to the banks of a river or a mountain top would be irrational and idiotic, judged by utilitarian standards; he is devoting himself to a silly or destructive pastime. In the view of formalised reason, an activity is reasonable only if it serves another purpose, e.g. health or relaxation, which helps to replenish his working power. (Horkheimer 1946/2004: 25)

Is going for a hike, or sitting down and reading a good book, or going out for a wild all-night party to be seen as an act of rebellion to be placed beside the Zapatista revolt or the uprising of December 2001 in Argentina? This is a crucial question that recurs repeatedly. It is clear that spending a quiet afternoon reading a good book does not have the same impact on society as organising the occupation of several towns by thousands of indigenous peasants, and yet we ignore the lines of continuity at our peril. Subcomandante Marcos makes a related point when he says:

> Marcos is gay in San Francisco, a black person in South Africa, Asian in Europe, a Chicano in San Isidro, an anarchist in Spain, a Palestinian in Israel, an Indigenous person in the streets of San Cristóbal, a gang-member in Neza, a rocker on campus, a Jew in Germany, an ombudsman in the Department of Defence, a feminist in a political party, a communist in the post-Cold War period, a prisoner in Cintalapa, a pacifist in Bosnia, a Mapuche in the Andes, a teacher in the National Union of Educational Workers, an artist without a gallery or a portfolio, a housewife in any neighbourhood in any city in any part of Mexico on a Saturday night, a guerrilla in Mexico at the end of the twentieth century, a striker in the CTM, a sexist in the feminist movement, a woman alone in a Metro station at 10 p.m., a retired person standing around in the Zócalo, a peasant without land, an underground editor, an unemployed worker, a doctor with no office, a non-conformist student, a dissident against neo-liberalism, a writer without books or readers, and a Zapatista in the Mexican Southeast. In other words, Marcos is a human being in this world. Marcos is every untolerated, oppressed, exploited minority that is resisting and saying 'Enough!'[13]

And yet the practice of the left is repeatedly to commit suicide by ignoring, denying or destroying these lines of continuity:

by condemning reformism, by using language that only the initiated understand, by the use of violence in a way that alienates many people.[14] Rather than creating sharp divisions (between the guerrilla leader and the housewife alone on a Saturday night, for example), we need to find ways of making visible and strengthening these lines of continuity that are often so submerged. This is the point of talking of cracks: to understand our multiple rebellions and alternative creations as being connected by invisible or almost-invisible (and rapidly shifting) fault lines in society.

The notion of the crack, unlike Bey's idea of the TAZ, keeps alive the perspective of a total transformation of society. While each rebellion has its own validity and requires no justification in terms of its contribution to the future Revolution, it remains true that the existence of capitalism is a constant attack on the possibility of determining our own lives. Although a crack should not be seen as a means to an end, there is always an insufficiency about it, an incompleteness, a restlessness. A crack is not a step on the path to Revolution, but it is an opening outwards. It is a lighthouse of dignity shining into a dark night, a radio transmitter broadcasting rebellion to who knows whom. It is never entirely closed, even when it is violently suppressed. The Paris Commune lives on, despite the slaughter of so many of its participants: an inspiration, an unredeemed debt. 1968 lives on too, a taste of freedom that becomes a craving. So many past struggles that are not past, but hang in the air, vibrations of unfulfilled hopes, promises of a possible future. So many unfinished experiments in what the world could be.

There is a drive outwards from these cracks. They are centres of transgression, radiating waves of rebellion, not according to some pre-determined model (for these do not work) but always experimentally, creatively. Our cracks are not self-contained spaces but rebellions that recognise one another, feel affinities, reach out for each other. The need to get rid of capitalism, the need for a lasting and radical transformation of society is more urgent than ever, but the only way of achieving this is through the recognition, creation, expansion and multiplication here and now of all sorts of cracks in the structure of domination.

The force of the cracks breaks dimensionality. Here we have mentioned three dimensions: spatial, activity- or resource-centred, and temporal. The aim, however, is not to establish a typology or a classification: what is important is rather to see the manifold forms of rebellion in everyday life. We live in a capitalist society, we are dominated by capital, and yet, all the time and in a million different ways, we try to break the logic of capital. To list different dimensions may help us to think of the many different ways in which we do this, but perhaps to revolt against capital is to revolt against dimensionality itself.[15] In this sense, surrealism is an aspect of the cracks: the breaking of dimensionality and projection into a different world, a world beyond capitalism.[16] There is a beautiful passage by John Berger in which he suggests the other-dimensionality of cracks:

> Yet it can happen suddenly, unexpectedly, and most frequently in the half-light-of-glimpses, that we catch sight of another visible order which intersects with ours and has nothing to do with it. The speed of a cinema film is 25 frames per second. God knows how many frames per second flicker past in our daily perception. But it is as if, at the brief moments I'm talking about, suddenly and disconcertingly we see between frames. We come upon a part of the visible which wasn't destined for us. Perhaps it was destined for night-birds, reindeer, ferrets, eels, whales …. (2001: 4–5)

I am not suggesting that anti-capitalist cracks are destined only for ferrets and whales, but that often their existence can be detected only by a special sensibility and that they take us into a world that breaks with the ordinary dimensions of life. Perhaps to rebel against capital is like walking through a looking glass and beginning to live in a world that does not yet exist (and therefore exists not-yet), a world with a quite different dimensionality, a world we are only beginning to understand.

To struggle not just against but against-and-beyond is always to cross a threshold into a beyond, a sort of counter-world,[17] that is both an experiment and a gamble, a beyond that is surreal in the sense that it projects us beyond existing reality. The Free Association express this point clearly:

By envisaging a different world, by acting in a different world we actually call forth that world. It is only because we have, at least partially, moved out of what makes 'sense' in the old world that another world can start to make its own sense. Take the example of Rosa Parks who simply refused to move to the back of the bus. She wasn't making a demand, she wasn't even in opposition, she was simply acting in a different world. (2007: 26)

That action, which sparked off the civil rights movement in the United States, now strikes us as the simple assertion of a human right, but in its moment it was a daring and experimental gamble, a crossing of a threshold into a world that might or might not come into existence.[18] That is in the nature of our cracks: they are the acting-out of a world that does not exist, in the hope that by acting it out, we may really breathe it into life; or rather, in the knowledge that this is the only way in which we can bring it into life.

7

Cracks are explorations in an anti-politics of dignity.

Cracks are explorations-creations of a world that does not yet exist. We walk over the threshold into a counter-world in which exploration is indistinguishable from creation: the only paths are those which we make by walking.[1]

What is important in the crack or counter-world is not the *what* but the *how*: 'no, we shall do not what money bids us do, we shall do what we consider necessary or desirable.' The 'what' in both cases is without content, the important thing is the way in which the decision is taken, whether as external imposition or constraint, or as the attempt to decide for ourselves what we should do. The crack is simply a push towards self-determination. This obviously precludes a pre-determination of the contents of the cracks, since the whole point is that the people involved determine the contents. The detailed description of utopias may be stimulating, but, if taken seriously as a model for how society should be organised, they immediately become oppressive.[2] Perhaps the most that we can say about the contents of the cracks is what can be gleaned from the struggles that already exist and, as we have seen, these struggles cover a huge range of different activities.

Rather than talk of the contents of the cracks, we should focus on the *how*. In general terms, the content is simply an empty content to be filled in a certain way: by self-determination. But what does self-determination mean and how is it organised?

Some of the examples mentioned (reading a book in the park, going to garden in the allotment) point us towards individual self-determination ('freedom' in a liberal sense). This experience of individual choice should not be dismissed lightly, but it is clear that it does not take us very far, simply because whatever we do is part of a social flow of doing in which it is difficult (or impossible) to separate the doing of one person from the doing of others. If the movement of this social flow of doing is not consciously shaped, then it will always appear as an external constraint: an external constraint, usually expressed in the form of money, that makes a mockery of our 'free self-determination'. The only real self-determination would be the social control of the social flow of doing and, since the social flow of doing is a global flow, this necessarily means world communism, that is, a form of organisation in which the people of the world would actively determine the flow of doing in the world. For the moment, this is hard even to imagine. It is a question now not of complete self-determination but a constant drive towards self-determination, a self-determination that can only be understood as a social process.

To speak of the cracks as pushes towards self-determination would make little sense if that were not reflected in their internal organisation. The crack is in the first place a break with capitalist social relations. There is no model to be applied, but there is a fundamental principle of *asymmetry* in relation to capitalist social relations. If capital is the negation of self-determination, then the push towards self-determination or autonomy must be fundamentally different in its forms of organisation. If our struggle is not asymmetrical to capital in its forms, then it simply reproduces capitalist social relations, whatever its content.[3]

Cracks, then, are explorations in asymmetry, explorations in the anti-politics of dignity.[4] Dignity is the immediate affirmation of negated subjectivity, the assertion, against a world that treats us as objects and denies our capacity to determine our own lives, that we are subjects capable and worthy of deciding for ourselves. Dignity in this sense means not only the assertion of our own dignity but also implies the recognition of the dignity of others. Central to the crack is the idea that mutual recognition does not have to wait till the end of history, but that we can already make a start on it now, by combating constantly the negation of our mutual recognition as persons. Where capitalism treats people as means to an end, or as abstractions, or as groups which can be labelled, the push towards mutual recognition means the refusal to accept sexism, racism, ageism and all those other practices which treat people not as people but as the embodiment of labels, definitions, classifications. Although not always observed in practice, the rejection of these forms of labelling has become a universal principle in anti-capitalist movements throughout the world. The creation of social relations based on mutual recognition and respect is at the core of the 'other politics' which the Zapatista movement and so many other movements throughout the world are struggling to develop. The 'other politics' means treating ourselves and others as doers, as subjects rather than objects, and finding appropriate forms of organisation to express this. In a world that constantly negates our dignity, this inevitably means a process of ever-renewed exploration and creation of organisational forms.

This ever-renewed creation of organisational forms builds, however, upon a long tradition. The idea that *our* forms of organisation are radically different from *their* forms of organisation is profoundly rooted in the whole history of anti-capitalism. Capitalist organisations are marked by hierarchy and the pursuit of efficiency. The anti-capitalist tradition of which we speak is characterised by respect for all those involved, the promotion of active participation, direct democracy and comradeship. This is the tradition of the commune, council, soviet, or assembly. This is a form of organisation celebrated in Marx's discussion of the Paris Commune in *The Civil War in France*, and one that recurs, with variations, in all the major uprisings against capitalism: in the soviets of the Russian revolution, the workers' councils of Italy and Germany, in the Spanish Civil War, recently in the communal councils of the Zapatistas, the *cabildos* in Bolivia, the *asambleas barriales* in Argentina and the forms of horizontal (or anti-vertical) organisation adopted by groups all over the world. These are non-instrumental forms of organisation that focus on the articulation of the opinions of all those involved in the struggles, working outwards from there rather than backwards from the goal to be achieved. The council, then, is quite different from the party, which is a form of organisation conceived as a means to an end, the end of winning state power. In the council, what is important is the effective articulation of collective self-determination; in the party, the important thing is to achieve a pre-determined goal.

The council is not only something that arises in revolutionary situations. The sort of relationship that it is at the base of the council is profoundly rooted in everyday struggle, that is to say, in everyday life. We go out for a meal with a group of friends and we take the decision on where to go through a discussion that aims to respect everyone's preferences. This sort of decision making is just an integral part of ordinary life. We think of it as friendship or comradeship. Comradeship is of course a concept with deep and strong roots in the whole communist, socialist, anarchist and anti-capitalist tradition: a pivotal concept, yet one that is often subordinated or lost sight of. In accounts of struggles against capital, comradeship is often given a subordinate place. Thus, one might say, 'In the great miners' strike in Britain, the miners struggled against the closure of the pits and in the process a great sense of comradeship was built up.' Comradeship, in other words, is seen as a by-product of the struggle. But, if you listen to the participants, the emphasis is often different: what they stress as the most important part of the experience is the sense of comradeship and community that was established among the strikers, and its loss as the strike was broken and the communities divided. Indeed, any strike generates new relations of friendship and solidarity and gives the strikers the practical experience of a world without bosses: the creation of a world of different social relations goes beyond what was foreseen at the outbreak of the conflict.

The centrality of the quality of social relationships (comradeship, in other words) is not new, but in recent years it has acquired a new recognition. Attention has shifted from the instrumental goal of taking power to the present creation or strengthening of social relations incompatible with capitalism. Dignity has become a central concept. 'Amorosity' (*amorosidad*) is another word sometimes used to express the relations being created in these struggles. The relations generated are relations of love that give the movement force and permit the participants to overcome and respect their disagreements. This is not easy, as one *piquetero* points out: 'It is hard. Just imagine in a neighbourhood in La Matanza, hard men who have to go through violent situations with a high level of machismo, it is not easy to talk of amorosity, or to practise it' (Sitrin 2005:

58–9; 2006: 64) The old comradeship has moved to the centre of the stage, but it has shed its masculine image and declared its name as love.[5]

This is what is being emphasised in very many struggles: that, over and beyond the immediate aims and their achievement (or not), there is a crucial residue of different social relations created or recovered. Thus, after the War of Water in Cochabamba, in which the people of the town came together to prevent the privatisation of water, one of the participants concludes:

> We learnt a lot of lessons really. I think that beyond conquering the water for the people of Cochabamba it has been a re-finding of life, a re-finding of solidarity, fraternity, and we have been developing very valuable, very lasting friendships. Sometimes between neighbours we look at each other and say 'how are you?' but now there was an opportunity to talk about our children, about problems – in so many hours of keeping watch. We became human again. (Ceceña 2004: 123)

Or again, from one of the participants in the uprising of the 19/20 December 2001 in Argentina:

> There is an important break. That is, I meet my neighbour and chat in the square of my neighbourhood or on some street corner, and we tell each other our problems ... There is a recovery of old spaces of sociability that had been lost ... One of the first things that is recovered with the nineteenth and twentieth is face-to-face interaction. It is the community itself. (Sitrin 2005: 5; 2006: 29)

The world we try to create is sometimes described in terms of contrasting value systems. We reject the de-humanising values that capital embodies and create a world according to different values, different ideas of what is good and bad. Massimo De Angelis describes the experience of the anti-G8 action in Gleneagles in July 2005 in these terms: 'the Stirling camp became a place in which *other* values were dominating social cooperation, or co-production' (2007: 19), and argues that 'the politics of alternative is ultimately a politics of value, a politics to establish what the value practices are, that is those social practices and correspondent relations that articulate individual bodies and the wholes of social bodies' (ibid.: 25).

The emphasis on value helps us to understand that the force of this 'other politics' lies in its overcoming of the distinction between ethics and politics. The Machiavellian distinction between means and ends which is so characteristic of the Leninist conception of politics is abandoned. Living now the world we want to create with its 'social practices and correspondent relations' breaks the instrumental separation of means and end: the means is the end. This view of struggle is often criticised as being naïve and un-realistic, but the experience of recent years suggests that it has a tremendous force. It is rather when movements slip back towards the separation of means and ends, between ethics and politics, that they weaken themselves considerably.

Comradeship, dignity, amorosity, love, solidarity, fraternity, friendship, ethics: all these names stand in contrast to the commodified, monetised relations of capitalism, all describe relations developed in struggles against capitalism and which can be seen as anticipating or creating a society beyond capitalism. They stand in contrast to the commodified relations of capitalism not as timeless alternatives, but as struggle-against. It is not that there is some trans-historical quality of dignity: dignity is nothing other than the struggle against and beyond its own negation. It follows too that to speak of cracks as explorations in the anti-politics of dignity does not mean that we hope one day to arrive at a pre-existing dignity, but that dignity is itself an exploration, a shifting process of creating social relations against-and-beyond capital.

There can therefore be no clear rules about how these principles should be translated into organisation, but one idea much emphasised in practice is that of 'horizontality'. Horizontality is part of the assertion of our own subjectivity, the rejection of vertical structures, chains of command which tell us what to do, which make us the object of the decision making of others, whoever those others may be. The idea of horizontality is that all should be involved in decision-making processes on an equal basis and that there should be no leaders. In practice, it is difficult to make this work in absolute terms, since informal patterns of leadership often grow up even where there are no formal structures, so it is probably more helpful to think of horizontality not as an absolute rule but as a constant struggle against verticality. Raquel Gutiérrez, in her study of the struggles in Bolivia (2009), emphasises that the important thing is not the adoption of any particular model, but the production of shared horizons of meaning through an effective process of collective deliberation. Or, as Colectivo Situaciones put it in an interview with Marina Sitrin: 'Horizontality is a tool of counter-power when it's a question. Horizontality is a tool of power when it's an answer' (2005: 49; 2006: 55).

A related, but slightly different idea is expressed in the Zapatista principle of *mandar obedeciendo* ('to command obeying'), the principle that those in a position of authority must always obey those over whom they exercise that authority. Here a degree of non-horizontality is accepted, but the classic council principle of accountability and instant recallability ensures that those who (temporarily) occupy positions of responsibility should obey the wishes of the community. In many cases (in the tradition of indigenous communities, for example), this is supplemented by the idea of a rotation of responsibilities: part of belonging to a community is to accept that one may be called upon by the community to assume certain communal responsibilities for certain periods, but always in obedience to the wishes of the community.

All of this expresses the rejection of representative democracy as a form of organisation that excludes the represented. All the organisational forms that we have mentioned can be seen as developments of direct democracy, not as a set of rules but as a constant process of experimenting with democratic forms, ways of overcoming people's inhibitions, ways of controlling people's aggressions or sexist or racist assumptions. The central challenge is how to articulate effectively the *we do* that is the core of the cracks: how to articulate the *we* that is the subject of the movement, as a cohesive and yet open *we*, and how to articulate the *do*, the *we* as subject, as doer. The Zapatista *mandar obedeciendo* ('to command obeying') not only presents a solution to these questions but indicates oxymoronically a real field of tension and challenge.[6] That the process must be understood as both exploratory and open is underlined by another central principle of the Zapatistas: *preguntando caminamos*, 'asking we walk'.

These can all be seen as examples of pre-figurative politics, the idea that the struggle for a different society must create that society through its forms of struggle. The term 'describes the idea that if you can embody the change you struggle for, you have already won – not by fighting but by becoming. Reclaim the Streets realized this beautifully, recognizing that if what the RTS activists opposed was privatization, alienation, and isolation, a street party was not just a protest of these conditions but a temporary triumph over them' (Solnit 2005: 23).

An enormous amount of experience has been gained, especially in recent years, in this pre-figurative or 'other' politics, this politics of dignity.[7] This includes both experience in the organisation of the great anti-summit events of the alter-globalisation movement and the organisation of the world and regional Social Forums, but also the less spectacular creation of community gardens, alternative schools, radio stations in resistance, street theatre, and so on. The idea is gaining ground that the only way to change the world is to do it ourselves[8] and to do it here and now. And yet, the attempts to create now the other world that we say is possible are never unproblematic: in a society based on the negation of dignity, a politics of dignity is always a struggle.

Part III
Cracks on the Edge of Impossibility

8
Dignity is our weapon against a world of destruction.

Cracks break with the logic of capitalist society. To that logic, we oppose a different way of doing things. We want to break the system, the social cohesion that holds us in place and obliges us to act in certain ways.

Dignity is a cutting edge shearing through the tight, tough, compact weave of capitalist domination. Dignity is an ice-breaker, its sharp bows cutting into an enormous mass of compacted ice, the apparently unbreakable horror that we call capitalism. Dignity is a pick-axe wielded against the encroaching walls that threaten to crush the whole of humanity. Dignity is a blade hacking at the strands of the spider's web that holds us entrapped.

The weapon of dignity is otherness, other-living, other-doing. The otherness of dignity is a weapon, an otherness-against, a misfitting directed (explicitly or not) against that which we do not fit into: a world of exploitation and destruction.

The spaces and moments we have called cracks are often described as autonomous spaces, or spaces of exodus or escape. We have tended to avoid these terms here simply because they draw attention away from the crucial issue: the conflict between these space-moments and the world that surrounds them. It is important to sing the glories of the worlds that are being created, the new social relations and the new ways of doing things: but we cannot go very far without talking of the clash with the world to which these dignities are opposed. There is a constant antagonism, a constant pressure to make the otherness yield to the enormous cohesive force of the society that surrounds us. The spaces are not autonomous, though they aspire to be. They are rather cracks, the sharp ends of a social conflict.

Dignity is an attack on capitalism, but not necessarily a confrontation. To confront capital is to allow it to set the agenda. Dignity consists in setting our own agenda: this is what we shall do, irrespective of capital. If capital chooses to repress us, to co-opt us, to imitate us, so be it, but let it be clear that we lead the dance. This certainly does not mean, cannot mean, that we cease to struggle against capitalism, but that, as far as possible, we take the initiative, we set the agenda, we make it clear that it is capitalism struggling against us, our lives, our projects, our humanity.

Dignity is to refuse-and-create: to refuse to make capitalism and to create a new world. In an article on the movement in Oaxaca, Gustavo Esteva comments, 'Thousands, millions of people assume now that the time has come to walk our own path. As the Zapatistas say, to change the world is very difficult, if not impossible. A more pragmatic attitude demands the construction of a new world. That's what we are now trying to do, as if we had already won' (Esteva 2007d: 7).[1] Building a new world does of course mean changing the existing one, but the shift in emphasis is crucial: instead of focusing our attention on the destruction of capitalism, we concentrate on building something else. This is an inversion of the traditional revolutionary perspective that puts the destruction of capitalism first and the construction of the new society second.

To make a new world means to cut the web that binds us into the cohering force of capitalist society, so that we can create something different. The enemy is the social synthesis of capitalist society.

9
Cracks clash with the
social synthesis of capitalism.

1. OUR CRACKS ARE VULNERABLE TO THE GELATINOUS SUCTION OF THE CAPITALIST SYNTHESIS.

We wield our dignity like a pick-axe against the encroaching walls of destruction, and then feel a little embarrassed and disheartened as it sinks with a splodge and a squish into a gooey jelly.

All metaphors are dangerous games that may have to be abandoned at some point. But not now. We want to break: that is what the idea of the crack expresses in the first place. We must not lose that. Rupture is what it is all about. We want to break, not just to make things a little better, not just to have Obama in place of Bush, the Kirchners in place of Menem, López Obrador instead of Calderón. We do not just want to build a movement or stop the privatisation of water or oil: that certainly, but we want more, we want to break capitalism, to break the dynamic of a system that is destroying us. It is precisely when the idea of breaking seems so hopeless that we need to reassert it.

It is just that at times it seems so terribly difficult. All our attempts to break seem to get sucked back into the system, if not openly repressed. It is not enough to celebrate the cracks. We must talk also about their problems.[1]

The argument is clear: the only way to think about revolution is in terms of the creation, expansion and multiplication of cracks in capitalist domination. This is not an empty abstraction because these moments or spaces of revolt-and-other-doing already exist all over the place and because they have been at the forefront of anti-capitalist struggle in recent years. But it has become increasingly obvious in the last few years that these cracks face big problems. Thus, the Otra Campaña initiated by the Zapatistas, the attempt to spread their movement beyond

Chiapas in an organised way, has not progressed as fast as many of us hoped; the great upsurge of alternative struggle in Argentina in 2001 and 2002 was not able to maintain its momentum in the face of the Kirchner government's strategy of cooptation and criminalisation. The 'popular-communitarian' struggle in Bolivia has been swamped by the 'national-popular' struggle and the government of Evo Morales;[2] the multifarious forms of the movement for another world have faced increasing state repression all over the world in the wake of 11 September 2001 and the police brutality in Genoa, with many small alternative groups ending in disarray and dissolution. There is certainly plenty of room for all those who maintain that the only way to change the world is by taking state power (or indeed those who say that there is no possibility at all of destroying capitalism) to pick on examples and say 'I told you so.'

It is hardly surprising that the cracks should face difficulties, since they are all revolts against the existing social synthesis, they are all attempts to break through the system of social cohesion that is currently destroying humanity. Any society is based on some sort of social cohesion, some form of relation between the activities of the many different people. In capitalist society, this cohesion has a particular logic often described in terms of the laws of capitalist development. There is a systemic closure that gives the social cohesion a particular force and makes it very difficult to break. To underline the close-knit character of the social cohesion of capitalist society, I refer to it as a *social synthesis*.[3]

There is a deep dilemma in any rebellion. Rebellion is always irrational, judged by the dominant rationality. And the dominant rationality is backed by the material conditions of survival: acceptance of that rationality is a condition of being able to live in reasonable conditions, or, in many cases, of being able to live at all. The movement against capitalist globalisation is often referred to as the movement for global justice, but we all know that, in anything more than a mockingly formal sense, it is nonsense to want global justice in the real world of capitalism. The *piqueteros* in Argentina say they want a meaningful activity, to dedicate themselves to what they consider necessary or desirable, but we all know that too is non-sensical, literally devoid of meaning, in the real world of capitalism. How, then, can this nonsense avoid being swamped by the rationality of capitalism?

The universal pressure to conform comes from the social cohesion of capitalist social relations. We can make a protest, we can scream, we can throw stones, but then the totality of capitalist social relations seems to flow around us and suck us back into the system. We go and hurl our fury at the meetings of the G8, but then what? We still must eat and we still must sell our labour power or otherwise bow to capital in order to get money to buy food. We can occupy a factory, but then what? We still must find a way of selling the products we make if we carry on producing, we still must bow to market forces. We can overthrow the government, perhaps, if we all go on the streets and protest enough, but then what? What happens after our moments of rebellion, our moments of excess? We still have to find a way of reinserting ourselves into the world order, and that world order is capitalist.

To fight the *but then what?* is to fight for the particular, for the particular that refuses to fit in. It is to fight for a world of particulars, a world of many worlds. We are hurling particulars against the totality. But often it seems that the totality, the social synthesis, just laughs back at us, absorbing it all. How do we avoid that, how do we avoid being reabsorbed into the everyday functioning of capitalism? How do we avoid our cracks becoming simply a means for resolving the tensions or contradictions of capitalism, just an element of crisis resolution for the system? How do we know that our cracks are not just like cracks in the side of a volcano, escape valves that secure the stability of the whole?

The enemy, we said, is the capitalist social synthesis, the peculiarly tight logic of social cohesion in capitalist society. This cohesion draws us back into its arms in different ways. The most obvious are perhaps the state and our own personal 'failings', but the most insidious and forceful is value. Let us look at each of these.

The most obvious force of social cohesion that confronts the cracks is the state. The threat of violent repression by the state is constantly present. A report in today's newspaper makes the point dramatically:

About 120 members of the Federal Preventive Police, armed with rifles, last night broke into the installations of the community radio *Tierra y Libertad,* transmitter with a power of 1 watt and with a radius of about 4 kilometres in the popular settlements at the west of the city ... The attorney general's office indicated in a bulletin that the operation was due to the fact that the transmitter operated without a legal concession in Monterrey. (*La Jornada,* 7 June 2008, p. 13)

The violence of this example is grotesque, yet it highlights the growing brutality and intolerance not only of the Mexican, but of all states. The violent repression of non-violent cracks, in the name of property or law and order, is a daily occurrence in every part of the world. The eviction of Ungdomshuset, the long-established commune in Copenhagen, made world headlines in March 2007, as did the destruction of South Central Farm in Los Angeles in June 2006, where the bulldozers moved in to 'destroy the corn, flowers, medicinal plants, vegetables, fruits and some of the 600 trees that have been cultivated for more than 14 years with dedication, love and hard work by the farmers – most of them Mexican immigrants'.[4] A similar fate met the Orgazmic Orchard in central Buenos Aires just a few months ago. And so on and on and on. Everywhere, the attempt to do things in a different way, the attempt to crack capitalist social relations, is seen as being a threat to society (as indeed it aims to be) and is liable to be met with various degrees of violent repression.[5]

This immediately raises the questions of legality and self-defence. The very notion of a crack implies disrespect for the law, since it is a force of cohesion of the society we reject. The law, by its form, whatever its content, is an alien imposition. Whether it makes sense to disobey the law in any given situation, however, can only be judged in the context of a particular struggle. People who come together to form a social centre as a centre of anti-capitalist opposition must decide whether to occupy a building illegally (and risk violent eviction) or to do it legally (by renting or receiving some form of state concession). This is not an abstract question of whether we should obey the law but a practical question of avoiding repression (or, possibly, hurt to other people): in some contexts, squatting is a perfectly practical option; in others it would probably be met by immediate police repression,[6] closure of the centre and arrest and possibly torture of those involved. The same may be said, probably, of any kind of anti-capitalist action: it makes no sense to obey the law as a matter of principle, but the practical consequences of any particular action will always depend on the context.

Legality is usually used as a reference point to justify violent state repression, but of course in many cases legality is no guarantee at all against repression. Legal or illegal, any crack that poses a significant threat to capital is likely to attract a violent response from the forces of order, at least if the social context permits it. How do we deal with state violence? Does revolution inevitably mean the violent overthrow of capitalism? Do we need to build an armed organisation?

Certainly violence is becoming more and more attractive as a means of confronting an increasingly violent capitalism. It is not surprising that demonstrations against such events as the meetings of the G8 have become more violent in recent years, with the violence coming not only from the police but often being initiated by demonstrators.[7] And yet there are many problems in thinking of our struggles against capital in terms of violence. For a start, we are probably not very good at violence. Violence is not part of the society that we want to create and we are unlikely to be able to match capitalist forces in violence. Violence is not a neutral terrain, but the terrain of the forces of domination: it draws us into the social relations and forms of behaviour that we repudiate: hierarchical structures dominated by men.[8] Dignity is our ground and violence is the negation of dignity, wherever it comes from.

Perhaps the key issue is not violence, but the setting of the agenda, seizing the initiative. The point of the crack is that it is a rupture: not just a response to capitalist aggression but the attempt to move beyond it, to create now a different set of social relations. Seizing the initiative means moving beyond confrontation: we determine our action according to our own needs. Let capital and the state run after us, let it try to co-opt or repress us. The question of how we defend and expand our crack without losing the initiative or being drawn into an alien terrain is a very difficult one. State violence is often a way of seizing back the initiative, forcing us to stop our revolt and campaign for the release of the prisoners.[9]

The argument here is not a completely pacifist argument, then, for we do have to think of how we defend ourselves against state violence. I write not long after the terrible repression by the Mexican state in Oaxaca, and the question is unavoidable. If we wish to think of breaking capitalist social relations, then we have to think of the question of self-defence. In many cases, there may be no danger of direct state repression, at least in present circumstances, but the tendency in the world is for violent repression to become a more and more common response to any sort of challenge to the existing system of domination.

Self-defence is, however, not the same as armed defence, and certainly not the same as the 'violent overthrow' of capitalism. Although there may be a strong argument for some form of armed organisation in some cases, it is probably a mistake to think of arms as being the key to self-defence. Certainly the fact that the Zapatistas are armed and organised as an army has been a significant element in deterring large-scale military repression of the uprising in Chiapas,[10] but probably the most effective form of defence has been the strength of the resonance of their movement in Mexico and throughout the world. For any movement, it is probably the quality of the movement itself, that is, the quality of the transformation of everyday life through the movement, that is the strongest form of self-defence, and this runs directly counter to armed organisation and violence. As Raoul Vaneigem puts it, 'every time that a revolution has failed to consider as its first objective the task of enriching the daily life of everyone, it has given arms to the repression.'[11]

State violence imposes certain social relations upon us and does so the more effectively the more we mimic its action by responding with violence. Violence is just one aspect of the way in which the state constantly draws us back into the social cohesion of capitalism by getting us to behave in certain ways, adopt certain categories of thought and forms of organisation. In the exercise of violence, as in all its activities, the state is a form of social relations, a way of doing things.

It is not only by direct physical repression that the state reacts to attempts to break the social cohesion of capitalism. Through the law and through all its forms of action, the state channels us into certain ways of behaving, encloses us within certain limits. It is difficult to avoid contact with this altogether.[12] Even if we are clear that we cannot change society radically through the state, it is still very difficult to avoid all contact with the state. Clearly, this contact is not neutral: it tends to draw us into certain ways of doing things. We go to a state school or university and it pulls us into a certain type of education. We receive a state grant for studying or some other purpose and it too tends to impose certain conditions. An occupied factory seeks to avoid repression by seeking legal recognition of its status, but to do so, it has to satisfy certain requirements, fill certain forms, adopt a certain language. We occupy an empty warehouse and set up a social centre and then find that we can apply for a state subsidy to improve the building – and that we are more likely to receive it if we do not antagonise the local government too much. And so on. In some cases, some sort of state funding seems necessary for realising our collective project of an alternative doing. How, then, do we relate to the state and state funding?

The Zapatistas take the radical position of refusing all state subsidies and avoiding all contact with the state in so far as possible: by creating their own schools and system of health care, for example.[13] Some other radical groups (some, but not all, of the *piquetero* groups in Argentina, for example) take the opposite view, namely that to receive money from the state is simply to recover a small part of the social wealth that we have created, and that the important issue is not where the money comes from (since all wealth comes from the workers), but to find ways of asserting effective social control over the money (refusing state conditions and organising forms of directly democratic control of the use of the money).[14] It is not necessary to say that either of these views is wrong or right. The important thing is probably the manner in which the decision is taken (and constantly subjected to question): its relation to the opening or closing of the crack in question will depend on the context of the struggle and should not be made a question of dogma. Above all, it can not be a question of purity. In a struggle in-against-and-beyond capitalism, there is no purity: what matters rather is the direction of the struggle, the movement against-and-beyond.

Is the answer, then, to take control of the state and either neutralise it or use it to spread our cracks? Can we not convert the state itself into an anti-capitalist crack? Indeed, should we not focus our activity on organising to gain control of the state and turn it into an anti-capitalist crack? Is this not what is happening in Cuba, Venezuela and Bolivia, for example?

The state is not just any organisation, but a particular form of organisation, and to focus the struggle for change on the state has profound implications for the movement against capital. The state is a way of doing things: the wrong way of doing them.[15] The state is a form of organisation developed over centuries as an integral part of the capitalist system. Capital is above all a process of separation: of the separation of the object of creation from the creating subject, of the subject from herself and those around her, of that which has been created from the process of creation, and so on.[16] The state is part of this process of separation. It is the separation of the public from the private, of the common affairs of the community from the community itself. The state is an organisation separated from society, staffed principally by full-time officials. Its language and its practices express that separation: the language of officialdom, the practices that follow set procedures and formalities. The separation from society is policed by rules and hierarchies that ensure the maintenance of the established forms of behaviour. The relation of the state to society is an external relation: it relates to people as citizens (or non-citizens), as individuals abstracted from their social context and the particularities of their doing. It is only as such abstract atoms that the citizens can be represented – the passions and particularities of real people cannot be 'represented'. The state, by its very form, and independently of the content of its action, confirms and reproduces the negation of subjectivity on which capital is based. It relates to people not as subjects but as objects, or – and this amounts to the same thing – as subjects reduced to the status of mere abstractions.

A political organisation which focuses its action upon the state inevitably reproduces these characteristics of the state as a form of relations. To gain influence within the state or to capture what appears to be control over the state, the organisation must adopt those forms of behaving and thinking which are characteristic of the state. Thus, political parties, however left-wing or indeed 'revolutionary', are characterised by hierarchical structures and tend to adopt certain forms of language and behaviour which dovetail with those of the state. The external relation to society is reproduced in the concept of the 'masses' – a quantity of undifferentiated, abstract atoms, with limited capacities and in need of leadership.

These left-wing parties may well be anti-capitalist in their intentions, but in their forms of organisation and action they tend to reproduce the objectification of the person which is the core of capitalist social relations. This is not a politics of dignity, because it does not start out from the recognition of the creative power of the oppressed subject. On the other hand, the commitment to radical change is often very genuine. This commitment is understood as the struggle for the liberation of the people – the 'people' being seen as an external other. Revolution through the eyes of the state or a state-centred organisation can only be a revolution on behalf of others, for the benefit of the people, not a revolution by the people themselves. This is not a politics of dignity, but a politics of poverty, not a politics of dialogue, but a politics of monologue (as reflected, for example, in the length of the speeches of political leaders). People are understood not as doers, but as victims:[17] poor people.

The attractiveness of this conception should not be under-estimated. It starts from the genuine perception of a world of terrible, appalling poverty and humiliation and sets out to resolve this problem by constructing a revolution on behalf of the victims of capitalism, for which the appropriate organisational form is certainly the state. There is no doubt that, even within the world capitalist system, much can be done to alleviate poverty and its effects. A headline in this morning's paper[18] tells me that

Cuba has the lowest rate of infant mortality in Latin America. To dismiss this as unimportant would be grotesque.

And yet it is not enough. It seems unlikely that a real break with capitalism can be carried out on behalf of the suffering masses, and, even if it could, the result would probably not be a very attractive society. To act on behalf of, or for the benefit of, the people inevitably involves a degree of repression. If the people do not have the same idea as the state, then some means has to be found to impose the well-being of the people even against their wishes. The revolutionary movement becomes repressive and is also weakened as it loses active support. No more need be said: the story has been acted out many times.

But then what do we say of Bolivia and Venezuela? Are they to be counted as cracks in capitalist domination?

Probably all revolutionary movements are a confluence of many movements, of people fighting for change in different ways and for different reasons. We have simplified this multiplicity by emphasising two forms of struggle; the politics of dignity and the politics of poverty, the politics of councils or assemblies and the politics of parties focused on the state. These two struggles are often interwoven, often mixed within the same organisation or indeed the same individual, but the way in which they interact will have profound consequences for the movement for change. The Russian revolution, for example, was a complex mixture of council (soviet) organisation and state-centred organisation. The tension between the two forms of organisation led to the suppression of the soviets and the development of an oppressive regime under the mocking title of the Soviet Union. In other cases, the development has been less disastrous and less bloody, but the politics of monologue has undoubtedly prevailed: Cuba is a case in point.

In the case of Bolivia and Venezuela, the processes are still open at the time of writing, but with a clear predominance of the state. Raquel Gutiérrez, in her profound analysis of the struggles in Bolivia (2009), distinguishes between the 'national-popular' struggle and the 'communitarian-popular' struggle.[19] The latter comes from and develops the traditional communitarian forms of direct democracy and has at its centre the affirmation of dignity and a refusal to accept alien domination. It was this that was the driving force of the struggles from 2000 to 2005. But this struggle of dignity was overlaid by the 'national-popular struggle', which focuses on the state and pushes for the concretisation of the achievements of the struggles in the form of a new government. This meant channelling the struggles into the party-form (the MAS) and led eventually to the election of Evo Morales as president of Bolivia. This brings significant reforms to the state, but involves a demobilisation and de-radicalisation of the original movement. The original uprising by the people themselves is converted into a movement on behalf of the people, and this leads inevitably to the reproduction of state practices and to accommodations with the interests of capital.

In the case of Venezuela, the course of the struggles has been different, but there too there is the coexistence of two movements: the movement of community-based struggle from below and the state-centred struggle from above. Here the struggle has been much more clearly state-dominated from the beginning, but, at least since the attempted coup against Chávez in 2002, it has been clear that the strength of the movement as a whole is very dependent on the strength of the movement from below. The process of transformation is seen as a movement from two sides, above and below, and the leaders speak of the need to overcome the bourgeois state and create a 'communal type of state'.[20] The creation and promotion of communal councils is at the core of this movement.[21]

This raises the question of how to think about the abolition or dissolution of the state. Does it have to come about by the creation of non-state forms of organisation (communal or council organisation) outside the state (this is basically what the Zapatistas are trying to do, and what has happened to some extent in Argentina, Bolivia and Ecuador)? Or can we think of the dissolution of the state as coming about from within the state itself: revolutionaries take state power in order to dissolve the state from within? Or some combination of the two processes? Many see the Bolivarian Revolution in Venezuela in these terms, as a combination of a movement from above and from below.

Can this be done? This is an important question that touches not only Venezuela, but also the attempts from within the state to overcome the state in other parts of the world (such as Porto Alegre, Venice, East Manchester, and so on) through the promotion of 'participatory democracy'.[22] Is it possible to re-signify the state (as Nicanoff (2007: 12) puts it), or to harmonise the dynamics of sovereignty and autonomy (Mazzeo 2007: 28)? This approach is sometimes discussed in terms of 'popular power' and the insistence that power comes from the people.[23] This is an attractive formulation, but the category of 'the people' actually conceals that the source of power is doing: it abstracts from the organisation of human activity and its antagonistic existence. It is this antagonism that is skated over in the formulations that look to an easy combination of a movement from above and a movement from below.

That the state should be dissolved from within, or as a coming-together of pressures from within and from without, is difficult, because of the weight of inherited structures and forms of behaviour, because of the separation of paid state functionaries from the rest of the population and because of the pressures to secure the functioning of 'the economy' (as though this were not a system of exploitation). If it were to be possible, then the crucial factor would be not the revolutionary commitment of the state functionaries or politicians themselves, but the force of the struggles outside the state apparatus for a different form of social organisation. The movement of 'from above' and 'from below' is inevitably an antagonistic process, although the contours of this antagonism may not follow institutional demarcations: it can be displaced into the state apparatus itself. Certainly the movement of history constantly defies theory, yet the term 'popular power' conceals the real antagonisms and difficulties.

A rebellion does not cease to be a rebellion just because it is channelled towards the state. The drive towards self-determination remains alive, although it is likely to be increasingly suppressed to the degree that the state structures become consolidated. A state-centred revolution is a highly self-antagonistic process, a crack that widens and plasters itself over at the same time. Whether, and at what point, the hand that plasters succeeds in suppressing the hand that opens the crack is always the outcome of struggle, the struggle for self-determination on the one hand and the struggle to contain it within forms of alien determination on the other.[24] Certainly in criticising state-centred rebellions, we should bear in mind that all rebellions are self-contradictory, that state-like practices can easily appear within anti-state movements and that there is no purity, there are no given answers.

The question, finally, is not one of intentions, but of forms of organisation, that is, of the real practices of organisation. Any form of organisation that focuses on changing society *on behalf of* the workers (the poor, the people, whoever) will tend, whatever its declared intentions, to weave acts of rebellion back into the social synthesis of capitalism. The state is the most obvious example of such organisation.[25]

The argument that the only way of conceiving of anti-capitalist revolution is as an interstitial process should be uncontroversial. In traditional revolutionary theory, the issue is obscured by the identification of the state with the totality of social relations. But once it is recognised that there are many states supporting one capitalist society, then it becomes clear that state-centred revolutions are also interstitial. The question is then not whether revolution should be understood as interstitial (for it must be), but what is the appropriate form of interstice. The discussion above leads us to conclude that the state is not an adequate interstitial form simply because, as a form of social relations, it is part of the social synthesis that we are rejecting: the state is part of the cohesive suction of capital. The only answer then is to think in terms of non-state interstitial forms: cracks.

3. CRACKS CLASH WITH OURSELVES.

We create our cracks, our spaces of dignity, and they are immediately threatened by the world outside us. But the external world is not only external: we carry it inside us.

We build our self-governing community in the Lacandon Jungle, we create our social centre in Edinburgh, we go to an all-night rave in Berlin. We say 'here no, here we do not accept the rule of capital, here we shall do something else, here we create a space of dignity, horizontality, love.' But obviously it is not so simple. We cut a slice out of capitalism, but our slice is not a slice of purity. Within our non-sexist, non-racist spaces, sexist and racist habits reappear. Within our horizontal assemblies, patterns of power emerge which are all the more disturbing for not being regulated or perhaps even recognised. Those who are most articulate find ways of imposing their will. In large assemblies, it is often the groups with experience of political militancy in the old left parties that are able to impose their line. Within our areas of shared responsibility, the work continues to fall on just a few people.[26] Old patterns reassert themselves:

> We find ourselves falling back into the same practices. It seems to be a problem that springs from our inner lives … It's as if there's an enduring memory of verticality of representation, of delegation, that plays out almost unconsciously. No matter how much we say we're autonomous, there always comes a point where we're waiting for someone else to act, for someone else to speak, or waiting for acceptance by another.[27]

New social relations are not created by decree: even groups that put at the top of their agenda the creation of different social relations between the members sometimes finish up with bitter quarrels and a strong sense of disillusionment. Sometimes the intensity of the effort to create something different is reflected in the intense bitterness of the animosities created.

Our cracks are not pure cracks, our dignities are not pure dignities. We try to break with capitalist society, but our break still bears its birthmarks. However much we try to do something different, the contradictions of capitalism reproduce themselves within our revolt. We are not pure subjects, however rebellious we might be. The cracks, both as spaces of liberation and as painful ruptures, run inside us too.

These problems are probably inevitable. The purpose of the cracks is not to create a community of saints but to establish a different form of relations between people. They cannot be based on purity, or on Puritanism. Any attempt to base them on an idea of self-sacrifice is disastrous: if they are not attractive spaces/moments, if they do not exert a magnetic attraction, they can never become cracks, for they will not spread.[28] To some extent, these problems can be dealt with by organisational means. Many, or perhaps most, alternative or autonomous groups have experimented with different forms of organisation that take human contradictions into account without falling back on authoritarian methods. Thus, the Zapatistas have a system of rapid rotation in the composition of their Juntas de Buen Gobierno not just to involve more and more people in the self-government of their communities, but also to eliminate the dangers of corruption. Cecosesola, the long-established cooperative in Barquisimeto, Venezuela, that coordinates the distribution of cooperative products and organises popular markets, sets aside a great amount of time to the collective discussion of the problems that arise from sexism, racism, authoritarianism and so on, and adopts trust as a central organisational principle.[29] The problems are very real and should not be overlooked, but they should certainly not be erected into some sort of unchangeable concept of 'human nature'.[30]

4. CRACKS CLASH WITH THE RULE OF VALUE.

Beyond the state, beyond our personal reproduction of the social relations that we reject, there is another force that pulls us back in, that reabsorbs our attempts to break.

It is not the state that creates the social synthesis that surrounds us, although it often presents itself as doing so. The state represses and co-opts in order to defend something else. We are repressed or co-opted into something other than the state. The real force of cohesion stands behind the state: it is the movement of money. Money makes the world go round, as the saying has it. More precisely, the social synthesis is established through that which is expressed in money: value.[31]

Value is what holds society together under capitalism. It is a force that nobody controls. Capitalism is composed of a huge number of independent units which produce commodities that they sell on the market. The social interconnection between people's activities is established through the sale and purchase of commodities or, in other words, through the value of the commodities, expressed through money. Value (manifested in money) constitutes the social synthesis in capitalist society, that which holds together the many different, uncoordinated activities.[32] The state presents itself as being the focal point of social cohesion, but in fact the state is dependent on money and can do little to influence its movement.[33]

It is the existence of money as the synthesising force that makes capitalism so gelatinous, so spongy. Money is the fine spider's web that holds us entrapped. When we hit it, it does not shatter into pieces but oozes back around our fist, mocking us.

Behind money stands value, the all-conquering drive of the cheap commodity, the commodity produced in the least amount of time. This is hard to resist. 'The cheap prices of [the bourgeoisie's] commodities are the heavy artillery with which it batters down all Chinese walls', as Marx and Engels put it (1848/1976). We do not have to go back to the time of Marx and Engels to see this. What happened to the Vietnamese revolution that inspired the world forty years ago? It could not be defeated by the most powerful army on earth, but it has been effectively undermined by value. The great Chinese revolution has been converted into the world-wide symbol of the cheap commodity. The destruction of all the revolutions of the twentieth century by value stands as a stark warning. We can declare independence for Scotland, or Euzkadi or wherever, but as long as value is not challenged, its effect will be very limited. We can occupy factories, set up our alternative systems of production, but we will not be able to match the prices of capitalist commodities, we will not be able to produce things as cheaply and as quickly, and, if we were, we would probably be producing them in just the same way as the capitalists.

Value is incompatible with self-determination, or indeed with any form of conscious determination. Value is the rule of necessary labour time, of the shortest time necessary to produce a commodity. Value is controlled by nobody. Capitalists are capitalists not because they control value, but because they serve it.

How can we resist the rule of the cheap commodity and all that it brings with it, especially when the struggle to survive shapes the lives of so many people in the world? The traditional answer is that the only way is a system of planned production that would be even more efficient than capitalism and would respond to people's real needs. Traditional socialist analysis contrasts the anarchy of the market with the rationality of central planning, but in practice central planning has never been either rational or central, and it certainly has not been an example of self-determination.[34]

From the perspective of our multiplicity of cracks in capitalism, how can we possibly think of a system of planning? Yet value preys on fragmentation: that is a real problem. If there is no central planning, then how do we coordinate our different processes of creation or production, if not through the market? And if we produce for the market, what distinguishes us from any other capitalist enterprise?

Whatever the crack, whatever the form of the struggle to break with capitalism, value lays siege, not just as an external force, but through the corrosive, destructive force of money. Money embodies the rationality of capitalism that stands against the non-sense of rebellion. In capitalism, it is the movement of value that determines what should be done and how it should be done: no human, not even the capitalist class, makes those determinations.

Value attacks as a force operating behind our backs, as the silent power of money, introducing cheap commodities, luring people away in the hope of escaping from poverty (the Zapatistas that migrate to find employment in Cancún, for instance). As market, it also stands against us as a palpable limit to what we can do.

Occupied factories, like the hundreds occupied in Argentina in recent years, face immediately the question of their relation to the market. In general, the factories occupied (or 'recovered') were faced with closure before the occupation – closure motivated by the inability of their owners to sell their products on the market. When the workers seize the factory, they are faced with the dilemma of having to produce the same commodities for sale on the market: that is the only way that they can ensure their own physical survival. It may be possible to introduce different working relations within the factory or workplace, to do away with hierarchies or introduce the rotation of tasks; it may be possible to use the workplace after working hours for political meetings or cultural activities, but all such changes (significant though they undoubtedly are) take place within the context of the pressures generated by the need to sell the products as commodities on the market. It may perhaps be possible to change the nature of the commodities produced, to produce things that are more obviously socially beneficial, but this will depend on the skills of the workers and the equipment at their disposal, and any alternative products will, in any case, normally require to be sold as commodities on the market.

The action of value may be very subtle and gradual. Fighting it is much more difficult than throwing stones at the police. Many radical groups have seen producing cooperatively for the market as an alternative to working for a capitalist company, or accepting funds from the state. It is an alternative, but at what point does the market impose itself to create the same sort of pressures as exist in any capitalist enterprise? Is there any escape?

It is not just the market in general, but also the labour market in particular that seems to have us firmly entrapped. Similar pressures face any individuals or groups who say no to capitalist employment and decide to dedicate themselves to an activity which they consider meaningful. If we do not sell our labour power, how do we survive? In some countries, it may be possible to do so by taking advantage of state systems of social assistance, but this is not the case in most countries and means, in the best of cases, acceptance of a life of poverty and surveillance. Many of the inhabitants of the more visible cracks, at least in the cities, survive on some combination of casual employment, state benefits and parental subsidies, but all of these undoubtedly impose limits on our capacity to develop our power to do things differently.

There are ways in which some of these problems can be dealt with. The most obvious is to look for funding of some sort, either from the state or some sort of non-state foundation. Many radical groups in Latin America receive some support from foundations connected with the Catholic or other churches, for example. It is clear that any such support carries risks, in the sense that it will probably, directly or indirectly, impose limitations on the activities of the recipient groups, or create certain social relations within the groups (between those with the skills necessary for fund-raising and others, for example).[35] A more traditional, perhaps superficially more radical, way of financing anti-capitalist activities is through bank robberies and kidnapping, yet, although such money generally comes free of conditions, the actual fund-raising itself will probably create patterns of behaviour and organisation that tend to reproduce the capitalism that we are fighting against. The point is surely that there is no purity here. In order to create a different world, we need to survive physically and, unless we cultivate our own food from the land (a real possibility in the case of peasant revolutionary groups, but difficult in the cities), this requires some sort of access to money, and money, whether it comes from external funding or crime or some sort of employment, always brings limitations and contradictions with it. The challenge is always to see to what extent we can use money without being used by it, without allowing our activities and our relations to be determined by it.

Funding can perhaps be seen as a particular way of building structures of mutual support. A more direct way of doing this is to construct links of mutual assistance between the different cracks. The Italian ¡Ya basta! group organise financial and practical support to install an electric generator in a Zapatista community. The workers in Zanón, the largest of the recovered factories in Argentina, buy their materials from mapuche cooperatives in Chile and in this way give their support to the mapuche movement.[36] The interconnections between rebellions in the world take the form of informal and constantly changing networks,[37] often providing important practical support.

These sorts of links are often contradictory. If the support flows in one direction, it may result in a loss of self-determination for the group supported, although it is not necessarily so. More generally, solidarity can mean dilution. If it is understood as support for the struggle of others, it is likely to contain the struggle within certain limits. It is only if the struggle is understood as *our* struggle that there can be a real joining of cracks.[38]

This building of links of mutual support between the different cracks in capitalist domination is sometimes seen in terms of the construction of an alternative economy or an economy of solidarity (*economía solidaria*). This refers to the construction of an economy that is not dominated by value or the pursuit of profit. This is an important development, but there are problems. First, the notion of an alternative *economy* already seems to impose a definition on the organisation of activities. If I say 'No, I will not follow the logic of capital, I shall do something else', then I do not consider my other-doing to be economic, but rather an escape from the economic. In addition, the notion of an alternative economy or economy of solidarity can easily obscure the fact that our other-doing is an act of rebellion, an against-and-beyond. If this against-ness is overlooked, the alternative economy can become simply a complement to capitalist production. If this is the case, then far from constituting a break in capitalist social relations, it helps to underpin them.[39] Certainly, at the end of the day what we want is a social connection based on trust, solidarity, generosity, gift, in place of the social synthesis of value, but for the moment this can only exist as an assault on value, not as a complement to value production.

Value is the enemy, but it is an invisible enemy, the invisible hand that holds capitalism together and tears the world apart. Value creates a powerful and complex field of tension around all our attempted breaks with capitalism, in which it is difficult to draw clear lines between what is 'revolutionary' and what is 'reformist'. Beyond the state, beyond our personal contradictions, it is value, the power of the market, of the cheap commodity, of money, that threatens all the time to overwhelm our cracks.

10

Cracks exist on the edge of impossibility, but they do exist. Moving they exist: dignity is a fleet-footed dance.

On the one hand, the drive to break the logic of capital: the push to create moments or spaces of refusal-and-creation, dignities. On the other hand, the enormous cohesive force of capital: the great sucking that pulls us back into conformity, that reabsorbs our efforts to break away, that tells us over and over again 'Run if you like, this is a free society, but there is no escape, there is no escape, there is no escape.'

A real and constant clash. We fling ourselves over and over again against the advancing walls, and we get hurt. We scream until the ice cracks, and then watch as it freezes over again. Our cracks exist, but they exist on the edge of impossibility. Disillusion and disappointment are never far away: they are written into the attempt to create another world.[1] That should not surprise us, for objectively that is where we are: always pushing at the limits, always trying to do the impossible, always trying to break the logic of the system, always half afraid that perhaps they are right, perhaps we are crazy. We spend years building an alternative space, then realise that it is not so alternative, that the other social relations we are building are not so other, after all. We throw all our energies into breaking the logic of capital, then look around three years later and ask 'where is the break?' This walking on the edge of disillusionment is what dignity means in a society based on its negation.

The logic of capital, that great destructive force of social synthesis, tells us that there is no room for dignity in a society based on the negation of dignity. Everything must fit together, and that is the glory of money: it is such a flexible form of fitting things together that all sorts of activities can be bent to its dominion.

And yet it is not so. The world is full of misfittings, of people who say 'we do not fit in, and we shall not fit in.' We have seen the enormous cohesive force of capital: how, through the state, through our own practices, above all through money, it draws us back in to its logic, finds a way of slotting our rebellions into the implacable jigsaw of the system. And yet, there they are, everywhere, these pieces that simply do not fit in. Over and over again, logic tells us that our rebellions are useless, that we must submit, and yet there they are, all over the place, these insanities that push towards a different world, these dignities that will not wait until after the revolution.

And there they are, and so it is, and so it must be. So it must be, because there is not only a logic of capital but an anti-logic of humanity, of refusal, of movement in-against-and-beyond capital. Rebellion is inseparable from obedience, misfitting from fitting.

We start from the momentum of rage and hope and creativity. We try to break the constraints of the society that oppresses us, to overflow the domination that suffocates us, to create something else. It is not a question of purity, for any crack will reproduce the cracked within it. It is a question of movement, of direction. *Movement is what matters. The possibility of the cracks is in their moving.*

Think of occupied factories or cooperatives, for example. In isolation, the taking of a factory into workers' control is of limited significance: all the pressures of the market will tend to impose constraints that limit the extent to which the workers can radically alter the nature of their activity within the factory or enterprise. It is as part of a movement of struggle that the occupation of the factory becomes important, because then it becomes possible to open up new forms of relations with the users of the products, so that work is not just for an anonymous market but oriented towards the satisfaction of certain social needs. The workers' occupation of the factory does not create a stable non-capitalist space, but it may be a significant part of a movement against capital and against the imposition of capitalist discipline. The important thing is to understand this present intensity, the factory occupation, as a moving and open present, not as a closed, isolated instant. Workers take control of the factory: that is important, irrespective of what happens later, but if a whole series of factory occupations take place, then the experience acquires a new dimension. We light a match: that gives light and heat, but if a spark flies and a whole forest catches fire, then the flame acquires a different meaning. I refuse to go to work and instead sit in a park reading a book: this is a pleasure that requires no justification; but if everyone else decides to do the same thing, then capitalism will collapse.

The validity of a rupture does not depend on the future, but being part of a movement can transform its significance. We throw a stone at the sheet of ice that covers the lake of possibility. The stone makes a hole in the ice, but the ice is thick, the day is cold and soon it freezes over again. We are left with the inspiring memory of something beautiful, we have caught a glimpse of a possible future. We throw another stone, and this time not only do we make a hole, but cracks shoot out in different directions, some of them connecting up with the cracks that radiate outwards from the hole made by a stone thrown by someone else. If the ice is to be broken completely, then that is the only way it can happen: by lots of people throwing stones and by the shooting out of cracks that sometimes connect.

Revolt generates shock waves, expanding waves of antagonism. The cracks that result are never straight, and their movement is rarely predictable. They run along more or less invisible fault lines, weaknesses in the structure of the ice. There is something about the way that society is organised that means that there are certain lines of weakness or particular fragility. The subjection of our daily activity to the rule of money (capital), means that there is a frustration that runs through our daily lives, an antagonism that takes many different forms and exists as a multiplicity of interconnected fault lines. This is the network of fault lines that we want to touch, the cracks and potential cracks that we want to open.

Look at a crack in the wall. At one end it is clearly visible, at the other end it is so fine, so tiny that we have to strain our eyes to see where it ends. But the crack extends and widens along that fine line that we can barely see. If we focus just on the end that is clearly visible, then we understand nothing about the potential of the crack, about how it can extend. There is a line of continuity between the obvious and the barely visible.

The lines of continuity are the lines of potential movement and possible confluence. The obvious end of the crack is the Zapatista uprising or the great counter-summit demonstrations. The fine end is the woman who sits at her kitchen table reading with enthusiasm of the latest anti-imperialist demonstrations or the girl who, instead of going to work, sits in the park reading a book, simply for the pleasure it gives her. Do these fine fissures have the potential to widen into big cracks? We do not know, cannot know in advance. The woman reading at her kitchen table may go out and join the next demonstration, or she may not. The girl reading her book in the park may conclude that there is something fundamentally wrong with a society that does not have pleasure as its principle, or she may not. But these are the lines of continuity upon which the future of the world depends. This is where the war is fought. Capital is a constant process of blocking these continuities, of dividing people into blocks, of telling the woman at the kitchen table that her frustration has nothing to do with the anger of the demonstrators against the G8 – and in this process, the left, with its definitions and classifications, often plays an active part.

But is there a problem here? Do we not also have to establish distinctions, lines of division? The book started with the anguished cry of 'what can we do, what can we do to change the world?' Is the answer 'go and sit in the park', or 'join the local choir', or 'go for a hike in the mountains'? No. The answer is rather 'Revolt in whatever way we can', but what matters most is not just the cry of revolutionary hatred for capitalism but the ways in which we try to develop in our everyday practice activities that misfit with the cohesive suction of capitalist activity.

But how do we know if our activity is a misfit or if it simply complements the development of capitalism? The difficult thing is that we do not know. We analyse it and think about it, but we cannot know for sure. Moreover, our evaluation of what breaks and what complements capitalism is shifting all the time. In the last century, thousands, perhaps millions, of people gave their lives to the struggle to break the logic of capital and create a different society. And now we look at the results – the Soviet Union, the People's Republic of China and so on – and suspect that their lives of struggle did more to strengthen capitalism than to harm it. Sometimes it seems that capitalism is infinitely flexible, infinitely absorbent and that any revolt will just be reabsorbed. Look at 1968, they say: all that rage, all that creativity, simply laid the basis for a new style of capitalism.[2] Look at all those autonomous groups that start off as rebellions against capitalism and, with the aid of a few gentle subsidies and a bit of professional advice and training, end up as non-governmental organisations, key elements in the governance of neo-liberalism.[3] Look at all those revolts against the rigid time-keeping of the working day which capital has simply absorbed by making flexible the working day and extending it to the whole of people's lives. Do not be so naïve, they say, there is no escape.

And yet it is not so. It is not so first because the validity and necessity of our revolt does not depend on its future. The event we know as 1968 released a joy and creativity that needed no justification in terms of its end results. And secondly, it is not so because it is not true that capitalism is infinitely flexible: it is a particular way of organising our social interrelations and our activity, and many of the examples that we have already seen suggest that it is becoming more rigid, less tolerant, less capable of absorbing revolt. Misfitting is becoming a more and more central part of everyday existence. And although it is difficult to say with certainty of any particular action that it breaks with capital, we do have a clear picture of that which we reject, of the actions and forms of behaviour that clearly contribute to the reproduction of capital – the treatment of people as a means to the end of making profit, the treatment of people as objects rather than subjects, as means to an end rather than as ends in themselves. Our dignities are always moving-againsts, exploring-beyonds, in which we risk our lives to break with that which we reject with certainty and create something that we aspire to with uncertainty. The uncertainty of our creation is no ground for giving up, for it is founded in the certainty of our rejection.

And third, it is not so because, even if capital can absorb most things with time, that does not matter, because by then we have already moved on. We lead the dance, and capital follows. Dignity is a fleet-footed dance. And the more fleet-footed it is, the harder it is for capital to follow. Identity is the constant identification of non-identity, but non-identity always remains one step ahead. Dignity is a leaping, gliding, swinging, dancing, never a marching: and that, for capital, is hard to follow and absorb.

We do not need hard lines, then, because hard lines and clear divisions hinder the dance of dignity. Certainly there is a difference between a great popular uprising and the girl sitting in the park reading her book. In the one case it is an open and public declaration of revolt, in the other it is a completely private, de-politicised moment of pleasure. But if we limit our gaze to that which is public and open, then we are doing just that: limiting our own vision, and with it the impact of our dignities. We are in fact reproducing the capitalist distinction between public and private, whereas our aim is to cut through that distinction. Perhaps we do want the girl in the park to rise up and fight with others for a world in which we can all spend much more time in the park reading our books or doing whatever we want, but unless we can recognise and respect the present potential of that struggle in the girl's reading of her book, then we are in effect closing our eyes to the potential movement of the crack. We are closing off the potential spread of our crack, enclosing ourselves within a ghetto.

This is the danger of militancy or activism. The great public displays of revolt or dignity (Gleneagles, Heiligendamm, and so on) are of course the outcome of dedicated militancy or activism, the result of the activity of a lot of people who devote much of their lives to organising anti-capitalist action. Most of them are not professional revolutionaries in the old style, but people who make the organisation of struggles against capital a high priority in their lives. Without such dedication, many of these great protests would not take place.[4] The danger, however, is that a self-referential world of militancy or activism can be created. This may take an obvious institutionalised form in the creation of a party or some other permanent organisation, but, even where this type of institutionalisation is rejected, the danger remains. The focus on the great public displays of dignity can easily lead to a lack of sensitivity or even a complete lack of respect for the less visible displays of revolt. If that happens, we are in a situation of vanguardism, however strong the anti-vanguardist commitment of the militants may be.[5] The world becomes divided into the world of those who fight for change on the one hand, and the great mass of people who must be convinced, on the other. The argument here is not an argument against the importance of what activists do. It is certainly not an argument against activists, but it is, crucially, an argument for 'breaking down the division between "activist" and "non-activist"' (Trott 2007: 231).[6]

The relation between the visible and the invisible (or barely visible) revolts can be thought of in two ways. In the first, it is only the visible, public revolts that are to be taken seriously. Beyond that there is a barrier or gap, outside which remain the vast majority of people. These people are to be reached by teaching, by explaining, by talking. The central issue is consciousness and the lack of it. The other way is to think that there is not a gap or barrier but lines of continuity that run from the great insubordinations to the tiny, apparently insignificant insubordinations. The central issue is not consciousness but sensitivity: the ability to recognise insubordinations that are not obvious and the capacity to touch those insubordinations. Consciousness or understanding certainly plays a role, but it cannot be a question of bringing consciousness from outside but of drawing out that which is already present in undeveloped form, of bringing different experiences into resonance with one another. This takes us to a politics not of talking but of listening, or of listening-and-talking, a politics of dialogue rather than monologue.

A politics of listening sits uneasily with any form of institutionalisation, whether as a party or not. Institutions tend to have rules or practices which define expectations and tune in to certain voices, but not others. Institutions are not very good at listening even when they try to do it. Lines of antagonism (class struggle, if you will) move faster than any institution and any attempt to institutionalise them or tie them down is likely to constitute an impediment and a deafness to such movement. There is an important distinction to be made between institutionalisation, which projects the present on to the future and imposes definitions and limits, and organisation, which has as its core the open and effective coordination of doing.[7] Certainly we need forms of organisation, but it is important that the organisational forms should be as open and receptive as possible. The

77

confluence of our dignities is important, but perhaps it should be thought of as a confluence of resonance, of trying to play in the same key: jazz musicians who come together for the fun of it without a leader, learn to join in the same tune, each with her particular style of developing themes and variations, moving together in a discordant harmony.

It might be thought that any attempt to listen to, or touch the experience of, the tiny fissures (the girl reading her book in the park, say) means a loss of radicalness, a conversion of the revolution into something soft and wishy-washy.[8] That is not so at all. The tiny, subterranean revolts may be far more radical in their potential than the noisiest demonstration. What the girl reading her book in the park is saying silently is 'Live for pleasure, not for pain', a slogan far more radical than the slogans of the huge anti-US demonstration taking place at the same time. The issue is not one of degrees of radicalness but of touching nerves, of channelling angers and dreams, of finding resonances.

Our dignities are dignities in movement, cracks that spread.[9] But the spreading is not a question of increasing membership or enrolling more adherents. Nor is it primarily a matter of preaching or talking, though that may play a role. It is probably more helpful to think of contagion, emulation and resonance. The social centre movement has spread basically in this way: not through the members of one social centre going to another town and convincing the people there to set up a social centre, but through the latter hearing of or seeing the first social centre, being impressed and deciding to set up something similar in their own town.[10] In this process of contagion, the speaker on the rostrum is being supplemented by, or replaced by, street theatre. If the central issue is not so much to convince or explain, but to touch discontents that are already there, then art, theatre and music play an especially important part. That is surely why the aesthetic element of the manifestations of revolt has come to play such an important part in recent years.[11] Theatre, poetry and humour have been a key element in the impact of the Zapatistas and other movements, not as instruments of the movement but as a central element of the movement itself.

The cracks in capitalist domination exist. Logically, perhaps, they do not and can not exist. But they do. They do exist and they often possess an extraordinary energy and creativity, taking us into new dimensions of understanding and perception.[12] Cracks in the pavement: we are the weeds pushing through. In a cold world, we are the sun shining on the ice, creating cracks that can move with terrifying and unpredictable speed. Or not.

The old revolutionary certainties have gone. We can no longer proclaim with confidence that our victory is inevitable. We accept that we live in a world of uncertainty and confusion, but can we find a way of understanding our uncertainty and confusion? There is no certainty in history, but is there some way in which we can understand the multiplication of cracks, or even the fact that we are here talking about cracks, as part of a powerful historical or anti-historical undercurrent? Can we understand the cracks not just as an endless series of attacks on the social synthesis of capitalism but as the crisis of that synthesis?

Part IV
The Dual Character of Labour

11

The cracks are the revolt of one form of doing against another: the revolt of doing against labour.

The focus on cracks carries us back and forth, from elation to despair, from despair to hope and determination, and back again. The breaks clash with the social synthesis and they are absorbed or repressed. We rage against the machine, but we want more than that: we want to break it and we want to create something else.

The tradition of orthodox Marxism tells us that the only way forward is to break the system as a whole, to take state power, dismantle capitalism and construct socialism. But that does not work, has not worked. Our only option is to fight from the particular, but then we clash against the force of the whole. It would be lovely just to forget about the force of the whole, but it is there, a real, crushing force of social synthesis.

We go back and forth between despair and hope. Ping, pong. Are we crazy to rebel or is there some real force in our drive against capitalism? Are we tragic Don Quixotes out of touch with historical reality, or are we the first swallows of a new summer? 'Before a time breaks up and moves on', wrote Ludwig Börne in the early nineteenth century, 'it sends capable and trusted people ahead of it, to suss out the new terrain. If these heralds were allowed to go their way, people would soon learn where time is heading. But that is not done, these precursors are called troublemakers, seducers and fanatics and held back with force.'[1] But how do we would-be heralds of a new age know that we are not crazy troublemakers? Maybe *they* are right. Maybe books like this are sheer nonsense or, worse than that, actually harmful.

This is a practical and urgent dilemma. The cracks exist. Many, many people are devoting their lives to breaking the rules, to trying to live in a way that does not fit in to the patterns of capitalist social relations. What do we say to them? Do we warn them that they will not go very far because sooner or later the system will prevail, and that the only way forward is to conform or to fight for the overthrow of the capitalist system as a whole? Or do we say to keep on pushing, to make the cracks as big as possible, because the cracks are the crisis of the system, the only way that the system can be overthrown? A frightening question, because people are playing their lives on the answer. Banging one's head against reality can be painful.

To try and find a way forward, we go back to that which we have already emphasised as being the core of the crack: '*a crack is the perfectly ordinary creation of a space or moment in which we assert a different type of doing.*'[2] We start from two antagonistic types of doing: that which we reject and that which we try to create. The cracks are revolts of one type of doing against another type of doing.

'We shall not do what capital requires, we shall do what we consider necessary or desirable.' That is the essence of a crack in capitalist domination. 'We shall not do *a*, we shall do *b*.' But no: this formalisation is completely wrong. The first option (*a*, what capital requires) is fundamentally different from the second option (*b*, what we consider necessary or desirable). 'Do' in the first case (do what capital requires) is absolutely different from 'do' in the second case (do what we consider necessary or desirable). To *do* something over which we have no control is a completely different experience from *doing* something that we choose to *do*.

We really need two different words for the two forms of doing. In English, we have the word 'labour' to indicate a doing that is unpleasant or subject to external compulsion or determination.[3] To find an adequate word for activity that is self-determined or at least pushes towards self-determination is more difficult, so we shall retain 'doing' as a general term to indicate an activity that is not necessarily subject to alien determination, an activity that is potentially self-determining.[4]

The essence of our crack can be rephrased: 'We shall not *labour* under the command of capital, we shall *do* what we consider necessary or desirable.' The crack is the revolt of doing against labour.

The revolt of doing against labour is the revolt of one form of activity, which we choose, against another form of activity, which we reject. We reject labour because it is unpleasant to do something as the result of external obligation, and also because we can see that it is labour that creates capital, that creates a world of injustice that is destroying humanity. The doing we choose is more agreeable by virtue of the fact that we choose it, and it is also an attempt to stop creating capitalism and create a different world.

The story of the cracks is the story of a doing that does not fit into a world dominated by labour. The cracks are mis-fittings, mis-doings. To say that cracks are quite ordinary rebellions is to say that the misfit is not someone or something that belongs to the margins of society, but is at its very centre. To mis-fit is a central part of everyday experience. We start from there because it is this failure or refusal to fit in to an oppressive society that is the basis for hoping that we can change it. If we look through the eyes of domination or start from the analysis of capital, these misfittings simply do not exist. To put cracks at the centre gives us a different vantage point: we start from that which does not fit in, that which overflows, that which is not contained, that which exists not only in but also against-and-beyond. We start not from the stillness of identity but from the moving of non- or, better, anti-identity. We start dialectically, but not with a dialectic understood as interaction but rather as the negative restlessness of misfitting, of insufficiency.[5]

The pivot, the central fulcrum, in all of this is our doing: human creation. One form of doing, labour, creates capital, the basis of the society that is destroying us. Another form of doing, what we call simply 'doing', pushes against the creation of capital and towards the creation of a different society. In both cases, our doing is at the centre. By focusing on doing, we put our own power at the centre of our understanding of society: our power-to-do (and therefore, our power not to do, and our power to do differently). By focusing on doing, we also state clearly that the argument of this book is not for 'more democracy' but for a radical reorganisation of our daily activity, without which the call for 'more democracy' means nothing at all.[6]

The insoluble dilemma of our cracks, the back-and-forth between hope and despair, is not composed of external forces but has to do with the organisation of our own practice. We create the society that we want to get rid of. That is terrible, but it is also the source of hope. If we create capitalism, then we can also stop creating it and do something else instead. Hope lies in the dual, self-antagonistic character of human doing.

12
The abstraction of doing into labour
is the weaving of capitalism.

Here we turn to Marx. We must. This is not an apology, but an acknowledgement that some readers (if such there be) may be reluctant to look at Marx. The current wave of struggle against capitalist globalisation has paid relatively little attention to Marxist theory, and much of the writing within the Marxist tradition has become divorced from the movement of struggle. In the argument so far, I have insisted on the importance of starting out from particular struggles – the cracks in capitalist domination – rather than starting out from an analysis of capitalism as a whole, as most work in the Marxist tradition has done. This is not because I reject Marxism but, on the contrary, because I understand Marxism as critique, a solvent, an acid which dissolves the social rigidities that confront us, the apparently unmovable system that we keep on clashing against. In the present stage of the argument, that is exactly what we need, an acid to dissolve the hardness of the social synthesis that repeatedly puts us down. In what follows, I shall suggest that the key to the solvent power of Marxism is the dual nature of doing.

The 'two-fold nature of labour' (as he called it) was central to Marx's critique of capitalism. At the beginning of the second section of the first chapter of Volume I of *Capital*, he states quite clearly: 'This point [the two-fold nature of the labour contained in commodities] is the pivot on which a clear comprehension of Political Economy turns' (1867/1965: 41; 1867/1990: 132).[1] After the publication of the first volume, he wrote to Engels (Marx, 1867/1987: 407): 'The best points in my book are: 1) the two-fold character of labour, according to whether it is expressed as use value or exchange value. (*All* understanding of the facts depends upon *this*. It is emphasised immediately in the *first* chapter).'[2] Despite the force and prominence that Marx gave to this point, it has remained almost unmentioned in the Marxist tradition (so that to insist on its importance is inevitably to propose a re-reading of Marx).

Marx introduces the idea of the dual nature of labour in his youthful work, the *1844 Philosophical and Economic Manuscripts*. One of the most famous (and important) passages in his writings is the section there on Estranged Labour. In order to understand the 'intrinsic connection' (1844/1975b: 271) between the phenomena of capitalist society, Marx turns to labour as it exists in capitalist society, which he characterises as alienated or estranged labour: 'The object which labour produces – labour's product – confronts it as *something alien*, as a *power independent* of the producer' (ibid.: 274). This alienation is not just the end result of labour but inherent in the process of labour itself:

> But the estrangement is manifested not only in the result but in the *act of production*, within the *producing activity* itself. How could the worker come to face the product of his activity as a stranger, were it not that in the very act of production he was estranging himself from himself? ... If then the product of labour is alienation, production itself must be active alienation, the alienation of activity, the activity of alienation. (1844/1975b: 274)

Labour, as alienated labour, is a separating of ourselves from ourselves, a tearing asunder of ourselves and our activity.

It is through our alienated labour that we produce our master. Marx says of the worker who performs alienated labour:

> Just as he creates his own production as the loss of his reality, as his punishment; his own product as a loss, as a product not belonging to him; so he creates the domination of the person who does not produce over the production and over the product. Just as he estranges his own activity from himself, so he confers upon the stranger an activity which is not his own ... The relationship of the worker to labour creates the relation to it of the capitalist (or whatever one chooses to call the master of labour). (1844/1975b: 279)

The worker produces the master, not by just any form of activity, but by performing alienated or estranged labour.

Marx focuses on alienated labour, but the very concept implies a contrast with non-alienated labour (or, as we might say, non-alienated doing). Marx does not use the term 'non-alienated' labour or 'non-alienated' doing, but he does speak of alienation as the alienation of man's conscious life-activity:

Free, conscious activity is man's species-character ... Conscious life-activity distinguishes man immediately from animal life activity ... Admittedly animals also produce. They build themselves nests, dwellings, like the bees, beavers, ants, etc. But an animal only produces what it immediately needs for itself or its young. It produces one-sidedly, whilst man produces universally. It produces only under the dominion of immediate physical need, whilst man produces even when he is free from physical need and only truly produces in freedom therefrom ... It is just in his work upon the objective world, therefore, that man really proves himself to be a species-being. This production is his active species-life ... In tearing away from man the object of his production, therefore, estranged labour tears from him his species-life, his real objectivity as a member of the species, and transforms his advantage over animals into the disadvantage that his organic body, nature, is taken away from him. (1844/1975b: 276–7)

Marx does not dwell on conscious life-activity: it is the other side, the dark side of the moon, the inevitable reference point of the concept of alienated labour, but a reference point that has rather a shadowy existence, as the lost truth of humanity, as potential future, as present struggle. It is alienated labour that is in the foreground. Labour (alienated labour) is what we reject: it is an activity that we do not control, an activity that produces the master, that produces capital. (Alienated) labour is the enemy: we do not want to labour. But in the background there is another possibility (potential, dream?): to engage in free, conscious activity, conscious life-activity. There is not just a contrast but an antagonism here: between alienated labour and conscious life-activity.

Marx does not discuss the present status of conscious life-activity.[3] Alienated labour is clearly visible as the present reality of capitalist society, but what exactly is the status of conscious life-activity: is it potential future (life in communism) or present struggle? Certainly the doing-against-labour that is characteristic of our cracks *aspires to* become conscious life-activity: a life-activity that overcomes the distinction between labour and non-labour and pushes in the direction of conscious determination.

In *Capital*, Marx no longer speaks of alienated labour and conscious life-activity, but, as we have seen, he does place the 'two-fold nature of labour' at the very centre of his critique of political economy. The 'two-fold nature of labour' refers to the distinction between useful or concrete labour and abstract labour.

Useful (or concrete) labour produces use-values, things that are useful. Useful labour is inseparable from its specific qualities:

The coat is a use-value that satisfies a particular want. Its existence is the result of a special sort of productive activity, the nature of which is determined by its aim, mode of operation, subject, means and result. The labour whose utility is thus represented by the value in use of its product, or which manifests itself by making its product a use-value, we call useful labour. (1867/1965: 41; 1867/1990: 132)

Useful labour is 'productive activity of a definite kind and exercised with a definite aim' (1867/1965: 42; 1867/1990: 133). This type of labour 'is a necessary condition, independent of all forms of society, for the existence of the human race; it is an eternal nature-imposed necessity, without which there can be no material exchanges between man and Nature, and therefore no life' (1867/1965: 42–3; 1867/1990: 133). Later, when speaking of the labour process (the process of useful labour), Marx says, more accurately:

The labour-process … is human action with a view to the production of use-values, appropriation of natural substances to human requirements; it is the necessary condition for effecting exchange of matter between man and Nature, it is the everlasting Nature-imposed condition of human existence, and is therefore independent of every social phase of that existence, or rather, is common to every social phase. (1867/1965: 183–4; 1867/1990: 290)

This self-correction is very important. If useful or concrete labour were *independent* of every social phase, this would imply a transhistorical concept, the idea that useful labour is something that can be studied independently of its historical forms. If, on the other hand, useful or concrete labour is *common* to all social phases, this implies a *historical* concept, that is, the idea that useful labour changes in each historical epoch and can only be understood in its historical context. While some sort of useful labour or productive activity is necessary in any society, it takes different forms in different societies: it does not stand outside the different social phases.

In a capitalist society, products are not produced simply as use-values: they are produced as commodities, that is, they are produced for exchange. What interests the producer is not the utility (or use-value) of the product but its exchangeability or value. The tailor produces a coat not because he wants to wear it but because he wants to exchange it. The weaver produces linen not because he wants to use it but because he too wants to exchange it. In the process of exchange between coat and linen, two qualitatively different concrete, useful labours are brought into contact and a proportional measure established between them, so that 1 coat = 20 yards of linen (say). What is measured in the equation is not a qualitative relation between two different types of activity but a quantitative relation between two labours considered *in abstraction from* their specific qualities. From the point of view of the exchange, that is, from the point of view of value, the only thing that matters about labour is its quantity, not its quality or particular characteristics. The labour that produces value is not useful, concrete labour, but abstract labour, labour seen in abstraction from its concrete characteristics. The commodity can no

> ... longer be regarded as the product of the labour of the joiner, the mason, the spinner, or of any other definite kind of productive labour. Along with the useful qualities of the products themselves, we put out of sight both the useful character of the various kinds of labour embodied in them, and the concrete forms of that labour; there is nothing left but what is common to them all; all are reduced to one and the same sort of labour, human labour in the abstract ... The labour ... that forms the substance of

value is homogeneous labour, expenditure of one uniform labour-power. (1867/1965: 38–9; 1867/1990: 128–32)

This is 'an abstraction which is made every day in the social process of production' (1859/1971: 129).

Useful or concrete labour exists, then, in any society. In capitalist society (or more generally, commodity-producing society), it acquires a specific social form, the form of abstract labour.[4] Useful labour continues to exist, but in relation to other labours it counts only quantitatively, as a certain quantity of labour abstracted from its specific qualities. When commodities exchange, what matters is the quantitative relation between them (measured normally by the amount of money I get for the coat I have made). This quantitative relation is determined by the amount of labour required to produce the commodity concerned: not just the amount of time that I actually spent on it, but the amount of labour time socially necessary to produce the commodity. The quantity of the value of the commodity is determined by the socially necessary labour time required to produce it: socially necessary labour time establishes the *measure* by which the different labours are compared. The worker may work with love and care and true dedication to her craft, but if the article produced does not sell (or does not sell at a price that secures the survival of the worker), she will have to change her relation to her work and produce what will sell and at a rhythm and in a way that will secure her own reproduction. The imposition through the market of the socially necessary labour time required to produce a commodity is at the same time the abstraction of labour, the separating of the worker from her process of production. The process of exchange (the operation of the market) imposes an abstraction which rebounds upon the way in which the concrete labour is performed.

I bake a cake. I enjoy baking it, I enjoy eating it, I enjoy sharing it with my friends and am proud of the cake I have made. Then I decide that I will try to make a living by baking cakes. I bake cakes and sell them on the market. Gradually, the cake becomes a means to gaining an income sufficient to allow me to live. I have to produce the cake at a certain speed and in a certain way so that I can keep the price low enough to sell it. Enjoyment is no longer part of the process. After a while, I realise that I am not earning enough money and think that, since the cake-making is in any case merely a means to an end, a way of earning money, I might as well make something else that will sell better. My doing has become completely indifferent to its content, there has been a complete abstraction from its concrete characteristics. The object I produce is now so completely alienated from me that I do not care whether it is a cake or a rat poison, as long as it sells.

This example can be discussed in terms either of alienation or abstraction. My doing (baking) is alienated or abstracted, and this alienation or abstraction converts it into labour: doing is alienated or abstracted into labour. Essentially, then, the abstraction of labour discussed in *Capital* is the alienation of labour discussed in the *1844 Manuscripts*.[5] All the characteristics of alienated labour – the fact that 'the worker is related to the product of his labour as to an alien object' (1844/1975: 272), the 'relation of the worker to his own activity as an alien activity not belonging to him' (ibid.: 275), the estrangement of the worker from his own species-being (that which makes him human), his estrangement from the other workers, and so on – all of these recur in Marx's critique of abstract labour in *Capital*. The argument of *Capital* rests on the same distinction between humans and animals which is so central to the *1844 Manuscripts*. It is purposive doing that distinguishes us from animals: 'a bee puts to shame many an architect in the construction of her cells. But what distinguishes the worst architect from the best of bees is that the architect raises his structure in imagination before he erects it in reality' (1867/1965: 178; 1867/1990: 284). Capitalism robs us of the unity of project and performance, purpose and doing: it robs us, therefore, of our distinctive humanity.[6]

And yet there is an importance in the shift from alienated to abstract labour. The notion of abstract labour confronts us more directly with the question that is central for us: the relation between the quality of what we do and its integration into the social context. Alienation tends to focus our attention on the experience itself, whereas abstraction draws our attention also to the social character of the labour: it takes us to the question of social cohesion.

The quality of our doing is intimately related to its social character. Abstraction is not external to the activity itself. The way in which our particular activity is brought into relation with other activities rebounds upon our activity, shaping it to its core. We have seen this in the example of the cake: here, there is a gradual process of abstraction, a gradual transformation of the pleasurable activity of baking into a labour totally indifferent to its content, an activity shaped by the pursuit of money. This is not a moral issue but a question of value and socially necessary labour time. In order to sell my cake, I must be able to produce it as fast and efficiently as other cake-makers: if I do not, I will be forced (by my own necessity to survive) to charge more than other bakers for cakes of the same quality, and my potential clients will buy their cakes elsewhere. The fact that I am producing for the market forces me to produce in a certain way. The abstraction is an abstraction of the activity itself, a process by which I become indifferent to the content of my own activity. The abstraction is not just an exchange-abstraction but a real abstraction. The relation between the abstraction implicit in exchange and the transformation of the activity itself into abstract labour is not a completely automatic process (think of cooperatives, for example, that struggle to transform their labour processes even while producing for the market), but it certainly exists as a strong tendency or pressure.

I make some cakes, sell them and with the money I buy a coat. My activity as a cake-baker and the activity of the tailor who makes the coat are brought together, but they are brought together through a process of abstraction, through the negation of the particular characteristics of baking and tailoring. This is an abstraction mediated through money, which is totally blind to the niceties of baking and tailoring. And so on, and on, and on. We are talking here not just of the relation between the baker and the tailor, but of the way in which the activities of all people are brought into relation with one another, and therefore the way in which those activities themselves are shaped. What makes it so difficult to punch a hole in capitalism is the way in which our activities (our lives) are woven together. This weaving is achieved not through the state (as appears to be the case) but through the abstraction of labour (the state is no more than a sort of protective coating that gives extra cement to the weave of abstraction). This is the way in which the totality of social relations is formed: the social synthesis is formed through the abstraction of doing into labour.

Abstraction is the peculiarly capitalist weaving of social relations, the peculiarly capitalist weaving of the particular into the totality. It is a process that nobody controls. It is the fact that nobody controls it that makes it absolutely essential to break it: not only is it the negation of human self-determination, but it is also clear that its dynamic is leading us towards human self-annihilation. At the same time, it is the fact that nobody controls it that makes it so difficult to break, for it confronts us as a seamless web. This totality of social relations woven by the performance of abstract labour is the social synthesis that constantly confronts our cracks, the synthesis that constantly pulls us back into conformity in practice, back into the reproduction of the system that we want to break.

And yet, it is our doing, our creativity that is at the centre. It is abstract labour that constitutes the totality of social relations. We could say that it is exchange that binds all our activities together, or value, or money, and all of these formulations would be correct. And yet Marx is right in insisting that it is the dual character of labour that is the 'pivot' of understanding. It is the pivot quite simply because *we* are the pivot. Our activity is the 'intrinsic connection' (Marx 1844/1975: 271) between the phenomena of capitalist society. It is by our activity that we humans create the society we live in, so it is important to understand the society and its potential in terms of our creative activity and its organisation, and not just in terms of the social relations we have created (value, money, capital, and so on): to go beyond value theory to a theory of that which creates value – abstract labour. This is what Marx calls critique *ad hominem* – a critique that brings all phenomena back to the human subject, to the way in which human activity is organised. If we make it, we can break it.[7]

Going to the root of things and understanding that root as our own activity is crucial. Think back to the previous discussion of the force of value and the way in which it imposes the social synthesis upon us (thesis 9, 4). That section was very depressing to write and should be depressing to read because we feel that there is no way out. It is when we open up value and ask what it is that produces value and see that it is our own activity, our abstract labour, then the skies begin to open, we begin to see a way forward, simply because it is not a thing (value), but our own activity that is at the centre. There is a world of difference, then, between an analysis that takes value as its pivot and one (such as this) that places the dual character of labour in its centre.

And yet. Analysing everything in terms of human action gives us a sense of our power to create a different world, but it does not (yet) free us. The abstract labour that we perform is real: it really creates a society that holds us entrapped, a social synthesis or totality of social relations that has such a cohesive force that it appears to run automatically, to operate according to the 'laws of capitalist development'. The abstract quality of capitalist labour means that the social interconnections are formed beyond any form of social control. The social synthesis or totality acquires an autonomy of its own and stands against us as an alien force: its uncontrolled and uncontrollable character expresses itself most visibly in the constant and frenetic movement of money, the medium through which the total social character of capital expresses itself. The existence of a social totality in this sense, as a cohesive law-bound force independent of any conscious human direction, is peculiar to capitalism.[8] We create this totality, we weave the web that holds us prisoner; to understand this helps us to see that we can stop weaving the web and do something else, but the totality retains its force: the web is still there.

Let us repeat the argument: we create the society that holds us entrapped. In capitalism, we do so because the way in which our activities are bound together, through exchange, imposes certain ways of behaving upon us that neither we nor anyone else controls. The way in which our activities are bound together gives us an illusion of freedom, but in fact our activities weave a web (what we have called a 'social cohesion' or a 'social synthesis') that is controlled by nobody, ruled by the necessity to produce things as efficiently as possible, in the socially necessary labour time. That is what Marx refers to when he speaks of abstract labour (which, it should be quite clear, has nothing to do with the concept of mental labour or immaterial labour).

But there is more to our activity than the creation of this social synthesis: we also act in ways that do not conform, that rebel, that misfit, that clash with the social synthesis. Our doing is not totally subsumed into abstract labour. At times, it seems that there is nothing more in life than the abstract labour of capitalism, but we know that it is not so, and all that we have discussed in relation to the cracks tells us that it is not so. Marx insists on the *two-fold* nature of labour, not just on abstract labour.[9]

The crucial question which we must explore in the rest of this book is the relationship between the two aspects of labour, between abstract labour and what we have called *doing*, for want of a better word. The young Marx refers to a contrast between alienated labour and conscious life-activity. This contrast can be understood in various ways: conscious life-activity can be understood as past (a lost paradise) or as future (communist activity). Neither of these interpretations is sufficient: the very concept of alienation would make no sense unless we had present experience of something that pointed beyond alienation. In other words, conscious life-activity must refer in some way to present experience. The contrast between alienated labour and conscious life-activity is a living antagonism. In relation to the present, however, the life-activity cannot be fully conscious, because we do not control our life-activity in capitalist society: it is rather an aspiration to conscious life-activity that clashes with the contrary movement, the alienation that deprives our activity of conscious determination. The antagonism expressed by the young Marx, so understood, can be seen as the clash between the push for self-determination and the social synthesis, which we have seen to be typical of the cracks.

In *Capital*, we take a step forward with the move from alienated to abstract labour. Here it becomes clear that abstract labour is the constitution of the social synthesis, that abstraction is simultaneously an alienation of our activity and the constitution of the social nexus, the weaving of capitalist society. The other side, however, is less forcefully formulated than the 'conscious life-activity' of the young Marx. He refers to

97

it now as 'useful or concrete labour'. This labour is 'common to every social phase of human existence', an 'everlasting Nature-imposed condition of human existence'. This confronts us immediately with a terminological problem, simply because we know that labour, as a distinct activity separate from other life-activities, is not characteristic of all societies. Labour, as a distinct activity, is in fact constituted by the abstraction typical of capitalism. If then, we want to maintain the notion of a human activity that is common to all forms of human existence, we must adopt a more general term, such as *doing*. The term 'useful' also comes up against similar problems, because the clear distinction between useful and non-useful activities is also characteristic of the instrumental reason typical of capitalism. It seems preferable, then, to think of Marx's two-fold nature of labour as consisting of a contrast between abstract labour and *concrete doing*. Concrete doing, then, is an activity that is common to all phases of human existence, but exists in different forms in different phases. In capitalist society, concrete doing exists in the form of abstract labour.

The central issue is not the terms we use, but the distinction between the two aspects of human activity and the relationship between them. The argument to be developed here is that the relation between the two aspects of labour (or doing) is one of non-identity, of misfitting, of living antagonism: there is a constant living antagonism between abstract labour and concrete doing. This point is central to the argument of this book and goes against the overwhelming weight of tradition, which, as we shall see later, regards this relation as unproblematic. The point rests, on the one hand, on the experience of the constant revolt of human activity against the constraints of abstract labour, the constant tension between our power-to-do and the way in which that power is moulded through the dominion of value (the rule of socially necessary labour time). On the other hand, it rests on an understanding of the dialectic relation between form and content, in Marx and in life. To say that something exists in the form of something else means that it exists in that form but is not contained in it without remainder: it overflows from the form, or exists in-against-and-beyond the form. To assume that concrete doing exists simply in the form of abstract labour is both to deny that dialectical relation and to close our eyes to the antagonism of everyday experience.

We can express this in other words by saying that the relation between concrete doing and abstract labour is ecstatic.[10] Concrete doing is the ecstasy of abstract labour: ecstasy as ek-stasis, standing outside abstract labour while existing within it, standing outside as actual and potential otherness. I am a teacher and produce labour powers for sale on the market, but at the same time I encourage my students to think critically about society. I am a nurse in a private hospital and produce profits for my employers, but at the same time I try to help my patients through some of the most difficult moments of their lives. I work on an assembly line in a car factory and every few seconds that I have free, my fingers are busy practising the chords that I'll be playing on my guitar tonight in the band. I work on a sewing machine making jeans, but my mind is somewhere else, building a new room for myself and my children. I am a student working hard to get good grades in my exams, but I want to find a way of turning my studies against capitalism and towards the creation of a better world. In all these cases, there is a standing outside capitalist labour, a projection against and beyond my entrapment within abstract labour. There is a concrete doing that exists in-against-and-beyond, that exists in ecstatic relation to abstract labour, that already pushes beyond abstract labour, both as project and as actual practice. This ecstatic relation is a matter of everyday experience, not the invention of left-wing intellectuals, not the privileged experience of dedicated militants. It is from this standing-out-beyond (this ek-stasis) that another world will be born, or it will not be born at all.[11] This ecstatic space is the space of dignity, the substance of the cracks.[12]

In what follows, we shall focus first on the meaning of abstract labour, that which weaves the social cohesion that holds us entrapped, before turning to the other side.

13

The abstraction of doing into labour is a historical process of transformation that created the social synthesis of capitalism: primitive accumulation.

Labour did not always exist. It is not in every society that a specific activity considered to be 'labour' is set aside from the general doing of people. Certainly, some sort of activity is required to provide food and the other basic requirements of life, but this is not necessarily an activity regarded as onerous or separated in time from other activities. Thus, Marshal Sahlins, in his *Stone Age Economics*, writes of 'that characteristic palaeolithic rhythm of a day or two on, a day or two off – the latter passed desultorily in camp. Although food collecting is the primary productive activity ... "the majority of the people's time (four to five days per week) is spent in other pursuits, such as resting in camp or visiting other camps (Lee 1969: 74)"' (Sahlins 2004: 23). He also quotes a nineteenth-century observer of the indigenous people of Australia: '"In all ordinary seasons ... they can obtain in two or three hours a sufficient supply of food for the day, but their usual custom is to roam indolently from spot to spot, lazily collecting it as they wander along (Grey 1841, vol. 2: 263)."' In such a society, there is clearly no separation between labour and leisure, which means that neither exists. In pre-capitalist societies, the activities required for social reproduction did not harden into something called *labour*, nor did they occupy the same amount of time. In fifteenth-century France, one out of every four days of the year was an official holiday of some sort, and Ehrenreich comments that 'despite the reputation of what are commonly called "the Middle Ages" as a time of misery and fear, the period from the thirteenth to the fifteenth century can be seen – at least in comparison to the puritanical times that followed – as one long outdoor party, punctured by bouts of hard labour' (2007: 92). The Krisis Gruppe argue:

> The working hours of a modern white-collar or factory 'employee' are longer than the annual or daily time spent on social reproduction by any pre-capitalist or non-capitalist civilisation inside or outside Europe. Such traditional production was not devoted to efficiency, but was characterised by a culture of leisure and relative 'slowness'. Apart from natural disasters, those societies were able to provide for the basic material needs of their members, in fact even better than has been the case for long periods of modern history or is the case in the horror slums of the present world crisis. (1999/2004: 24, s.9)[1]

In pre-capitalist societies, social relations are woven in a different way. People's activities are brought together socially on the basis of the quality of the specific concrete characteristics of the activities performed, not on the basis of abstracting from those specificities. If one thinks of a simple communal society, for example, there is a socialisation of activities. Tasks are distributed, people do things for the benefit of others, but the principle of sociality is the particular skills of the carpenter or the smith or the cook: 'In this case the social character of labour is evidently not effected by the labour of the individual assuming the abstract form of universal labour or his product assuming the form of a universal equivalent' (Marx, 1859/1971: 33–4). The same is true of a feudal society or a society based on slavery: the distribution of tasks is hierarchical but based on the particular qualities of the activity undertaken.

Labour and the abstract sociality of labour is not given by nature. It is the result of a historical process, involving the monetisation of social relations and the spread of the market that at times took place without open conflict,[2] but that was at its core a bloody and even genocidal process.[3] As Marx put it, capital came into the world 'dripping from head to foot, from every pore, with blood and dirt' (1867/1965: 760; 1867/1990: 926).

The process is described by Marx at the end of the first volume of *Capital*, in his analysis of primitive or original accumulation, where he talks of the origins of capitalism. The essence of the transition from feudalism to capitalism is a movement of separation. Through the process of enclosure of land, people are separated from the means of survival (of producing and consuming). They are torn from the old, feudal forms of socialisation, in which they produced for and depended on a very limited number of people, and forced into a new form of socialisation in which they depended directly or indirectly on the market for their survival. Often this process of separation of people from the land was accomplished with great brutality, although sometimes it was the result of serfs fleeing from the feudal community: serfs fled from the lords just as lords expelled the serfs – both fled from the old form of social relations. Either way, the result was the interstitial creation and expansion of a new form of socialisation in which people related to one another through the market, through the exchange of commodities.

This meant the transformation of people's activity, the abstraction of doing into labour. The separation of people from the land was simultaneously the separation of labour from other forms of doing, the learning of a new form of activity called 'labour'. This was not an easy matter: 'The imposition to waste the most of one's lifetime under abstract systemic orders was not always as internalised as today. Rather, it took several centuries of brute force and violence on a large scale to literally torture people into the unconditional service of the labour idol' (Krisis Gruppe 1999/2004: 21, s.9). The closing of the commons, the abolition of traditional rights of hunting, fishing and wood gathering, the series of laws against vagrancy, the poor law and the creation of the workhouses, the armed suppression of one revolt after another: these were the steps that created a society based on labour, this was the reality of the abstraction involved in the creation of abstract labour. The enclosure of land was also an enclosure of bodies in the factories, the creation of a prison of labour.

The imposition of labour often involved the elimination of whole populations. Néstor López (2006) mentions the example of the Yámana, the original inhabitants of Tierra del Fuego, who had lived there, fishing and hunting, for ten thousand years before the arrival of the Europeans. The Europeans killed the seals which had been the main staple of the Yámana diet and put sheep on the land, now defined as private property. Many of the

Yámana were killed simply because they stood in the way of this development, others were turned into labourers. That they were not very good at 'labour' is suggested, however, by this report:

> The Yámana are not capable of continuous, daily hard labour, much to the chagrin of European farmers and employers for whom they often work. Their work is more a matter of fits and starts, and in these occasional efforts they can develop considerable energy for a certain time. After that, however, they show a desire for an incalculably long rest period during which they lie about doing nothing, without showing great fatigue ... It is obvious that repeated irregularities of this kind make the European employer despair, but the Indian cannot help it. It is his natural disposition. (Gusinde 1961: 27, quoted in Sahlins 2004: 28)

By the second half of the twentieth century, the Yámana were completely extinct, a whole people wiped out by the violence of labour.

In general, the imposition of labour took the form of the imposition of wage labour. The serfs who were driven from the land found that the only way that they could survive was by selling things on the market, but very often the only thing they had to sell was their own capacity to perform labour. They integrated themselves into the market not by selling coats or linen but their own labour power, to those with sufficient money to buy it. They became the workers employed by the new capitalists. This put them under the direct command of their new employer: they were compelled to obey the orders of the capitalist. What liberal theory hails as the liberation of the serfs was a change in the nature of their servitude: from being serfs under the dominion of their lord, they became workers under the dominion of the capitalist. It is true that they could change from one capitalist to another, but it was (and is) difficult for most people to survive for long without selling their labour power. Historically, this meant the imposition – through centuries of capitalist struggle, the enactment of legislation regulating labour, the use of police violence, the support of religion and education, the use of ever more sophisticated management techniques – of a new discipline in the workplace, the creation of labour as a social habit. The former serfs learnt to labour.

Labour was imposed through the expansion of wage labour.[4] This is important because it makes clear that what is at issue is not just the shaping of people's activities but the whole structure of socialisation. When I sell my labour power to the capitalist, my labour power becomes a commodity. But this carries in its wake a radical commodification of all aspects of social relations. I no longer have the time (nor the means) to grow my own food or make my own clothes, so the only way I can acquire them is by buying them with money from someone who specialises in producing and selling food. It is when labour power becomes a commodity and capitalist production is born that there is a general commodification of social relations. Everything in society tends to be transformed into a commodity and the connection between the different processes of work is a purely quantitative connection, measured in money. The connection is established through abstracting from the particularities of each activity. The transformation of our doing into labour is at the centre of a new complex of socialisation.

The fact that labour was imposed through the wage relation is also extremely deceptive, in various ways. Most important for our argument, it has created the illusion within the anti-capitalist tradition that the problem with capitalism is the wage relation rather than labour itself. As the Krisis Gruppe put it, 'It was not labour that was regarded as a scandal, but its exploitation by capital' (1999/2004: 16, s.6). In the classic communist tradition, the revolutionary struggle came to be seen as the struggle for the abolition of the wage relation, but not as the struggle for the abolition of labour. Quite the contrary (as we shall see in more detail), the struggle came to be seen as the struggle *of* labour against capital, whereas our argument here is just the opposite: the creation of labour and the creation of capital are the same process,[5] and the struggle against capital is the struggle against that which produces it, the struggle against labour.

Labour creates capital and it creates capitalism, a world structured on labour. Labour is cruel and dehumanising, the very opposite of that conscious life-activity which is potentially the basis of our humanity, but it is more than that. Labour is a spider that weaves an intricate web of social relations. As we perform labour, we weave a complex prison for ourselves.

This is what makes it so difficult to simply walk away from capital, to *serve no more* and let the tyrant topple. The term 'abstract' reminds us of that. The labour that we perform in the factory, in the office, in the university, is not just drudgery: it is a web-weaving activity, a process of self-entrapment. But the term *abstract* labour also reminds us of something else: that it is just one face of the dual character of doing, and that the other face still awaits us in the shadows. In what follows, we shall look at the web of abstract labour before turning to the dark, to ourselves. In looking at the different faces of the domination of abstract labour, it is important to bear in mind that there is another side, one that is gathering strength.

Part V
Abstract Labour:
The Great Enclosure

14
Abstract labour encloses both our bodies and our minds.

The argument is simple. We make capitalism: we must stop making it and do something else. This means setting doing against abstract labour: this we must, can and already do.

The argument is simple and yet it has its complexities. Abstract labour weaves a complex world, and it is important to recognise the complexity of this weave in order to understand the underlying unity of apparently unrelated struggles against the world as it exists and to see what it is that we are trying to unravel and to weave differently. In this part of the book, we focus on the complexity of the weave, before turning to its unravelling.

Labour imprisons our bodies in an obvious way: it shuts them up in factories or offices or schools for a large part of our waking life, or binds them to computers or mobile phones. But, in a less obvious way, the abstraction involved in capitalist labour also creates an equally profound prison, a prison that encloses our minds – the way we think, the concepts we use. There is a tearing-apart at the core of our existence, the separation of ourselves from the determination of what we do, and this tearing-apart affects every aspect of our lives.

Marx spoke of this enclosure as fetishism, and made its critique the central theme of *Capital*. When we produce a commodity, we produce something for sale on the market. What we produce and the way in which we produce it (our cakes, for example) are determined by the market. The market is the negation of self-determination. When I sell my product on the market and buy someone else's product, I establish a relation between our two different creative activities, but I do not establish the relation directly. The relation is established through things, as a relation between things: 'the relations connecting the labour of one individual with that of the rest appear, not as direct social relations between individuals at work, but as what they really are, material relations between persons and social relations between things' (Marx 1867/1965: 73; 1867/1990: 166). When I buy a car, say, my relation with the people who made it is a relation between my money and the car, not a relation of love and gratitude between those who made the car and me who am able to enjoy the benefits of their careful activity. We begin to think of the whole world in terms of things, not in terms of relations between people.

It is not a mistake or a mere illusion when I see my relation with the workers who built my car in terms of things. The relation between my doing and their doing really exists in the form of a relation between things. Social relations really exist in the form of things. The car in this case is a social relation between the activity of the car workers and mine. The money I pay for the car is likewise a social relation between my doing and theirs. We are surrounded by things that seem to (and do) hem us in. To think of changing the world, we need to dissolve the thing-ness of these things, understand them as social relations, understand them as the forms of existence of our social subjectivity, our doing. This means criticising these things as *forms* of social relations, subjecting them to what Marx called a critique that brings everything back to human doing and its organisation.

The existence of the relations between human doers as things (reification) means that the world around us acquires a fixity, a permanence. Social relations acquire a rigidity. Whereas we are aware in our daily lives that our most intense relations with friends and lovers are constantly changing, at a more general level, once those relations are converted into things, once they are reified or fetishised, then they appear to be permanent. They acquire the character of just being there and it becomes difficult to even imagine a society without them. Money, or the state, or capital, for example: instead of being seen as social relations with other people which we have created (and which we create and re-create each day and can stop creating), money and the state appear to be unavoidable facts of life and we find it hard even to imagine a life without them. Or labour, to take another example, is seen as a timeless, trans-historical category, the inevitable accompaniment of our existence on this earth, rather than a historically specific form of acting and relating to others.[1] These apparently timeless things hold our minds in captivity, limit what we can think, just as surely as the factory or the office or simply the need to sell the products of our labour imprisons our bodies and limits what we can do each day.

Reification can be seen as a process of identification, of creating identities. The abstraction of doing into labour constrains what we do. We do, but our doing is channelled into strict lines, lines that prolong the present. We are converted from doers into beings. The world of things is a world that is. All aspects of life acquire an 'is-ness', an identity. Identity becomes the key category for conceptualising the world, the key category of bourgeois thought. Identity is the core of the prison that holds us tight, the key ingredient in the web of entrapment that we ourselves weave.

Doing is a flow, a flow of life, in which there are no clear dividing lines, in which the doing of one person flows into the doing of another and is inconceivable without the doing of others. Your reading of this book (if indeed you are reading it) would be impossible without the doing of the writer (me), but that would be impossible without a whole world of previous reading, writing, computer-making, electricity-generating, desk-making, language-teaching, and so on and on and on. The abstraction of labour converts a part of that doing into a separate action, breaks that flow of doing. By breaking the social flow of doing, it breaks too the social-doer, the We, into a multiplicity of individual subjects, a multiplicity of identities. The breaking of social cooperation into a system of commodity exchange produces the individuals that exchange those commodities: in order for exchange to take place

> ... it is only necessary for men, by a tacit understanding, to treat each other as private owners of those alienable objects, and by implication as independent individuals. But such a state of reciprocal independence has no existence in a primitive society based on property in common, whether such a society take the form of a patriarchal family, an ancient Indian community, or a Peruvian Inca State. (1867/1965: 87; 1867/1990: 182)

The very concept of the individual is product of the spread of commodity exchange and the growth of capitalist society. But capitalism does not just produce the individual: it breaks the We-Doer and breaks the flow of social doing. The flowing together of social doings becomes converted into a noun, Society, with its defined forms of social cohesion. And Society, then, is composed of a multitude of fragmented persons-that-are, identities, all limited and defined in their doing.

Identities give rise to identitarian thought, the form of thinking that starts from the unquestioned existence of identity and identities and constructs on the basis of being rather than doing. To start from identities means to create a positive basis for thought, whereas to understand those identities as historically specific forms of social relations immediately puts thought on a negative footing. To start from identities is to start from the idea that we are, or *they* are, women, workers, Irish, Mexicans, gays, Jews, capitalists, and to construct a world from there. To understand these different identities as forms of social relations, on the other hand, is to say that we are formed as women, Irish, gay, and so on, and this immediately leads us to look behind these identities, to ask what has constituted us as women, gay, workers and thereby to pose the inadequacy of these forms, the possibility of being more. To proclaim an identity without simultaneously proclaiming its inadequacy, to give ourselves an identity without simultaneously saying that we exist in-against-and-beyond that identity, is to strengthen the walls of the capitalist prison.

Identitarian thought acquires a particular solidity in structuralist thought, the understanding of the world in terms of structures which rest on the 'bearers' of these structures, people understood simply in terms of their roles, people understood as personifications of their social functions. This approach can be attractive in the sense of offering a complex portrayal of the structures of oppression, but it offers no way out, since the subject is reduced to a bearer of capitalist social relations. Structuralism is the ideology of Cassandra, the left intellectual who bemoans the world and its fate but assumes there is nothing to be done about it.

Identification or reification is an enormously destructive force in everyday struggle. We give our protests a name, a label, a limit. Our struggle is the struggle of women, of gays, of workers, of the unemployed, it is the struggle for indigenous rights, for uncontaminated food, for peace. It may be that we are at least vaguely aware that our struggles are part of a wider whole, perhaps even that they are the product of the way in which human doing is organised in the world, but, precisely because that form of organisation seems permanent ('it is easier to imagine the end of the world than the end of capitalism'), we enclose our struggles within limits, within an identity. And so we have a world full of protest, a world of people aware in some way that there is something fundamentally wrong with the way society is organised, and yet so many walls separating these struggles, so many dykes preventing them from flowing into each other. And all these walls are identifications, the grand framework identification of the capitalism-that-is-and-always-will-be, and the lesser identifications of 'we are gay, we are women, we are indigenous, we are Basque, we are Zapatistas, we are anarchists, we are communists'. And all these identities become so easily the basis for sectarianism, the perennial self-destruction of the left that makes life easy for the police. Far more effective than any system of secret police, identity is the reproduction of capital within anti-capitalist struggle.[2]

15
The abstraction of doing into labour is a process of personification, the creation of character masks, the formation of the working class.

The creation of labour is the creation of the labourer. It cannot be otherwise: labour cannot be performed if there is no labourer to perform it.

Think of the Yámana of Tierra del Fuego who, after any concentrated effort, would lie around for ages doing nothing. They could not perform labour because they were not labourers. Even an effort in the early nineteenth century to take a group to England, teach them to speak English and drink tea, dress them properly and generally civilise them, did not produce results, because they simply took off their clothes and reverted to their savage customs when they were taken back to their native land.[1]

The labourer, just like labour, is the product of centuries of struggle. The doers, the savages, are forced by starvation, by repression, by education, by discipline to adopt certain ways of behaving, to learn to labour.[2] They become labourers, people who labour for certain hours of the day, who obey the orders of their employers or otherwise accomplish what is required by the market. People were forced to adapt to fit the function thrust upon them by the new form of socialisation. Those who did not adapt (like the Yámana) became extinct.

This adaptation to the social function thrust upon us can be seen as personification.[3] We come to personify a social relation. Marx insists on seeing the capitalist and the worker as personifications of capital and labour: 'The capitalist functions only as *personified* capital, capital as a person, just as the worker is no more than *labour* personified. That labour is for him just effort and torment, whereas it belongs to the capitalist as a substance that creates and increases wealth' (1867/1990: 989–990). The capitalist may be a very nice person and kind to his children, but if he does not dedicate himself to the function of capital, to maximising his profits (ultimately maximising surplus value through the exploitation of labour), then he will go out of business and cease to be a capitalist. Similarly with the worker: if he does not labour and obey the orders of his employer, he will soon lose his job and cease to be a labourer. Whatever our personal inclinations, we are forced to adopt a role, a persona, to don a 'character mask'[4].

It is not just the worker and the capitalist who are forced to assume certain roles. The abstraction of labour, as we have seen, is a separation of activities from their context, the rupture of the social flow of doing, so that each activity acquires a particular identity, and each performer tends to assume the corresponding character mask: as teacher, student, bureaucrat, social worker, security guard, whatever.[5]

These roles have real force. They are not just a matter of personal choice but are imposed upon us by the structure of social relations. The teacher who does not measure the performance of her students will soon confront problems. Likewise the security guard who does not raise the alarm when something is stolen or the state official who does not participate in the process of exclusion inherent in the state. The compulsions arising from the structure of social relations are then often assumed by us as a personal choice: we want to be a successful capitalist, an efficient bureaucrat, and so on. We identify with our role, we assume it as an identity, we blend in to the mask that we have put on our face. What are you? I am a university professor, a student, a social worker.

These personifications limit us. In so far as I am a university teacher, I do certain things and not others. Our identity is limited and also classifiable. Within my limits as a university teacher, I fall within a certain class, the class of university teachers. The world of personification is an ordered world, a world that can be classified, a world in which people perform their social functions, a world that can be understood in functionalist terms. A world in which revolution has no place.

We have a problem, then. How can we think of changing the world radically in a world in which people are personifications of their social function? If we are entrapped in roles generated by capitalism, how can we think of breaking the pattern of social relations formed by those roles? This touches particularly the question of class and the revolutionary nature of the working class. If we think of the working class as people who fit into a certain classification (as wage earners, as producers of surplus value), then we treat them as being inherently limited, as personifications of the social position that they occupy, as bearers of certain social relations, capitalist social relations. How can workers, as personifications of labour, constitute a revolutionary class, a class that would overthrow labour?

There are three simple answers to this dilemma, but none of them is satisfactory. The first is a structuralist argument. The structuralist concept of the world sees society as the interaction of these character-masks, as the structural antagonism of these bearers of social relations. People are reduced to that which capitalism makes them. Or rather, from the structuralist perspective, there is no reduction here: people are that which capitalism makes them. We are the subjects created by capitalism. The working class is the changing face of abstract labour, the character generated by the changing forms of capitalist organisation. The only possibility of revolution lies then in a change in the structure as a whole which leads to a change in the significance of the social *personae*. Thus, a crisis of capitalism may lead to a change in the character of the working class that would lead to radical change. The working class would then be able to perform its historical function of overthrowing capitalism. The difficulty with this argument is that, as long as people are understood as being defined by their position in capitalism, it remains difficult to see how they can, through their own movement, break free of those definitions.

The second response, the classic Leninist argument,[6] is much more straightforward. It still sees the workers as being determined by their structural position: the working class is limited in its understanding and its consciousness, because it is effectively enclosed within the character mask of labour.

Therefore, the only way in which we can think of revolution is in terms of the intervention of an external force, a group who, for one reason or another, are not enclosed within the *personae* of capitalism. In other words, we need a revolutionary Party. It is a perfectly logical solution: if the workers are the personification of abstract labour, then the only possible way of thinking of them as a revolutionary force is under the leadership of a group who have not been subject to this personification.[7] The problem is, first, that it is not clear where these revolutionaries who have broken free from the constraints of abstract labour come from, and, secondly, that it is an inherently hierarchical conception of revolution in which the workers ('the masses') are understood as the object rather than the subject of the revolution. The historical experience of this type of revolution is not encouraging.

A third answer is simply to say that the working class is not (or is no longer) a revolutionary class. The personification inherent in abstract labour has reached the point where the worker has become a 'one-dimensional man', in Marcuse's graphic phase. The one-dimensional man is obviously incapable of revolution, so that the only way of thinking of an agent of radical social change is to look elsewhere, to the margins of society. This view is possibly more influential in recent anti-capitalist struggles than the Leninist position, but the problem is that it shares the same starting-point: the identification of the workers with their class persona. This can easily lead to the recrudescence of elitist, vanguardist positions even in groups strongly committed to an anti-vanguardist politics.[8] When the vast majority of the population are forced to sell our labour power in order to survive, any conception of revolution that excludes us on the basis of our being one-dimensionalised is highly problematic.

In all of these answers, it is assumed in different ways that there is an identity between people and the structural position that they occupy in society, that people really are subsumed within their character mask. The only other way forward would be to question the strength of personification, to try and prise the character mask away from the face of the wearers and see if there is something behind it, to see the wearer as existing not

117

only within, but also against-and-beyond the mask. The working class, then, can be considered revolutionary only to the extent that it exists not only in but also against-and-beyond itself as working class, only to the extent that it succeeds in throwing off its character mask, that it fights against its own existence as working class.

16
The abstraction of doing into labour is the creation of the male labourer and the dimorphisation of sexuality.

Labour is constituted by its separation or abstraction from life-activity. This separation is supported by a radical subordination of life-activity to the requirements of labour. Life-activity (having children, bringing them up, getting food and preparing it, and so on) continues to exist outside the *immediate* domination of value-production, but its subordination to labour is secured by its dependence on the labourer's wage (or the sale of other commodities produced).

The constitution of labour is the constitution of a new hierarchy between labour and other activities.[1] The creation of the labourer is at the same time the creation of a new hierarchy between him and those whose primary responsibility is the performance of those other activities of reproduction. In other words, primitive accumulation is the brutal and bloody creation of a new hierarchy between men and women.

This is not to say that patriarchy did not exist in pre-capitalist societies, but there did not exist the same separation of labour and other activities, nor the same dependence of the other activities upon the wage of labour. Thus, Federici says of the feudal village:

> Female serfs were less dependent on their male kin, less differenti-ated from them physically, socially, and psychologically, and were less subservient to men's needs than 'free women' were to be later in capitalist society ... In the feudal village no social separation existed between the production of goods and the reproduction of the work-force; all work contributed to the family's sustenance. Women worked in the fields, in addition to raising children, cooking, washing, spinning, and keeping an herb garden; their domestic activities were not devalued and did not

involve different social relations from those of men, as they would later, in a money-economy ... If we also take into account that in medieval society collective relations prevailed over familial ones, and most of the tasks that female serfs performed ... were done in cooperation with other women, we then realise that the sexual division of labour, far from being a source of isolation, was a source of power and protection for women. (2004: 25)

This changes radically in the centuries that follow. One particular activity (labour) was separated off from the others, generally being located in a different place (the factory) and this was seen as an activity for men. Women continued to take charge of the activities of reproduction, but they no longer had direct access to land for growing crops, nor to common land for grazing animals, nor to the same collaborative support of other women. In a money economy, the man's wage defined the conditions of the family and the work of reproduction came to be seen as unimportant. Women were excluded from the wage in various ways: by being excluded from paid employment, by receiving much lower wages when they did perform wage labour, and even in many cases by the woman's wage being paid directly to her husband (Federici 2004: 98).

The creation of the new hierarchy was not achieved easily. It meant a redefinition of women's role in society and a redefinition of the meaning of being a woman. This took centuries of struggle involving the passing of laws to restrict the rights of women, the intervention of the churches, the insensitivity, brutality and at best collusion of the masculine (and masculinised) wage labourers and, crucially, the slaughter of more than a hundred thousand women condemned as witches, the torture of many, many more and the intimidation of millions. That is how women were reduced to invisible non-persons. Capitalism was built on a brutal and bloody misogyny.

This too was an enclosure: not just of the bodies of women,[2] but of their doing. The woman/housewife created did not have her doing contained directly in wage-labour, but it was contained just as effectively, within the constraints of servicing and reproducing wage labour. Primitive accumulation involved a double personification: the personification of labour and the personification of the labour's helper. This double containment was (and is) a double mutilation,[3] the creation of two personas, of two identities (to be accepted or struggled against).

The mutilation is hierarchical. The creation of labour is the creation of the male labourer. This refers not to the sexual composition of the workforce but to the process of mutilation involved in the creation of the capitalist labourer. The woman who enters the world of wage labour enters a world where male logic and the logic of capital are often hard to distinguish.

The mutilation goes even farther: it is not just the establishment of a hierarchy between men and women but the very creation of women and men. Sexuality was central to the witch hunts which were such an important element in the transition to capitalism. One element of this was the war against women's control of their own bodies and their own fertility: anything to do with contraception or abortion or even the knowledge of herbs and their uses was sufficient to lay the basis for a charge of witchcraft. Sexual perversion also figured prominently in the charges brought against witches.[4] One can see these charges as being just part of the spectacle and legitimation of the horrific slaughter of so many women (men too, but mainly women), but it can also be argued that the suppression of sexual perversion was an important and necessary part of the abstraction of doing into labour, the transition to capitalism.

Perversion refers to anything seen as abnormal, so prosecution of perversion meant at the same time the constitution by violence of a new normality. This normality is focused on sex as procreation or potential procreation, so that any other form of sexuality comes to be defined as perversion:

> The witch trials provide an instructive list of the forms of sexuality that were banned as 'non-productive': homosexuality, sex between young and old, sex between people of different classes, anal coitus, coitus from behind (reputedly leading to sterile relations), nudity, and dances. Also proscribed was the public, collective sexuality that had prevailed in the Middle Ages, as in the spring festivals of pagan origins that, in the 16th century, were still celebrated all over Europe. (Federici 2004: 194)

The new sexual normality was undoubtedly connected with the promotion of the procreation of a plentiful supply of labour power (ibid.: 85ff.), but it was also part of the creation of the *labourer*, that mutilated personification of abstract labour. The creation of the labourer involved the necessary subordination of the pleasure principle to the reality principle, and not just to the reality principle which is part of living in any social context, but to the reinforced reality principle or 'performance principle' (as Marcuse dubs it) that is inseparable from a society based on labour: 'The pleasure principle was dethroned not only because it militated against progress in civilisation but also because it militated against a civilisation whose progress perpetuates domination and toil' (Marcuse 1956/1998: 40). In this context, what is important about sexual perversion is not the particular content of the acts, but simply that it proclaims pleasure to be the end of sex, and this is what is incompatible with the creation of the labourer: 'Against a society which employs sexuality as a means for a useful end, the perversions uphold sexuality as an end in itself; they thus place themselves outside the dominion of the performance principle and challenge its very foundation' (Marcuse 1956/1998: 50).

The normalisation of sex in terms of procreation inevitably means the genitalisation of sexuality: sex comes to be defined in terms of the genital contact that leads potentially to procreation. Sexuality, from being polymorphous and spread throughout the body, becomes focused in the genitals. There is a 'desexualisation of the body: the libido becomes concentrated in one part of the body, leaving most of the rest free for use as the instrument of labour' (ibid.: 48).

The genitalisation of sexuality leads to sexual dimorphism,[5] the idea that there are two and only two sexes. If sexuality were thought of (and enjoyed) in terms of polymorphous pleasure, the touch of skin on skin, for example, then there would be no reason to think of people as being divided into two sexes:

The interpretation of human bodies according to precisely two categories, neither more nor less than two, is logically an effect of reducing the perception of erogenous areas of the body to those that are functional in reproductive activity: the sexual responsiveness of body areas that are irrelevant for reproduction is denied, and may be tabooized. These 'desexualized' body areas are thus made irrelevant for the sexual classification of bodies, too. The concept of 'the two sexes', the one sex and the other sex, is therefore an effect of heterosexuality as a societal norm. In European societies before the modern era, sexuality seems to have been less clearly dichotomized into hetero- and homosexuality. Everybody was assumed (or, rather, suspected) to perpetrate homosexual acts along with heterosexual ones, the former of which would be more or less severely persecuted and punished. Since the nineteenth century, however, homosexual acts are automatically considered to be expressive of a homosexual nature of the actor who is not anymore a human being perpetrating sinful homosexual (or, rather, 'sodomite') acts, but who is 'a homosexual', i.e. a member of a particular human species. The discourse moves from whether, or how, homosexual acts need to be punished to whether the homosexual as such, as a different species, is persecuted, psychiatrized or tolerated. (Stoetzler 2009: 165–6)

This suggests, then, that *woman* and *man* should be seen not as trans-historical categories, but as specifically capitalist forms of social relations, akin to value or money or state.[6] *Man* and *woman* (and indeed *homosexual* and *heterosexual*) are identifications, aspects of the society of identity, part of the mutilation involved in the creation of the *labourer*, the performer of abstract labour. A classification to be fought against.

Labour is an abstraction, a separation of labour from the world of doing or life-activity. This fragmentation of our life-activity is a fragmentation of our lives in every aspect. The separation of sexuality from the body as a whole and its concentration in the genitals was imposed historically at the same time as the abstraction of labour, made a fundamental contribution to the creation of the body as a machine for labour and is part of the general process of abstraction or separation, the process of limitation, classification and identification.[7]

The particular patterns of domination, then, are not something that *happens* to us or that *they* (men, capitalists, whoever) impose on us, but patterns of domination that *we* create through our activity and the way in which it is organised. That is the importance of the critique *ad hominem* (or *ad mulierem*, or *ad humanum*): it is only by bringing everything back to our own doing, our own creative power, that we can open up the question of how we do differently. It is not that we *are* women or men, or homosexuals or heterosexuals: we *do* women and men, masculinity and femininity and homosexuality and heterosexuality, not just as individual choice, but as social practice. This social practice is part of a complex weave of practice, a web of abstraction; but, however complex it is, the core is that *we do*. We create the world that is killing us, and if we create it, then we can stop creating it and do something else instead.

17
The abstraction of doing into labour is the constitution of nature as object.

The driving of people from the land laid the basis for the creation of a proletariat cut off from the means of production and survival, and with it for the generalisation of abstract labour and the rise of capitalism. At the core of Marx's discussion of primitive accumulation is the 'forcible driving of the peasantry from the land' and 'the usurpation of the common lands', starting in the last third of the fifteenth century (1867/1965: 718; 1867/1990: 878).[1] This was (and is) a violent process. Marx cites the infamous Highland clearances in Scotland:

> As an example of the method obtaining in the nineteenth century, the 'clearing' made by the Duchess of Sutherland will suffice here. This person, well instructed in economy, resolved, on entering upon her government, to effect a radical cure, and to turn the whole country, whose population had already been, by earlier processes of the like kind, reduced to 15,000, into a sheep-walk. From 1814 to 1820 these 15,000 inhabitants, about 3,000 families, were systematically hunted and rooted out. All their villages were destroyed and burnt, all their fields turned into pasturage. (1867/1965: 731; 1867/1990: 891)

We now, possibly city dwellers for generations, read this and we are shocked. 'Poor people, how they suffered', we think, and we do not understand. We do not understand that the 'poor people' are we.

The tearing of people from the land is perhaps the original and irredeemable sin of capitalism. It is a tearing asunder, a violent separation of humans from the natural conditions of their existence: 'Man *lives* on nature – means that nature is his *body*, with which he must remain in continuous interchange if he is not to die. That man's physical and spiritual life is linked to nature means simply that nature is linked to itself, for man is a part of nature.'[2] The constant interchange, or metabolic relation, between humans and nature is central to human existence. When Marx speaks of useful labour (the labour process as opposed to the valorisation process), he says that 'labour is, first of all, a process between man and nature, a process by which man, through his own actions, mediates, regulates and controls the metabolism between himself and nature' (Marx 1867/1990: 283).[3] The interaction with nature is a central aspect of human doing.

In pre-capitalist societies, the relation to the living and non-living world around us was generally based on the idea that it was important to maintain some sort of equilibrium. Before cutting down a tree, the woodcutter might ask it for forgiveness: absurd though it may seem to us, this was a recognition of the interdependence of the different forms of life on this planet. Often this relation was understood in magical or religious terms: 'At the basis of magic was an animate conception of nature that did not admit to any separation between matter and spirit and this imagined the cosmos as a living organism, populated by occult forces, where every element was in "sympathetic" relation with the rest' (Federici 2004: 142). These were certainly enchanted, fetishised forms of thought which interposed gods, goddesses and other spirits as mediators in the relation between humans and the non-human world (and an integral part of the patterns of domination in those societies). Nevertheless, these magical or religious forms gave anchorage to a certain equilibrium between humans and the surrounding world. Human doing, before the rise of capitalist labour, was generally based in a respect for this equilibrium.

The driving of people from the land is the forceful separation of humans from their natural surroundings, the breaking of the equilibrium necessary for human survival. This is the creation of what Marx referred to as the 'metabolic rift'[4] between humans and the nature of which we are part, the metabolic rift that now so obviously threatens the very existence of humanity.[5] This rift is inseparable from the abstraction of doing into labour: the former peasants, driven from their land, have no alternative but to sell their labour power to the owners of the means of production. The very meaning of human activity is transformed: from the daily dialogue with nature it is transformed into the empty carrying-out of instructions – doing becomes labour. The alienation of labour is at once alienation from nature (Foster 2000: 72).

The rift is a dis-enchantment of nature.[6] Nature becomes an object for humans, an object of scientific study, an object of labour, separated from magic and religion. This was not just a shift in thinking, but in fact a long and violent process closely bound up with the suppression and redefinition of women. The witch hunts that were such an important part of primitive accumulation were an attack on the magical vision of the world and the practices associated with it. (Federici 2004: 200ff.) This was accompanied by the rise of a new scientific rationalism that had at its base the constitution of nature as an object quite separate from humans, an object governed by laws that could be discovered by reason.[7] Our relation to the world around us came to be seen as a relation of separation, of distance, of knowledge-about and use or exploitation.

This has profound consequences. Marx and Engels spoke of the resulting 'idiocy of rural life' (1848/1976: 188) and the cutting-off of the rural population from 'all world intercourse, and consequently from all culture' (1845/1976: 401), but the more serious problem is perhaps not so much what the separation did to the rural population as what it did to the urban population, those deprived of the contact with the land. The separation 'makes one man into a restricted town-animal, another into a restricted country-animal' (1845/1976: 64), and it is perhaps the restricted town-animal that does the greater damage, and suffers the greater loss.[8] Ehrenreich (2007: 129ff.) speaks of an 'epidemic of melancholy' in Europe in the seventeenth century, which she sees as an aspect of the repression of collective joy, but it does not seem fanciful to connect both the widespread melancholy and the repression of collective joy to the separation of people from the land, the loss of the therapeutic effect of contact with other forms of life and the loss of vitality of the village communities. The enclosure of the land does not just provide an abundant supply of available labour power for the nascent capitalism: it creates a world of city dwellers depressed, impoverished and desensitised by their loss of contact with nature.

The enclosure of land is far from being just a past episode: in world terms, the elimination of peasants from the land has never been so torrential as it is today:

> The global forces 'pushing' people from the countryside – mechanisation of agriculture in Java and India, food imports in Mexico, Haiti and Kenya, civil war and drought throughout Africa, and everywhere the consolidation of small holdings into large ones and the competition of industrial-scale agribusiness – seem to sustain urbanisation even when the 'pull' of the city is drastically weakened by debt and economic depression. (Davis 2006: 17)

All of this means not only misery for the people involved but that the metabolic rift between humans and nature is constantly growing.

By producing and reproducing the separation between humans and the rest of nature, we produce and reproduce the destruction of our own conditions of existence; in other words, we produce and reproduce the conditions of our own destruction. In this, humans bear a peculiar responsibility that separates us from other forms of life. The metabolic rift that threatens not only our own existence but also the existence of very many (possibly all) other forms of life is the consequence of human action and can be overcome only by a transformation of the ways in which humans live.

It has become very clear that our metabolic interaction with other forms of life and our natural environment is a precondition of human existence and that the future of humanity depends on our ability to overcome the rift we have created. This does not mean, however, that we are the same as other animals. It has become popular to assert that there is no essential difference between humans and other forms of life. This seems to me to be both wrong and dangerous. It is we humans (not the pigs, not the ants) who are destroying the prospects of life on earth and this reflects our peculiarly creative and destructive power. The doing which is central to this book is distinctively human doing, not animal doing. It is necessary to recognise our difference from animals in order to assume fully our peculiar responsibility in overcoming the metabolic rift: we cannot rely on the pigs or ants to do it.[9]

It is little wonder then that many of the movements of recent years have placed at the centre of their struggles the overcoming of the separation between humans and other forms of life. This is the substance of many of the cracks: the development (through organic gardening, permaculture, the creation of botanic gardens, dry toilets, whatever) of a form of living, a form of doing, based on a different relation with nature.[10] The revolt of doing against abstract labour echoes the cry of the sixteenth-century revolutionary, Thomas Müntzer: 'all living things must also become free.'[11]

18

The abstraction of doing into labour is the externalisation of our power-to-do and the creation of the citizen, politics and the state.

Abstraction is a removal, a displacement, a taking away. All that, and something even more terrible: abstraction is a giving away.

I bake a cake, for myself and my friends. Part of the pleasure of doing it is the feeling of my power. I realise that I am able to make a delicious cake, that I have a power to do something I enjoy. The next time I call in my friends and we make cakes together: again we delight in our abilities, our power-to-do. We feel our power as a verb, as a being-able-to.[1] Then, as we have seen, I decide to make cakes for selling them on the market. After a while I realise that in order to live I need to produce in a certain way and at a certain rhythm. The market measures my baking and that measurement rebounds upon my activity. My doing, we saw, has been transformed into labour and at the same time my power-to-do has been transformed into something else: into an impersonal power over us. We no longer exercise power over our own activity. We have externalised our own power and by doing so we have converted our power-to-do into its opposite, power-over us. Our power as a verb, our being-able-to, has been transformed into power as a noun, a thing outside us. When we see what we have done, we wail and gnash our teeth, but the terrible thing is that we keep on doing it, we repeatedly externalise our power, convert our creative power into an impersonal, alien power over us. We do it repeatedly because we see no other way to survive.[2]

The conversion of doing into abstract labour takes place largely through the expansion of wage labour. The externalisation of power is the same, but even more palpable. I bake a cake, enjoy doing it, feel my power-to-do. I decide this time that I shall not sell my cakes directly on the market, but I shall sell my capacity to bake cakes, my power to bake, to a large bakery, and in return I receive a wage. This time it is not the market but my employer who measures my work and imposes the rhythms necessary for him to be able to sell the cakes on the market. The power-over has a personal face, but the capitalist is simply the personification of impersonal forces that he does not control. Again we have externalised our own power and by doing so we have converted our power-to-do into a power-over us. Again we do it again day after day: we externalise our power-to-do and convert it into an alien power-over us. What else are we to do when we have been cut off from the means of production, the means of survival?

And after a while we forget the pleasure of creative doing. We even forget that our power-to-do is the substance of power-over, that the power-over of capital depends totally upon our power-to-do, that it is we who create the power that is exercised over us. Our power-to-do becomes invisible: 'power' becomes a noun, synonymous with the power of the powerful, the power of capital, the power of the system.

The repeated and multiple externalisation of our power (and thereby the metamorphosis of power-to into power-over) creates a complex web of social cohesion (capitalist social relations). This web of social cohesion is produced and re-produced by the myriad processes of abstraction of our doing, the externalisation of our power-to-do, and it comes to constitute a complex network of power-over, a web of obligation, compulsion, domination. This is the capitalist society that stands over against us, the social cohesion or synthesis that makes a mockery of our attempts to do something else, tells us that our cracks are the cracks of insanity.

The society that is constituted by abstract labour, by the repeated transformation of our being-able-to into a power-over us, is an antagonistic society. It is based on the frustration of our doing, our thrust to do what we consider necessary or desirable. This fundamental frustration is at the same time a class antagonism, an antagonism between those who are created by and benefit from abstract labour (the capitalists) and those who are forced to perform the abstract labour (the labourers). The 'dull compulsion of economic relations' (Marx 1867/1965: 737; 1867/1990: 899) is never enough to contain this antagonism: it must be backed by the use of force. Our externalisation of power acquires an extra dimension. Power-over, that monster created by the metamorphosis of our power-to-do, duplicates itself. It comes to exist in two distinct forms: the economic and the political. There develops over time an instance separated from society that seeks to secure the social order necessary for the rule of abstract labour. This instance is the state.

It was not always so. In feudal society, for example, there was neither the same externalisation of our power, nor the same separation of the economic and the political. The serf was forced, under pain of punishment, to exercise her capacities on behalf of the lord but there was no loss of the specificity of the activity, and there was no separation between exploitation and the use or threat of force necessary to maintain it. Domination was directly personal and overtly hierarchical. A feudal society is a 'parcelised' society, in which social cohesion is established in the community and under the personal and traditional domination of the lord.

This changed as the lords drove out the peasants to make way for sheep, and as the peasants fled from the tyranny of the lords. Personal bondage no longer held the society together. The new cohesion centred on the abstraction of doing into labour created a new, abstract subject. The serfs, subordinated as a community to their lord, were transformed into individuals, sellers of commodities and especially of the central commodity, labour power. As individual sellers of commodities, they necessarily enjoyed equal rights, rights as equal property-owners, without which the contract of exchange would be impossible. They were transformed into legal subjects.[3] They became (through a process of struggle) equal citizens enjoying equal rights. This is a formal, abstract equality, that tells us nothing of their real situation in life. Citizenship is an abstraction, the consolidation of the abstract individuality inherent in the abstraction of doing into labour. As abstract labourers, we are all equal, all partakers in the social production of the commodity society, a society based upon abstraction, upon indifference to meaning and particularity.

As abstract individuals (and only as abstract individuals) we are citizens and can be represented.

The state is characterised by its separation from society. It does not establish the social cohesion, but acts as a necessary complement to the establishment of that cohesion through the process of exchange. It is a derivative form of abstract labour, constituted by the abstraction of doing into labour. The constitution of the state is at the same time the constitution of the economic and the political as separate spheres, from both of which the abstraction of doing into labour, the transformation of our being-able-to into a power-over us, disappears from view.

The political draws our fire, distracts our attention from the fundamental question of our power-to-do. The state, by its very existence, says in effect, 'I am the force of social cohesion, I am the centre of social determination. If you want to change society, you must focus on me, you must gain control of me.' This is not true. The real determinant of society is hidden behind the state and the economy: it is the way in which our everyday activity is organised, the subordination of our doing to the dictates of abstract labour, that is, of value, money, profit. It is this abstraction which is, after all, the very basis of the existence of the state. If we want to change society, we must stop the subordination of our activity to abstract labour, do something else.

Yet the siren call of the state is enormously forceful. Over and over again, it calls to us that if we want to achieve anything, if we want to change society, we must look at it. It diverts our efforts. The existence of the state as a separate or particular instance is a constant calling to us, a constant seducing of us into a separate sphere of politics. Even if we reject the party as a form of organisation, even if we say we do not want to take power, there is still the constant voice saying 'it is the political that is important, forget the content of your everyday activity, it is politics that matters.' Even many autonomist groups get drawn into this: they focus on the construction of an 'other politics' without seeing that an 'other politics' must be based on the critique of the very separation of politics from the rest of our everyday activity, on the overcoming of the separation of politics from doing.[4]

The state draws us on to a false terrain. But that means that politics draws us on to a false terrain: the very acceptance of politics as a distinct sphere leads us down the wrong road. Bring it all home, bring it home to our activity, our own doing and the way it is organised, what we do each day. The more we advance in our argument, the more we see the importance of Marx's insistence on critique *ad hominem*, the understanding and the changing of the world from the perspective of human activity.

The state, and therefore politics understood as a distinct sphere, is a removal, a displacement, a drawing away of our struggle for a different world. But more than that: it is a creation, a giving away by us. The existence of the state is part of the externalisation of power inherent in the abstraction of doing into labour, part of the transformation of our power-to-do into their power-over. We create and re-create it by paying taxes, by obeying the laws, by voting in elections: but also, by constituting a distinct sphere of the political separate from everyday life. The state is not an external force but an externalised force. We create the state by externalising our power: its power over us is the transformation of our power to do. The critique of the state, then, is the critique of the externalisation of our power, of our own constant creation and re-creation of the state as an authority standing outside us, and of politics as a distinct sphere separated from our daily lives, from our doing and eating and loving.[5]

19
The abstraction of doing into labour is the homogenisation of time.

One of the most subtle and yet most powerful elements of the web that we weave to entrap ourselves is time itself. Abstract labour produces abstract time, abstract labour produces the clock.

Clocks speak of duration, the homogenisation of time. From the perspective of the clock, one minute is just the same as the next. The clock goes round and round, quantifying time, treating minutes of happiness in the same way as minutes of despair, projecting the past into the future. For the clock, tomorrow will be just the same as today or yesterday. For the clock, the only revolution conceivable is the one that goes round and round, changing nothing.[1]

Any system of domination depends on duration, on the assumption that, just because something exists in one moment, it will continue to exist in the next. The master assumes that because he ruled yesterday, he will continue to rule tomorrow. The slave dreams of a different tomorrow, but often locates it beyond death, in heaven. She assumes in that case that there is nothing she can do to change the situation. The power of doing is subordinated to that which is. She is a slave and will still be a slave tomorrow. And tomorrow. And tomorrow.

We look around us. We see the politicians and the capitalists. We see their big buildings and their police and their armies. We see a world of great complexity and corruption. We know it is unjust, violent, destructive and we want it to be different. But we assume that it will still be there tomorrow. And tomorrow. And tomorrow.

And the clock ticks on, telling us that it is so, that time is a life of tomorrows, all repetitions of today. Life is so, things are so, that is the way things are. For the clock there is no past that was different from the present, no future that can be different from the present. The clock tells of an everlasting present, but it is a present that is totally empty, because it contains no possibility of a different future. There is no doing in clock time, only empty being, only the endlessly repeated *is*.

The clock tells us of duration, continuity, the impossibility of radical change. Duration seeps into our minds. We expect things to continue as they are. We know, perhaps, that it is not true, that disasters hang over us of which we have no control – war and its mirror-image terror, 'natural' and social disasters. The clock numbs us: numbs us to the danger of disaster, but numbs us above all to the possibility that we ourselves could change things radically.

It has not always been so. The clock has not ruled for ever. Before the rise of the clock, doing was at the centre of time, the principal means for measuring time. This is sometimes referred to as task-orientation. Thus, Thompson tells us that

> ... in Madagascar time might be measured by 'a rice-cooking' (about half an hour) or 'the frying of a locust' (a moment). The Cross River natives were reported as saying 'the man died in less than the time in which maize is not yet completely roasted' (less than fifteen minutes) ... The Oxford English Dictionary gives us English examples 'pater noster wyle', 'miserere whyle' (1450) and (in the New English Dictionary but not the Oxford English Dictionary) 'pissing while' – a somewhat arbitrary measurement. (1967: 58)

Doing-time (or task-orientation) is the prevalent form of time in societies in which doing has not yet been transformed into labour: 'a community in which task orientation is common appears to show least demarcation between "work" and "life". Social intercourse and labour are intermingled – the working-day lengthens or contracts according to the task – and there is no great sense of conflict between labour and "passing the time of day"' (ibid.: 60).

The rise of the clock accompanies the rise of the abstraction of doing into labour. It is a long process, involving centuries of struggle. The spread of clocks from the fourteenth century onwards is at first connected with the spread of commodity exchange, with a 'merchant's time' distinct from the time of the medieval church.[2] The spread of clocks and later watches of growing accuracy (minute hands became common only in the eighteenth century)[3] was closely associated with the imposition of labour-discipline, first in the countryside and later in the factory. Task-orientation or doing-time is not adequate when the doing is a doing for someone else, a resisted doing. When the doing becomes labour, when the activity becomes external to the doer and imposed, then time itself becomes external and imposed. Time no longer arises from the doing but must be imposed upon the doing to ensure that the doing gets done. The clock is the means by which this is achieved. As Thompson insists, the spread of the clock is not just the expression of a need for the synchronisation of increasingly complex times but simultaneously the imposition of discipline: 'We are concerned simultaneously with time-sense in its technological conditioning, and with time-measurement as a means of labour exploitation' (1967: 80).

The imposition of clock-time was not accomplished easily: it required a long struggle, involving not only the assertion of discipline at work and punishment for late-coming, but also the constant affirmation of the virtues of punctuality by moralists and preachers and, to crown it all and inculcate good habits from an early age, the introduction of public education. The enemy to be vanquished was time-wasting, the refusal to accept the urgency of the tick-tick of the clock. One eighteenth-century clergyman observes with horror that '"the Churches and Streets [are] crowded with Numbers of Spectators" at weddings and funerals, "who, in spight of the Miseries of their Starving Condition ... make no Scruple of wasting the best Hours in the Day, for the sake of gazing ..."' (Thompson 1967: 83). Yet Thompson notes a gradual change in the resistance to time as the workers start to organise against capital: 'The onslaught, from so many directions, upon the people's old working habits was not, of course, uncontested. In the first stage, we find simple resistance. But in the next stage, as the new time-discipline is imposed, so the workers begin to fight, not against time, but about it' (ibid.: 85). The workers begin to fight, in other words, for a shorter working day and no longer for the right to waste their time in gazing or to measure their day simply in terms of

137

what they want to do. This is surely the birth of the struggle of abstract labour: there is an acceptance of the forms and rhythms of work within the factory or other workplace. The struggle against capital goes on, but it is within the ground-rules established by capital. Thompson concludes:

> The first generation of factory workers were taught by their masters the importance of time; the second generation formed their short-time committees in the ten-hour movement; the third generation struck for overtime or time-and-a-half. They had accepted the categories of their employers and learned to fight back within them. They had learned their lesson, that time is money, only too well. (ibid.: 86)[4]

The new time is the time of alienated, abstract labour. Abstract time is inseparable from abstract labour. When different products are compared on the market, a quantitative relation is established between them (the exchange value of the commodities) and this relation is determined by the socially necessary labour time required to produce the commodities. To speak of the abstraction of doing into labour is necessarily to speak of the abstraction of doing-time into the external, de-subjectified socially necessary labour time. The rule of socially necessary labour time is inevitably the rule of a time outside us, abstracted from the quality of our doing. When we say that abstract labour weaves capitalist society, we affirm that abstract clock time is an essential and inevitable part of that weave.[5]

This is the time of duration, the separation of time from our doing. Clocks represent not just labour discipline, not just punctuality, but a whole way of living and understanding the world. Clock-time, the time of duration, is the time of the separation of subject from object, of constitution from existence, of doing from done. We create something and the thing we create detaches itself from us. It takes on a new existence in which our constitution or creation of the thing is negated and our doing-time obliterated. We make a chair with love and dedication and the chair stands there as a commodity to be sold, our loving creativity forgotten, the time we spent in its creation obliterated in its price. The time of constitution is forgotten, the time of existence takes over: the chair is two years old, ten years old, a hundred years old. This is the time of existence-separated-from-constitution, the time of things, for which one day is the same as the last, or the next. The chair does not create, it does not fall in love, it does not rage and scream. Chair-time is clock-time, thing-time, object-time. Thing-time is the negation of person-time, object-time is the denial of subject-time. Clock time is the time of our helplessness, of our subordination to things. It is the time not of living, but of survival, of plodding on from day to day, the time of dullness.

Clock-time is the time-in-which we live. We live and act within time: 'From the tick to the tock, clock time measures human activity regardless of specific contents. In clock time, the expenditure of labour does not occur in time. It occurs within time' (Bonefeld 2010). Time contains our lives, a framework over which we have no control. With luck, we will live for eighty or even ninety years: that is the measured span within which we live. This is the time of identity. Time, separated from doing, is made up of identical units, units of identity: self-contained units separate from one another, units in which we are contained.[6]

Clock-time is the time of institutionalisation. Institution-alisation is an extension of the separation of existence from constitution. We create something and it acquires an existence independent from us, a 'life' of its own. We constitute a political party and the party goes on existing, claiming that it represents us, that it still has the same relation to us as in the moment of its creation. We create a state and the state exists independent of us, with its own time, history, commemorations. We get married and our relationship of love acquires its own existence separate from the feelings of the moment, acquires a temporality measured by anniversaries and no longer by seconds of infinite fragility. Prison is the supreme expression of the separation of time from meaning: prisoners simply 'do time'. The time they 'do' is totally outside their control.

Clock-time is the time of a world we do not control, a world that does not respond to our passions and intensities. It is time-outside-us. It is historical time, but the time of a history-outside-us, the history of a world that is alien to us. This is real history, the real history of a world we really do not control: a history measured in years, a history of successive structures, a history divided into periods that have a beginning and an end, a history with a clear division between past, present and future. This is the time of Progress, a time that runs forward along predetermined tracks. This is real time, this is real history, but it is not our time and it is not our history.[7]

This is the time of deferred gratification.[8] The clock tells us that this is not the hour for standing in the street and gazing. If we work hard during the hours of labour, then perhaps afterwards we can allow ourselves the pleasure of gazing. In the meantime, we must sacrifice our desires.[9] Sacrifice now, enjoy later. But the clock is above all the time of sacrifice now, of measured labour, of labour that cannot be enjoyable simply because it is measured by the clock. The deferred gratification is beyond the clock, over the rainbow, pie to be eaten in the sky. This is the time of Future Revolution: a logical absurdity because it is founded in the abstract time of abstract labour.

20
The abstraction of doing into labour is the creation of totality.

Any society depends on some sort of interconnection between people's activities. There must be some sort of knitting together of what people do:

> Their activities must interrelate in order to fit into a society, and must contain at least a minimum of uniformity if the society is to function as a whole. This coherence can be conscious or unconscious but exist it must – otherwise society would cease to be viable and the individuals would come to grief as a result of their multiple dependencies upon one another. (Sohn-Rethel 1978: 5)

In pre-capitalist societies, this knitting-together is established on the basis of the concrete characteristics of the activity. It may be on the basis of custom, or of communal decision, or of command, but the custom, command, or communal decision relates to a specific activity: the slave-owner tells the slave to build a wall, the custom in the village is that the woodcarver should make a statue for the church each year, or whatever. The social coming-together of activities takes place on the basis of some combination of perceived social needs and existing social skills.

Under capitalism, all this changes. The knitting together is not achieved by custom, command, or communal decision but through the exchange of products. Certainly within capitalist enterprises, coordination is by command, but in society as a whole, the only command is the uncontrolled and unconscious movement of money, the medium of exchange. The fact that I bake cakes for other people is the result not of custom, command, or communal decision, but simply the outcome of my perception that I can sell them (exchange them for money). If I find that I can no longer exchange them for money, I will be forced to turn to some other activity. The social weaving of activities takes place, then, not on the basis of the concrete characteristics of the activities but on the basis of abstraction from those characteristics, on the basis of all the different activities being treated as homogeneous, abstract labour. The social cohesion is achieved through treating all activities, all our particular doings, as homogeneous, quantifiable, measurable and interchangeable labour. The socialisation of labour is at the same time the homogenisation of labour, unlike in previous societies.[1]

This has important consequences for the meaning of social cohesion. There is a much tighter integration between a person's particular activities and the society as a whole. Whether I produce cars or cakes or do nothing at all is the result of the movement of money (the market) over which I have no control at all. The blind connection flings people from one sort of activity to another: from making cars to assembling computers to making hamburgers. The establishment of social cohesion through abstraction also means that the social connections are unlimited in space and time. Whereas in a feudal society, the social connections are established within a limited space, the mediation of exchange means that there is no limit at all. My cake (if it is frozen) can be consumed in China or Germany, tomorrow or in three weeks' time. A fall in the labour time that is necessary to produce a car in China will throw car workers in the United States into unemployment.

Social cohesion, then, is qualitatively different from that which existed in pre-capitalist societies. It covers the whole planet, it determines the contents of people's activity much more thoroughly and it exists as an external force independent of any conscious control. We can mark this difference by saying that social cohesion exists in capitalism as a social synthesis or a *totality* in a way that is not the case in non-capitalist societies.

Abstract labour constitutes a totality that is independent of conscious determination. It has its own logic, its own laws of development: the logic of capital, with its laws that operate behind the backs of the producers. I bake cakes, but if I take more than the socially necessary labour time required to bake those cakes, then I will not be able to sell my cakes (at a price that reflects my labour). How do I know whether I have met the requirements of socially necessary labour time? Only by seeing if I can sell my cakes or not: the laws of abstract labour operate behind my back. The interaction of people's activities is beyond their control, operates according to its own logic.

Like all other aspects of the transformation of doing into abstract labour, the constitution of the totality is a historical process and an extremely violent one. The constitution of the world market was (and is) not a smooth, rational process but a process that has condemned millions to misery and a sense of social redundancy, a process that has wiped out whole cultures and peoples. The totality (that is, the social cohesion peculiar to capitalism) is the elimination of alternative ways of doing and alternative ways of living, of anything that does not fit in with the blind laws of abstract labour.

Abstract labour constitutes a totality, but it does it in a way that is not obvious. Precisely because the social cohesion is not the result of any conscious process, society appears to be a mass of incoherent particulars, of unrelated phenomena. At first sight, the connection between sexual dimorphism (say) and the destruction of other forms of life is not obvious. They appear to be two unrelated phenomena. It is only by understanding both as part of a society formed by abstract labour that we can understand how the struggle against sexual dimorphism is related to the struggle against the destruction of other forms of life and the struggle for the abolition of abstract labour. In the face of a world that presents itself as a mass of particulars, *totality* is a fundamental category of critique. This is crucial because it throws light on the interconnectedness of capitalist domination (the connection, say, between development aid and arms sales) and on the unity-in-separation of our own struggles.

Totality, then, has been a central category of Marxist critique, pointing out the relation between apparently unconnected phenomena in capitalist society. There is, however, a great danger here: from being a *critical* category, totality can easily be transformed into a *positive* category.[2] This happens if totality is understood as a trans-historical category.

This is important because if we convert totality into a positive, trans-historical concept, then we tend to view it as something that must be liberated from its unconscious, fragmented capitalist form.[3] This slippage from totality as a critical to totality as a positive concept is associated especially with Lukács and his book, *History and Class Consciousness*. In this book, he famously asserted that Marxism is the 'point of view of totality'.[4] In so far as totality is the critique of fragmentation and of all phenomena that obscure the central role of human creation, this is very important, but Lukács himself goes further and interprets totality to refer to the proletariat as the subject-object of history. The struggle against capitalism becomes the struggle for the emancipation of the totality from its fragmentation and this is closely associated with the idea of the Party (as representative of the totality) and central socialist planning. At present, the totality is fragmented and anarchic: what is needed is a unified and socially controlled totality. It is little wonder that many regard such a perspective as frightening.

If, however, we see the totality as the product of abstract labour, then the struggle against capitalism is not only a struggle against fragmentation and lack of social control, but the struggle against totality as such. This opens up very different perspectives, both in the short and long term. The cracks of which we have spoken are not a struggle to establish an alternative totality, but rather to break the existing one. If abstract labour totalises, then the struggle against abstract labour is a struggle against totalisation.[5] This is an important practical point, simply because the positive concept of totality is an objection raised time and time again against the autonomist movements of recent years: where is your programme, your national plan, your strategy, your theory of transition? Over and over again we are invited to conceptualise our struggles from the perspective of totality, positively understood, that is, to incorporate them into the logic which we reject.

21

Abstract labour rules: the abstraction of doing into labour is the creation of a cohesive law-bound totality sustained by the exploitation of labour.

Much of the story recounted in the previous sections could have been (and has been) told in different ways. The creation of our modern society with all that it implies in terms of labour, rational-scientific thought, dimorphous male-dominated sexuality, the objectification of nature, the homogenisation of time, enclosure in an all-embracing system, and so on, and so on: all this can be (and has been) seen simply as modernisation, the creation of a modern industrial society. More critically, it can be discussed in terms of the establishment of a disciplined society,[1] or in terms of the critique of the Enlightenment,[2] or, fascinatingly, as the 'struggle between Pentheus and Dionysus' for the suppression of collective joy.[3]

Here we insist that the establishment of the society in which we live should be seen as being created by abstract labour (the abstraction of doing into labour). This is an attempt to bring it home to us, to put our activity, what we do from day to day, in the centre of analysis. This can be seen as critique *ad hominem*, or simply as materialism: materialism is quite simply the understanding that we humans create the world in which we live.[4] It is not culture, it is not an external force, that creates the society that is destroying us: it is we ourselves, through our peculiarly deformed activity, abstract labour: 'Human beings produce, through their own labour, a reality which increasingly enslaves them.'[5] And if it is we who create this society, then we can stop doing it and do something else instead.

Abstract labour rules, then.

We create a society that systematically conceals the fact that we create it. We create a society that moves according to a dynamic logic that neither we nor anyone controls. We create a society that is based on our exploitation. Each of these statements is a source of despair, a source of hope. We shall take them one by one.

First, we create a society that systematically conceals the fact that we create it. This we have seen already: we create a fetishised, reified world, a world of things. We, as subjects, create a world that turns us into objects. And backwards: this world in which we are treated as objects is the product of our subjective creation.

Secondly, we create a society that moves according to a dynamic logic that neither we nor anyone controls. The reified world that we create does not move according to anyone's volition. It follows its own logic. To the extent that social relations are really transformed into relations between things, it follows its own laws of development. The totality we create is a law-bound totality. This is what makes the study of economics possible, and indeed any other discipline that tries to understand the laws of social development. The social totality has a certain structure, a certain logic, a certain dynamic, summed up in Marx's exclamation: 'Accumulate! Accumulate! That is Moses and the prophets!' (Marx, 1867/1965: 595; 1867/1990: 742). In order to exist, capital must accumulate, must expand itself. The capital that we create is self-creating, self-expanding value. Capital, although it is created by humans, acquires a force independent of any human volition. It is not controlled by capitalists: capitalists are capitalists only to the extent that they succeed in obeying the logic of capital. Capital (the object of our creation) is an 'automatic subject' (as Marx called it),[6] the Subject of capitalist society. It is the story of Frankenstein, the story of the sorcerer's apprentice. By constituting capitalism, we create a system that we do not control, a system with its own laws of development. We create capitalism and thrust ourselves into a terrifying world. We enclose ourselves in an 'enchanted, perverted, topsy-turvy world' (Marx 1894/1971: 830), ruled by death.

The totality constituted by abstract labour is a totality without meaning. There is a linking of activities, but the activities themselves are abstracted from meaning: the content of the activity (whether baking or making rat poison) is a matter of indifference. The chain of connections is a quantitative chain, established through money. Each activity acquires significance only in relation to another activity, as a means to an end. Baking for its own sake, for the fun of it, makes no sense in the world of abstract labour. In this world, baking makes sense only as a means to an end, the end of making money: its end is a senseless sense, devoid of meaning (so that baking cakes can be substituted by making poison, writing books, whatever). The concatenation of activities is purely instrumental, but the instrumentality is empty. This formal, instrumental series of connections gives rise to a formal instrumental reasoning.[7] Abstract labour is the basis of instrumental reason, the formalisation of reason that emerged from the Enlightenment to become the basis of modern bourgeois thought, in which truth has meaning only as a measurement of the effectiveness of means to achieve an end, in which people themselves come to be seen simply as means to an end. In this totality, the only meaning is a quantitative one: the rate of economic growth, the number of bridges constructed, the number of kilometres of highway, the number of criminals imprisoned – Progress, in other words.[8]

The fact that capitalism is a law-bound society, a society with its laws of development, means that it is characterised by rigidities. It is not the infinitely flexible society it sometimes seems to be. Sometimes it seems that it is capable or absorbing anything we throw at it, of turning Che and Marcos into designs for t-shirts, of turning the great revolt of 1968 into a new style of domination. And yet it is not so. Capital has its limits, must follow certain rules, of which the basic one is Accumulate, accumulate! It does make sense, then, to speak of breaking or cracking capital. It is not a pane of glass, but it does have a rigidity, however flexible and adaptable that rigidity may appear to be: capital is a set of rules that channel the flow of our activity: to break capital, we break the rules. How do we break the rules? There used to be some rules on how to do it, but fortunately they were broken.

We create, thirdly, a society that is based on our own exploitation. The world that we create has at its centre the exploitation of labour by capital. The abstraction of doing into labour is generalised throughout society only when labour power itself becomes a commodity. In other words, as we saw, it is through the expansion of wage labour that abstract labour becomes established as the organising principle of society. Wage labour means that the worker sells his[9] labour power to a capitalist in return for a wage (the monetary equivalent of the value of his labour power); the capitalist puts the worker to labour and he produces more value than that of his labour power, the surplus value which is appropriated by the capitalist. This is the process of capitalist exploitation. The generalisation of abstract labour is simultaneously the generalisation of capitalist exploitation. Exploitation existed in pre-capitalist societies: in feudal societies, for example, the serf is forced to work to supply not only his own needs but also the demands of his lord. With the transition to capitalism (the bloody process of primitive accumulation), exploitation is re-constituted on the basis of abstract labour. The transformation of doing into abstract labour is a pre-condition of capitalist exploitation. Without abstract labour, there can be no production of capital; without value production there can be no production of surplus value. The production of surplus value and capital is in turn necessary for the reproduction of doing as abstract labour, but it is the abstraction of doing into labour that is logically prior.

Abstract labour creates, therefore, a class-divided society. Class antagonism, like exploitation, existed before capitalism, but it is reconstituted on the basis of abstract labour. The process of surplus value production creates two antagonistic classes: the class of those whose labour creates surplus value (the proletariat, the working class) and the class of those who exploit this labour. The antagonism inherent in the process of exploitation (the capitalist process of production) structures the whole of society and infuses it with the same antagonism. This division of society, this process of class-ification, is one aspect of the fetishisation/ identification/classification of society which we have already seen as one of the moments of the process of abstraction.[10]

Abstract labour, then, constitutes a system of social cohesion that is governed by objective laws of development outside our control, and that has as its core a relation of exploitation, the production of surplus value. This relation is a relation of antagonism, between the abstract labour that is being exploited and the capital that is produced by that exploitation: this antagonism is personified as an antagonism between the personifications of abstract labour (the proletariat) and the personifications of capital (the capitalists). It is important to keep hold of these two dimensions: if we see abstract labour simply as constituting a system of law-bound social compulsion, then we can easily lose sight of the antagonistic dynamic that is at the centre of this system;[11] if, on the other hand, we focus purely on the relation of exploitation, we fail to see the abstracting of doing into labour that is the pre-condition of the whole system of exploitation.

There are two crucial antagonisms here. Within capitalism, this world created by abstract labour, there is the central axis of exploitation, the antagonism between labour and capital. But the process that creates this world, the abstraction of doing into labour, is also an antagonistic process, a bloody, violent process. The existence of capitalism (a social system based on the exploitation of labour and with its own antagonistic dynamic) is based upon a pre-condition: the antagonistic conversion of doing into abstract labour.

From this point, there are two ways forward, two ways of thinking about radical social change. The meaning of primitive accumulation, long treated as a marginal issue by Marxist theory (and indeed in Marx's presentation in *Capital*) becomes a central issue.

The first approach sees primitive accumulation as a past event, so much water under the bridge. What's done is done: we now live within the world constituted by the abstraction of doing into labour. Consequently, the abstraction of doing into labour can be taken for granted, and indeed there is no need to talk of the dual character of labour since the only relevant labour in capitalism is abstract labour: we can just speak of labour and forget what Marx said of the importance of the dual character of labour. Primitive accumulation was a violent episode in the past, which created a capitalist world in which there is one central antagonism, that between labour and capital. It is from there that we have to think about the possibilities of change.

The second approach is to argue that if we take abstract labour for granted, then we already enclose ourselves within the world constituted by abstract labour, and then there is no way out: both logic and tragic historical experience tell us that it is so. The alternative is to question the abstraction of doing into labour: primitive accumulation should not be seen as a closed process, something that happened in the past, but as something that is open, a live antagonism.

Abstract labour rules, but there is more to be said. From the beginning, abstract labour announces its own antithesis. Abstract labour is one face of the 'dual character of labour'. But we have not spoken yet of the other face, the dark face, the face for which we really do not even have a satisfactory name, though for the moment we shall stick with 'concrete-creative doing'.

The dark side creeps in through the cracks. Abstract labour is, as we have seen, a constituted form of social relations,[12] a constituted form of human activity. Centuries of struggle have led to the constitution of abstract labour. But if that were all, we would not be able to criticise it, we would have no standpoint from which to gaze critically. The fact that we criticise suggests that there is more than abstract labour, that the transformation of doing into abstract labour is not closed, is not complete. We are more than the perverted performers of abstract labour. It is this 'more than', this remainder, this misfitting, that is the source of hope.

We cannot speak of abstract labour without talking of that misfit, concrete-creative doing, that which fits into and yet does not fit into abstract labour, that which is contained in and yet overflows from abstract labour. This is what we must move on to: the other face of the dual character of labour. But first we must look at the terrible hold of abstract labour over the anti-capitalist movement.

22

The labour movement is the
movement of abstract labour.

1. IN THE MARXIST TRADITION, THE ANTAGONISM BETWEEN USEFUL DOING AND ABSTRACT LABOUR ALMOST DISAPPEARS.

It is at first sight extraordinary that, although Marx attached such importance to the two-fold character of labour, the question is almost entirely ignored in the huge body of literature that takes *Capital* as its point of departure. The same point was made by I.I. Rubin in the early 1920s[1]: 'When we see the decisive importance which Marx gave to the theory of abstract labour, we must wonder why this theory has received so little attention in Marxist literature' (1928/1973: 131). However, his comment did little to change the situation.

Possibly, this has something to do with Marx's method. In his critique of political economy, Marx focuses his gaze on the object of criticism: abstract labour and the categories of political economy to which it gives rise. He looks at the world through the eyes of the concrete doing or conscious life-activity which the abstraction of labour negates. It is obvious, then, that concrete doing does not loom large in his critique: attention is directed to the abstract labour that is the object of critique. And yet this does not seem an adequate explanation, for Marx's comment at the beginning of Chapter 1 is obvious enough: 'this point is the pivot on which a clear comprehension of Political Economy turns' (1867/1965: 41; 1867/1990: 132). It seems difficult to overlook such a striking statement, and yet this is exactly what the whole Marxist tradition, and particularly the tradition of Marxist economics, does.

In Howard and King's two-volume *History of Marxian Economics* (1989, 1992), there is just one passing mention of the distinction between abstract and concrete or useful labour, and the point is not developed at all. This seems to be an accurate reflection of the work of those who have tried to develop a Marxist economics (rather than a critique of political economy). Thus, for example, Ernest Mandel, in his highly influential *Marxist Economic Theory*, makes no mention of the contrast between abstract and useful labour: he does have a small section on free labour and alienated labour (1962/1971: 172), but he does not make the connection with abstraction and the point does not play an important part in his argument. Similarly, Paul Mattick, a council communist and constant critic of Leninism as well as being one of the outstanding Marxist economists of the last century, also has nothing to say about the two-fold nature of labour.[2] The tradition of Marxist economics is dominated by a unitary and trans-historical concept of labour. This is not surprising perhaps, for the very notion of a Marxist economics implies the total subordination of concrete to abstract labour: it is only to the extent that this subordination really takes place that it is possible to speak of an economy bound by laws. The very idea of a Marxist economics closes the category of labour that Marx had opened.

We must look to those who have emphasised the importance of understanding Marx's work not as political economy, but as a *critique* of political economy, to find some mention of the two-fold nature of labour. But, even here, something strange happens: the two-fold nature of labour is treated as being just *one*fold, as referring exclusively to abstract labour. Here the field is led, as we have seen, by I.I. Rubin, who published his *Essays on Marx's Theory of Value* in the Soviet Union in the early 1920s and who later disappeared in Stalin's purges. Rubin insists that 'Marx attached decisive importance to the difference between concrete and abstract labour' (1928/1973: 131) and devotes a whole chapter to abstract labour: the chapter is devoted not to the two-fold nature of labour, but to abstract labour. He assumes that concrete labour is effectively subordinated to abstract labour and does not understand the relation as an antagonistic one.

In recent years, other authors have followed the same path as Rubin in emphasising the two-fold nature of labour and then focusing exclusively on abstract labour. Derek Sayer, in his book *Marx's Method*, does devote a section to useful labour/abstract labour, but he has very little to say about useful labour: 'This concept [useful labour] is not one which produces particular difficulty, for the simple reason that what it describes is labour in its natural form. The same, however, cannot be said of the other term of the distinction [abstract labour]' (1979: 18). Similarly, Michael Heinrich in his clear and influential exposition of Marx's critique of political economy, draws attention to the importance for Marx of the two-fold nature of labour (2005: 45), but he does so in a section devoted to abstract labour that pays little attention to the other side of the two-fold, concrete or useful labour.

We leave some of the more recent discussions aside for consideration in the context of the crisis of abstract labour, but, even taking these into account, it remains true that almost without exception, the Marxist tradition, contrary to Marx's clear statement in the opening pages of *Capital*, treats labour as a unitary category. Where the two-fold nature of labour is mentioned, it is assumed that the relation between the two aspects of labour is non-antagonistic and unproblematic.[3]

In the mainstream tradition of orthodox Marxism, this unproblematised 'labour' then comes to be seen as a positive force, the source of hope. The struggle against capital is seen as the struggle *of* labour against capital. Labour is treated not only as a unitary but also as a trans-historical category. Labour, in this view, is seen 'as an activity mediating humans and nature that transforms matter in a goal-directed manner and is a condition of social life. Labour, so understood, is posited as the source of wealth in all societies and as that which constitutes what is truly universal and truly social' (Postone, 2003: 5)[4] The problem with capitalism, then, is not that labour exists, but that labour is shackled, not allowed to reach its full development. The purpose of the revolution is to free labour from its chains.

It might be thought that this is merely a question of words, that the intention of the mainstream tradition is to argue that the revolution will emancipate useful labour from its abstraction. However, since the two-fold nature of labour is overlooked in that tradition, that distinction cannot be made. And it certainly has not been made in practice: the 'communist' revolutions did nothing to transform labour.

We are forced back and back to the same question: why is it that the two-fold character of labour, to which Marx attached such importance, effectively disappeared from the discussion of *Capital* and from the communist movement? Why is the category of useful labour (or doing) effectively suppressed? This was not because the authors in question had not read Marx carefully enough or reflected on the text. To find an explanation we must look to the development of class struggle itself.

2. THE THEORETICAL SUPPRESSION OF THE ANTAGONISM BETWEEN DOING AND LABOUR IS A MOMENT OF THE DOMINANCE IN PRACTICE OF THE STRUGGLE OF ABSTRACT LABOUR.

To understand the effective suppression of the category of concrete labour to describe an activity both subordinated and antagonistic to abstract labour, it is necessary to distinguish between two levels of struggle, those which we signalled already in the previous thesis.

First, there is the conflict which we have emphasised throughout this book, and which Marx portrayed as 'the pivot on which a clear comprehension of Political Economy turns' (1867/1965: 41; 1867/1990: 132), that is, the conflict between abstract labour and creative or purposeful doing. This is an irreconcilable conflict. Conscious doing is the negation of abstract labour, while the abstraction of labour is the subordination of conscious doing to production for the market: on the one hand, the potentially socially self-determined doing, on the other, labour subject to alien determination.

This abstraction of doing into labour generates a second level of conflict, that between labour and capital. Abstract labour is generalised as a principle of social activity only when labour power is converted into a commodity and there is a generalisation of the wage relation, and therefore of exploitation. We generally experience the loss of control over our own activity not as a direct result of selling our products on the market, but rather as a result of the fact that we have to sell our capacity to labour in return for a wage and perform the labour that is assigned to us. Abstract labour, which in the first place takes the form of value production, now takes the form of surplus value production (producing a surplus value which our employer realises as profit). The initial conflict between useful labour (doing) and abstract labour is overlaid by a conflict between wage labour and capital, centred on exploitation. The interest of capital is to exploit the wage labourers as much as possible: by lengthening the working day, reducing wages, increasing productivity and so on. The struggle of the wage labourers is to increase wages, shorten the working day, win better working conditions, ultimately, to abolish exploitation altogether.

Are we talking here of two different levels of class struggle or two different conceptions of class struggle? Both.

There are really two different levels of class struggle. Capitalist production is based both on the abstraction of doing into labour and on the exploitation of abstract labour. Without the abstraction of doing into labour, exploitation would not be possible. On the other hand, it is through the process of exploitation that the abstraction of labour is imposed and reimposed (or not, as the case may be). The two forms of struggle are closely intertwined, and yet distinct. The distinction is important because in the one case we are talking of the struggle of doing *against* labour, and in the other case of the struggle *of* labour against capital.[5]

There really are two different levels of class struggle, but these two different levels also give rise to two different understandings of class struggle, with far-reaching consequences for the struggle against capitalism.[6]

The dominant understanding, without doubt, centres its attention on the relation of exploitation, on the struggle *of* labour against capital. In terms of reading *Capital*, it sees the analysis of surplus value production as central and tends to regard the discussion of the commodity and the two-fold nature of labour (if it sees it at all) as a prelude to the important discussion. This approach sees labour as the revolutionary subject and understands labour as the working class, defined as those who produce surplus value or as those who sell their labour power to capital. The term 'labour' is used as a general term without making any distinction between abstract and useful labour. In this perspective, primitive accumulation, the transformation of doing into abstract labour, is an episode in the past, a sad story that is closed, so that there remains only one contradiction, that between labour and capital.

The alternative approach, far less widespread and less developed, focuses on the conflict between concrete doing and abstract labour, on the struggle of doing *against* labour. In terms of reading *Capital*, it attaches great importance to the first chapter and sees the later analysis of surplus value production as a development of the fundamental struggle between doing and abstract labour.[7] In this approach, the transformation of doing into labour is not a closed book but a living antagonism. The revolutionary subject is doing (conscious life activity) and the enemy to be abolished is abstract labour: the struggle of doing is the struggle of the working class against its own existence as working class, and it is not possible to define the working class since the antagonism between doing and labour is one that traverses every aspect of our existence – and indeed because the process of definition is one moment of the process of abstraction of labour.[8]

In one sense, the two approaches are diametrically opposed, since one sees anti-capitalism as the struggle *of* labour, while for the other it is the struggle *against* labour, yet we should not be too hasty to draw clear lines: in practice, there is a constant fudging of the separation, a constant overflowing from the more restrictive to the broader form of struggle.

The understanding of class struggle as the struggle *of* labour against capital has dominated both the practice and the theory of the struggle against capital, at least until very recently.[9] This has had enormous consequences for the theory and the practice of struggle. Among other things, it has led to the total neglect of the 'two-fold nature of labour', the theoretical and practical suppression of useful doing, the relegation of the antagonism between doing and labour to the historical past, the olden days of primitive accumulation. The Marxism of the late nineteenth and most of the twentieth century was part of the class struggle, but part of a particular form of class struggle in which the antagonism between doing and abstract labour was relatively obscure, with the result that the theory of this struggle was blind to the two-fold nature of labour. Traditional Marxism (not only Leninism in all its varieties but a whole spectrum that goes way beyond that) was the theory of the struggle *of* labour against capital.

It is this form of Marxism that is now in crisis, simply because this form of struggle is in crisis. This is what we need to explore. The crisis of the forms of class struggle pushes us to explore a new revolutionary theory, a new Marxism: the theory not of the struggle *of labour against capital*, but of the struggle *of doing against labour (and therefore against capital)*.

3. THE DOMINANCE OF ABSTRACT LABOUR IS THE SELF-INCARCERATION OF THE ANTI-CAPITALIST MOVEMENT.

The movement of abstract labour against capital is the aptly named 'labour movement'. In the labour movement, the existence of abstract labour is typically taken for granted, so that there reigns a unitary concept of labour. The dichotomy between useful doing and abstract labour is ignored completely, both in theory and in practice: the overcoming of abstract labour, if discussed at all, is projected into the future.

From the early days of industrial capitalism, the workers employed by capitalists have joined together to fight for better conditions, higher wages, shorter hours, and so on. The typical form of organisation is the trade union, a hierarchical and generally bureaucratic form of organisation. The struggle of abstract labour is first and foremost a struggle over employment: a struggle for better conditions of employment, for higher wages, for more employment, a struggle against unemployment. These struggles are important, they affect the living conditions of millions and millions of people throughout the world. But they are also struggles that take for granted the reproduction of capitalist domination, the subordination of our doing to alien control, the continued abstraction of doing into labour.

Trade union struggle is not the only form of struggle of labour against capital. Revolutionaries have always argued that trade union struggle is not sufficient, that trade union struggle does no more than defend the conditions of wage labour, whereas it is necessary to struggle for the abolition of wage labour and of exploitation. Trade union struggle is an economic struggle that needs to be complemented by political struggle. Political struggle is the struggle to take state power and, using state power, to socialise the means of production and abolish wage labour. This is the classical model of revolution of the Second, Third and Fourth Internationals. It is the model not just of Lenin but of all the leading revolutionaries of the late nineteenth and the first part of the twentieth century. The separation between trade union or economic struggle on the one hand, and political, revolutionary struggle on the other is a cornerstone of Lenin's theory of revolution, as sketched in *What is to be Done?* (1902/1968) But it is not just Lenin: Rosa Luxemburg is an interesting example to take, not in order to single her out for criticism, but simply because she is perhaps (and understandably) the most widely admired revolutionary of the classic period. Even in her pamphlet on *The Mass Strike* (1906/1970), Luxemburg maintains the separation between economic and political struggle.

In the separation between the economic and the political struggle, the transformation of our doing into abstract labour which is at the centre of capitalism, simply gets lost. It is not present in the idea of economic struggle, because economic struggle is about improving the conditions of wage labour. And it is not present in political struggle, because the political struggle takes the economic struggle for granted, as a basis on which to construct a revolutionary movement. In political struggle, abstract labour appears only (if at all) as something to be abolished in the future, after the taking of power, but not as present struggle. In practice, however, the taking of power by revolutionary movements has never led to the transformation of the labour process, to the emancipation of doing from labour. The very idea of socialist or communist revolution simply became uncoupled from any notion of liberating doing. The concept of the two-fold nature of labour disappears not only from theory but also from practice. Notorious is the support of Lenin for the adoption of Taylorism in the USSR: the open proclamation of the continuing rule of socially necessary labour time.

A struggle divided into economic and political struggles cannot question abstract labour simply because abstract labour is the basis of the separation between the economic and the political. Abstract labour is already pre-supposed when we make a distinction between economic and political struggle, so that the complementing of economic struggle by political struggle does not challenge the existence of abstract labour but confirms it. It does not overcome the limits of the trade union movement, but consolidates them. Abstract labour is the basis of the fetishism on which the separation of economic and political is based: the very separation of the economic and the political is a moment of the abstraction of labour.

To take wage labour (or simply labour) as the basis of the anti-capitalist movement is quite simply to entrap that movement within capital. All the features of abstract labour which were singled out in the previous discussion are characteristic of the labour movement: the reification of social relations, the reproduction of the hierarchy between men and women and the dimorphisation of sexuality, the objectification of nature, the acceptance of the capitalist concept of time, and above all, the orientation towards the state and the idea of influencing the state or taking state power. We could go on, and on, but the point is clear. As long as abstract (or wage) labour is taken as the unquestioned basis of the labour movement, or the revolutionary movement, then that movement will carry forward all the reified concepts and forms of behaviour that arise from the abstraction of doing into labour.

We can now see that the non-recognition of the dual character of labour is the core of a larger problem in the Marxist tradition. In the same way that abstract labour creates a closed world of things and laws of development, so a theory that takes the abstraction of doing into labour for granted and bases itself upon a unitary concept of labour encloses itself conceptually within the same world. In this conceptual world, people become converted into the bearers of social relations; classes become definable and defined groups of people: money, capital, interest and so on become the key categories of a new political economy centred on understanding the laws of capitalist development. This is the Marxism of Marxist economics, Marxist sociology, Marxist philosophy, Marxist political science and so on. Critique is forgotten and Marxism is treated as a positive science, a sort of structural functionalism,[10] dedicated to the study of the structures of capitalist society and the functional connections between them. Since the crucial category of labour is unidimensional, we are led into a unidimensional Marxism which focuses on the analysis of capital and its logic, or the structures and movements of capitalist domination. Marxism, from being a theory of struggle, becomes a theory of domination. It is not that struggle is forgotten, but it is seen as lying outside the central categories of Marxism. Capital accumulation, for example, is understood not as struggle but as the context within which struggle takes place; capitalist crisis is understood not as intensification of struggle but as providing opportunities for struggle. The categories are understood as closed categories rather than as conceptualisations of antagonistic relations, as relations of struggle, and therefore open. All this has been said before, and is indeed central to the argument of 'open Marxism'. What is new for me, perhaps, is the realisation that the central category in all this is labour. A closed, unitary concept of labour generates a closed understanding of all the categories, while an understanding of labour as an open antagonism gives rise to an understanding of all categories as open antagonisms. If labour is to be understood as concealing a live antagonism between doing what we want and labouring under the dictate of capital, then so must all the categories be understood as concealing related struggles: these are the battlefields on which we all live and die.

Abstract labour has incarcerated the movement against capitalism for 150 years. To say this is not to belittle the struggles of all those people who have dedicated and often sacrificed their lives to the struggle for a better world. Quite the contrary. If the dream of a better world lives on, it is thanks to their struggles: a book like this is necessarily a declaration of profound gratitude and admiration for their lives of rebellion.[11] The tragedy is that those rebellions were entrapped within an organisational and conceptual framework that arose on the basis of abstract labour.

There has, however, always been an overflowing of anti-capitalist struggle from the labour movement, there has always been an 'other labour movement'.[12] The struggles against capitalism have always been in-against-and-beyond the labour movement, but in recent years the against-and-beyond has become more important. As abstract labour becomes less capable of containing the force of doing, so the movement built on abstract labour, the labour movement, becomes less capable of containing our rage against the existing world. The crisis of abstract labour is the crisis of the labour movement.

Part VI
The Crisis of Abstract Labour

23

Abstraction is not just a past
but also a present process.

We are enclosed, locked in, entrapped. Enclosed by money, locked in by violence, entrapped by the logic of the social cohesion of capitalism.

It is we ourselves who create the prison. It is the product of abstract labour. Abstract labour is the labour we perform as a result of 'the transition to capitalism', those centuries of historical struggle that brought about a transformation of the way in which humans act and think.

The fact that we build our own prison is a source both of hope and of profound depression. The fact that we make the world that holds us entrapped means that we can unmake it. This is why it was so important for Marx to show that the apparently eternal facts of life like money, capital, or state, are historically specific forms of social relations, moments of the way in which our activity is organised. On the other hand, if we make our own prison, then clearly there is something wrong with us. This is perhaps why critical theory is sometimes linked to a deep pessimism: we are so profoundly crippled by abstract labour and all that it implies that there seems no hope at all for radical change.

The focus on abstract labour is a great leap forward compared with the simple assumption of a unitary labour. It allows us to see that the enemy is in the first place the abstract labour that creates capital, rather than some external force, and also allows us to open up a much richer picture of capitalist domination, as we have seen. But the very richness of the picture encloses us: as we explore this process of prison-building, we become aware of its immense complexity and force. The fact that our activity is organised in a certain way (the fact that we perform abstract labour) creates a complex weave of identity, sexuality, clock-time, destruction of nature, and so on. Changing social relations cannot be reduced to changing the ownership of the means of production: it means a transformation of all aspects of our lives. The complexity of domination seems to overwhelm us.

The only way out of this dilemma is to attack time itself.

The story that we have told so far is the orthodox tale of primitive accumulation. The historic transition from feudalism to capitalism created a new organisation of human activity as abstract labour, and this brought with it a transformation of time, of sexuality, of the person, of every aspect of life. This is a past process that has created a society of identity, a one-dimensional society, a society ruled by the clock. The capitalist forms of social relations will not necessarily exist for ever, but for the moment they rule.

But supposing it is not so? Supposing the past is not the past but also the present? Supposing primitive accumulation is not just a past process but also a present one? That would open the door to a very different politics and a very different theory.

Primitive accumulation is usually seen as a past process of violent struggle to establish the social bases of capitalism. Marx himself seems to have thought of it in that way, speaking of it as 'the pre-historic stage of capital' (1867/1965: 715; 1867/1990: 875) and suggesting that the initial violent establishment of capitalist conditions gives way to the 'dull compulsion of economic relations' and that now 'direct force ... is of course still used, but only exceptionally' (1867/1965: 737; 1867/1990: 899). And yet it cannot be so: there are certainly changes in the form of accumulation, but it is surely wrong to suggest that at some moment the direct violence of early accumulation is succeeded by a new stage in which the 'dull compulsion of economic relations' is sufficient to maintain capitalist order.[1]

At its core, primitive accumulation is the separation of producers from the means of production. (Marx 1867/1965: 714; 1867/1990: 874–5) But this separation is not a closed process. It is something that is repeated each and every day. On the one hand, there is a constant struggle to extend the enclosure of property: think of water, genetic resources, or intellectual property, for example. Think of the massive and accelerating expulsion of the peasantry from the land throughout the world and the huge growth of the cities in the last fifty years.[2] However, it is not just a question of the creation of new private property, and it is certainly not only on the margins of capitalism that primitive accumulation is relevant.[3] The old, past, established property is also constantly at issue. Even the property of land enclosed three hundred years ago is constituted only through a process of constant reiteration, constantly renewed separation, or enclosure. Capital accumulation itself, the amassing of profits, is a constant process of separation of the producers from their own product and hence from the means of production. The actual and threatened violence required to produce and reproduce the separation of the producers from the means of production is possibly now far greater than anything that Marx even imagined. The enclosure of land and the respect for private property require an enormous army of people for their enforcement. If we count not only security guards, police and army, but also judges, lawyers, social workers and teachers (not to mention parents), then a very significant part of the world's population is engaged in the constantly reiterated separation of people from the means of production. The term 'dull compulsion of economic relations' does not do justice to the active and constantly contested nature of capitalist appropriation.[4]

The same can be said not only of primitive accumulation in its narrow sense but of all the forms of social relations that are moments of the abstraction of labour. As Marcel Stoetzler (2009: 169) puts it in an article on the creation of the separation between women and men, 'When Hegel pointed to the daily reading of a particular paper as one of the reiterative acts that produce what looks like it has always been there, the same can be said of Renan's "daily plebiscites" and Judith Butler's daily acts of "performative reiteration" that produce the (real) illusion of sex.' Primitive accumulation can perhaps be said to be performative reiteration: in the same way as the separation (and thereby definition) of girls and boys is a product of constant repetition, so too the separation of people from the means of production is the result of the daily reiteration that constitutes private property as such.

The abstraction of doing into labour, then, is not just a past process: it is present, everyday struggle, the struggle on which the existence of capital depends.

The same point can be made in terms of constitution and existence. Fetishism is the separation of constitution and existence. We make a commodity and, once made, the commodity acquires an independent existence, negates the process of its own constitution. The shirt we buy in a shop tells us nothing of how it was made. The separation of constitution and existence is the establishment of a clear break between past and present, central to the homogenisation of time. This means that to take as given the separation of constitution and existence, or to take as given the homogenisation of time, is to place ourselves squarely on the grounds of fetishised thought. To take primitive accumulation simply as a past historical event is to fall into the real, but illusory, view of history that is produced by the same primitive accumulation. To criticise primitive accumulation is to criticise the temporality which it produced, to criticise the separation of constitution and existence, the separation of past from present. The constitution of capitalism is not a closed episode in the past: capitalism exists through its constant reconstitution.

The same point can be made yet again – and if I make the point repeatedly in slightly different ways, it is because this is the pivot of the book – by saying that the forms of social relations must be understood as form-processes. All the different forms of social relations that we have mentioned (money, state, capital, commodity, clock-time, woman, man, and so on) are not just forms that are established in the transition to capitalism but processes of forming social relations that are constantly active, and constantly at issue. Money is not just an established form but a process of monetisation of social relations that is constantly repeated and constantly contested (by those who take commodities without paying for them, for example, whether children or shoplifters). The state is not just there, but a constant process of statification, of channelling social conflict into certain forms, a process constantly at issue as those in struggle seek to maintain or develop other forms.[5] *Man* is not an established form of social relations but the result of constantly repeated practices, which are also constantly under attack. All the social relations are active battlegrounds, live antagonisms.

Form-determination, then, is never total: it is always a struggle. The determination of our activities by the forms of capitalist social relations is not given, but a constant battle. Rebellion is always an option, in any situation. The teacher can always refuse to teach what capital seeks to impose. The student can always criticise. The worker can always refuse to obey. The soldier can always refuse to kill. That is why capital invests so much energy and resources in trying to ensure that it does not happen. Yet finally the choice, and the responsibility, is ours: not as individual, free choice but as part of the struggle over the future of humanity. Rebellion is always an option, but much more than that, it is an integral part of everyday life. That is why the existence of capitalism is based on its own constant reconstitution, the constant recreation of its forms of social relations.

All the forms of social relations are processes, processes of struggle, live antagonisms. Our creative doing exists in alien forms, forms that deny its existence. As Richard Gunn points out, to say that something exists in the form of something else means that it exists 'in the mode of being denied' (Gunn 1992: 14). But to understand form as form-process is to insist that that which exists in the mode of being denied exists in constant revolt against its own denial: the relation between doing and abstract labour is one of tension and rebellion.

The issue is not new: it was posed in theological terms by Eriugena, the heterodox theologian of the ninth century. He argued that God created man, not just at the beginning of human history, but as a constantly repeated process, that he constantly creates and re-creates man. What this does is to open an enormous fragility in our lives: our existence depends from one moment to the next on the active process of divine creation.[6]

The point can be rephrased yet again in terms of 'the *truth value* of memory' (Marcuse 1956/1998: 18). The imposition of abstract labour required centuries of often violent struggle. The struggles of the women, men and others who resisted lie in the past, but also live on in the present, as memory. The present force or truth value of memory, whether of the individual or of society, 'lies in the specific function of memory to preserve promises and potentialities which are betrayed and even outlawed by the mature, civilised individual, but which had once been fulfilled in his dim past and which are never entirely forgotten' (ibid.: 18). Freudian psychoanalysis makes us very aware that, through memory, the past lives on in the present. The same is true socially: the unredeemed struggles of the past, the unfulfilled promises and potentialities, are a present force.[7] 'Fear the Wrath of the dead', as Elytis puts it.[8] And similarly, one can say of the possible future that the world that is not yet but could be, exists not-yet as real anticipation in the struggles of past and present.[9] The witches live on: not a rhetorical phrase, but the real force of memory and possible future in the present.

Other-doing is repressed but not extinct. According to Irish mythology, when the Milesians invaded Ireland, the previous inhabitants, the Tuatha Dé Danann, were not wiped out but driven under the ground, where they continued to live and do magic. The victory of abstract labour did not extinguish other forms of behaving but merely drove them underground, where they live on, repressed and rebellious. What interests us is the *return of the repressed*, which, according to Marcuse, 'makes up the tabooed and subterranean history of civilisation' (1956/1998: 16): not the repressed past, but that which is unredeemed in the past, the potentiality of a different future.[10]

All of these formulations point to the present existence of an *other side*. If money is a process, then it is a process of monetising *something*, just as the state is a process of statifying *something*, just as primitive accumulation is the constantly reiterated transformation of *something*. Behind money, state, man, woman, and so on, there is something hidden, a dark side, an invisible, a something that is being processed, something that is being formed, something that is not (yet) entirely absorbed into the capitalist forms, not entirely monetised, statified, commodified, sexually dimorphised. There is something that does not fit in: ourselves. The very fact that we criticise these forms means that there is something that exists beyond them. As Ernst Bloch puts it in relation to alienation: 'alienation could not even be seen, and condemned of robbing people of their freedom and depriving the world of its soul, if there did not exist some measure of its opposite, of that possible coming-to-oneself, being-with-oneself, against which alienation can be measured' (Bloch 1964 (2): 113).

This *other side* is not mere potential or possibility. The *other side* is potential, it is an anticipation of the world that might exist, but to treat it as mere possibility leaves us dangerously in the air, postpones yet again the realisation of this potential to some vague and undetermined future. A potential that is not a live antagonism, a living struggle, is worth nothing. We all have the potential to become famous basketball players or distinguished neurosurgeons, but if this potential has no material expression it becomes a self-deceptive dream. To understand abstraction as present process means that that which is abstracted exists not just as potential, but as real force in the present.

It is this dark side, not just as mere potential but as present force, that we are interested in. This brings us back to our starting-point: the dual character of labour, as abstract labour and useful or concrete labour, or as alienated labour and conscious life-activity. In the previous sections, we have focused on abstract labour as the force that weaves the web of domination. Now it is time to turn to the other side: useful or concrete labour, conscious life-activity, concrete doing. This is the turning-point in the argument.

24

Concrete doing overflows from abstract labour: it exists in-against-and-beyond abstract labour.

Abstract labour rules. It is a form of behaving and interrelating established at the beginning of capitalism. It is the basis of a system of social cohesion independent of human volition which, once established, 'acquired a necessary and systematic character' (Postone 1996:, 148).

Abstract labour is the historical form in which concrete doing exists under capitalism. As we have seen, even by the few authors who mention the dual character of labour, the relation between abstract and concrete labour (or concrete doing) is universally considered to be unproblematic: concrete labour is simply seen as being contained within the form of abstract labour. Abstract and concrete labour, it is said, are simply two aspects of the same process.[1]

And yet it cannot be so. Even if we walk alone in our argument, it cannot be that there is a total subordination of concrete to abstract labour. Both experience and theoretical reflection tell us that it is not and cannot be so.

At its simplest, the tension between concrete doing and abstract labour is a matter of everyday experience. If we are teachers, we feel the tension between teaching well and grading or producing the necessary number of graduates. If we are carpenters, we feel the contradiction between making a good table and producing a commodity that will sell. If we work in a call centre, we feel the tension between the possibility of having a friendly chat with someone on the telephone and the disciplines of the job. If we work on an assembly line, we feel the push of other-doing as an unbearable frustration. In the first part of this book, we saw that this tension leads many people to refuse to subordinate their activity to the demands of abstract labour and to find ways of liberating it from the demands of money.

It is true that in capitalism concrete doing exists in the form of abstract labour, but the relation of form and content cannot be understood as one of simple identity or containment. As we saw in the previous thesis, the forms of capitalist relations should be understood as form-processes: abstract labour is an active process of forming our activity, of abstracting concrete doing. That means that there is necessarily a relation of non-identity between them, a misfitting, a tension, a resistance, an antagonism. Concrete and abstract labour may be two aspects of the same labour, but they are contradictory, antagonistic aspects.

Concrete doing is not, and cannot be, totally subordinated to abstract labour. There is a non-identity between them: doing does not fit in to abstract labour without a remainder. There is always a surplus, an overflowing. There is always a pushing in different directions. The drive of abstraction is money: what matters is the social validation of labour through money. The drive of concrete labour is towards doing the activity well, whether this be teaching, or making a car, or designing a web page. This implies a drive towards self-determination: doing something well means trying to exercise our own judgement as to what is well or ill done. In so far as we recognise that our activity, like any activity, is a social activity, our drive towards self-determination is necessarily a drive towards social self-determination. Abstract labour involves a drive towards determination of our activity by money, whereas useful labour implies a drive towards social self-determination.

We can think of the antagonism in terms of socially necessary labour time. In order for the commodity-producer to sell his commodity, he must have produced it with socially established levels of efficiency: the value of the commodity is determined by the socially necessary labour time required to produce it. That which creates value is 'undifferentiated, *socially necessary general* labour utterly indifferent to any particular content. For that very reason ... it is defined in a manner common to all commodities and is distinguished from others only quantitatively', as Marx puts it (1867/1990: 993). In other words, the imposition of socially necessary labour time is one with the abstraction of labour. Abstraction, the determination of labour by money, means in practice the necessity to produce things in the shortest time possible. This means a constant restructuring of the labour process and a constant conflict with concrete labour, which knows no such time constraints. In the individual commodity producer, this conflict will be experienced as a conflict between market requirements and the established habits of the producer. Where it is wage labourers who produce the commodity, the conflict will obviously become an open one between the demands of the employer and the struggle of the workers to do things at their own rhythm.

Abstraction, then, is inseparable from conflict. Where abstract labour exists as wage labour, the conflict takes the form of a conflict between workers and capitalists:

> What we are confronted by here is the *alienation* [*Entfremdung*] of man from his own labour. To that extent, the worker stands on a higher plane than the capitalist from the outset, since the latter has his roots in the process of alienation and finds absolute satisfaction in it whereas right from the start the worker is a victim who confronts it as a rebel and experiences it as a process of enslavement. (Marx 1867/1990: 990)

The struggle is a struggle *against abstract or alienated labour* and this struggle comes from those who suffer most this abstraction or alienation.

If abstraction is a conflictive process, then its relation to concrete doing cannot be understood as other than antagonistic. The rebellion against abstraction is a 'No, we shall not do that, we shall not do it that way. We shall do it the way we think best. We shall do what we want to do, what we consider necessary or desirable.' The rebellion against abstract labour is concrete doing in movement.

Concrete doing, then, is not totally subordinate to abstract labour, as most of the literature assumes. Certainly it exists *in* abstract labour: abstract labour is the form in which concrete doing exists in capitalist society. The doing that is involved in any sort of production is subjected, directly or indirectly, to the requirements of having to produce for the market, the requirements of value production. The qualitative aspect of the work is subordinated to the quantitative: what matters is that the workers should expend no more than the socially necessary labour time to produce the commodities. The qualitative aspect of the work counts just as productivity, the workers' ability to produce efficiently.[2] We are palpably aware of that, of all the time that we devote to activities that we do not determine, whether it be tightening a bolt on an assembly line, marking examinations, or selling hamburgers.

But doing exists also in revolt against abstract labour: in every refusal of alien authority, in every attempt to gain control over the work process, in every attempt to develop meaningful activities either outside the hours of employment or as an alternative to employment, occasionally too as explosions of refusal (carnivals, riots, rebellions). There is a constant tension: useful doing is not only dominated by, but also in constant rebellion against, its own abstraction. This tension is manifested in the neuroses, the frustrations and the constant struggles of any worker who tries to work creatively, or just to do things well, against the constraints of time and money.[3]

Doing is a shadowy figure, but it exists, and it exists not only in labour (in the form of abstract labour), but it exists against labour, and also beyond labour (in our dreams, in our alternative practices). Abstraction is a process, constantly repeated, but much of what we do escapes or overflows from the process of abstraction. When we do things we enjoy or consider important, when we have a good time with those we love, when we relax and think 'yes, this is the way life should be!', all these are moments when our doing is not abstracted from its quality nor from our purposive determination. There are also many, very many people in the world whose doing is not converted into abstract labour, either because their established modes of living have not (yet) been completely overturned by capitalist organisation, or because they simply do not fit within the framework of capitalist exploitation.[4] Many who are excluded or only occasionally (and precariously) included in the exploitation and abstraction of labour consciously try to turn their exclusion to the development (often collective development) of activities that they consider desirable or important. One thing is to criticise the subjection of useful doing to abstract labour (as Marx does), another is to

175

assume that there is no useful doing other than that which has been subsumed into its own abstraction.

This is not to say that all these activities are untouched by abstract labour, or that they are in some way *outside* the process of abstraction.[5] All are contradictory, part of a society dominated by capital. Certainly it is tempting to think that our spaces-moments of other-doing exist outside capital, that when we sit with our friends in the garden, or dance all night with those we love, we are living outside capital. The spaces of otherness appear as differences, rather than contradictions. Yet this is dangerous. Capital (abstract labour) is far more voracious than we may think, invading every aspect of the way in which we act and think. Our spaces of otherness are always threatened, always in danger of being eliminated by the movement of abstract labour. Whether we are conscious of it or not, our other-doings exist in defiance of the claims of money, the demand that all human activity should be converted into abstract labour. Our moments or spaces of non-subordination are insubordinations, defiances. Apparent differences are contradictions.[6] This is important if we are to understand the unity of our variegated desires to live as we want: the unity is negative, anti-capitalist.

In the earlier anticipation of the present argument, we characterised the relation between concrete doing and abstract labour as ecstatic.[7] Doing is the ecstasy of abstract labour: ecstasy as *ek-stasis*, standing outside abstract labour while existing within it, standing outside as actual and potential otherness. It is quite true to say that abstract labour and concrete labour (or doing) are aspects of the same process, but the relation between the two aspects is an ecstatic one, a relation of containment-rebellion-and-overflowing, a relation of in-against-and-beyond. We must be careful not to give a false positivity to useful doing, or to attribute to it an essential a-historical character. It exists as struggle, as the struggle to escape from its abstraction. Its moments of freedom are often both contradictory and evanescent, sandcastles built on the ocean shore. The 'freedom' should be thought of not in terms of stable autonomies but rather as the force of that which is not-yet, lightning flashes of a world that could be. But, however evanescent these escapes may be – whether they be that of the assembly-line worker fingering his imaginary guitar, the university professor dreaming that he can do more than train the functionaries of abstract labour, or the indigenous people of Chiapas creating and maintaining for years their own autonomous municipalities – however evanescent these overflowings of concrete-creative doing may be, let us be clear that that is where we live, that is where we stand, that is the point from which we must think the possibility of creating a different world. These overflowings are the cracks from which we started.

25
Doing is the crisis of abstract labour.

There is a constant struggle of doing in-against-and-beyond abstract labour. But are these struggles just romantic outbursts doomed from the beginning to be reabsorbed into the unstoppable flow of value-abstract-labour-capital? Or is there some way in which these struggles, pathetic though they may seem at times, constitute the crisis of capital and the beginnings of a new society?

1. THERE IS A CONSTANT TENSION
BETWEEN DOING AND ABSTRACT LABOUR.

We all strain at the leash. We pull all the time against alien activity, either trying to escape from it (by illness, retirement, strikes, absenteeism, and so on, and on) or by reshaping it as much as we can. Doing is the fragility of abstraction, a constant threat to the discipline of labour. In this sense, we can speak of doing as the permanent crisis of capitalism. Frustration is the core of capitalism, its central, explosive contradiction.[1]

Normally this frustration, this drive of doing against labour is rendered invisible. It is more evident in the forces designed to contain it. The whole of management aims at containing the tension, bending the energy of doing to the disciplines of labour. The expansion of credit in the last fifty years plays an important part too in holding frustration in check. And then there are the police, the psychiatrists and psychologists, the teachers and social workers and parents: a whole world that tells us that there is no alternative to labour. When we leave school, we are not advised that we have a choice, that we can devote our lives either to labour under the dictate of money or to some activity that we, perhaps together with those around us, choose as being pleasurable or significant. The choice is invisible: we are simply told that now we are adults we must earn our living by labour. Abstract labour imposes itself through the invisibilisation of doing. Labour rules by being unitary, by presenting itself as labour-without-alternative, so that even to speak of the dual character of labour or the antagonism between doing and labour suggests a touch of madness.[2] And yet it is at the centre of our preoccupations, all the time.

2. THE TENSION BETWEEN DOING AND LABOUR IS INHERENTLY AND CRUCIALLY UNSTABLE.

The abstraction of doing into labour is, as we have seen, inseparable from the drive to produce commodities in the socially necessary labour time. What determines the saleability of commodities on the market is the amount of time that is necessary to produce them. Through competition, there is a constant drive to reduce the time necessary to produce the commodity: if I (as a capitalist) can produce my commodities faster than my competitor, then I will make more profit. If I cannot keep up with my competitors in the time required to produce my commodities, I will soon be driven out of business. The activity that produced value a hundred years ago, or even twenty or ten years ago, is quite likely to be useless for capital now, simply because the meaning of abstract labour has moved on. I am driven therefore constantly to reduce the labour time required to produce my commodities by intensifying the labour process and also by expelling labour and replacing it by machinery. The abstraction of doing into labour is a constant turning of the screw, a constant destabilisation of the tense relation between doing and labour.

The constant turning of the screw of socially necessary labour time intensifies social misfitting. As capital demands more and more, it becomes more and more difficult to fit in to its demands. The intensified misfitting expresses itself in a double flight from labour. From the perspective of capital, the constant drive to reduce necessary labour time leads to the expulsion of labour from the labour process and its replacement by machinery. This leads to what Marx calls the 'rising organic composition of capital', the progressive increase in the ratio between expenditure on machinery and expenditure on labour power in the capitalist production process. Capital depends on labour for its production, but it constantly flees from this dependence by replacing labour by machinery, by replacing living by dead labour. It flees from the dependence, but it does not escape from it, for it still depends on labour for the production of value and profit. On the level of capital as a whole (though not necessarily for the individual capitalist), the flight from labour leads to a fall in the general rate of profit, and this translates itself for the individual capitalist into an intensification of competition and an ever more frenetic attempt to reduce the necessary labour time by intensifying the labour process and replacing labour by machinery.

On the other side too there is a flight from labour. But, whereas the flight of capital from labour is a flight into a vertiginous void, because it cannot exist without labour, on the side of the workers the flight from labour is a flight to doing. This may be voluntary, as people try to escape from the pressures of the capitalist labour process, or it may be involuntary: those expelled from the labour process, or who are never absorbed into capitalist employment in the first place, have to find other ways of surviving. Often this struggle to survive involves an even more direct subjection to the market (selling chewing gum, balloons, toys, anything, at the traffic lights of the big cities, for example), but it also generates structures of mutual support among families, communities, or groups of friends, and in that sense a moving away from abstract labour and the growth of a socially self-determined doing.

The constant intensification that is inherent in abstract labour tends to undermine its own existence. There is a progressive expulsion and repulsion: workers are expelled and repelled. Labour (and not just capital) comes to be seen as the enemy and people, by choice or necessity, seek different ways of living, different ways of organising their activity. The doing contained within labour and made invisible by labour starts to assert itself. *The unitary character of labour is split open.*

The dynamic of capitalism is a double flight from labour. On capital's side, the flight can only end back in labour and its intensification. On the workers' side, the flight from labour opens up perspectives of a different world organised on the basis of a consciously controlled doing. On both sides, the flight from labour means crisis of capital, for it is abstract labour that produces value, the substance of capitalist profit, and it is abstract labour that provides the social cohesion that holds capitalism together. But there are two ways out of the crisis: the capitalist solution (intensification and expulsion of labour) digs the hole deeper and prepares the way for an even more profound crisis the next time around, while the anti-capitalist solution splits doing from abstract labour and opens directly and immediately the perspective of a very different world.

3. THE CRISIS OF CAPITAL IS THE SPLITTING OPEN OF THE UNITARY CHARACTER OF LABOUR: THIS IS THE CRISIS IN WHICH WE ARE LIVING.

The high point of abstract labour was the high point of the labour movement. The period after the Second World War was characterised by rapid accumulation of capital made possible by the massive defeat of the working class by fascism and war, which permitted in turn the widespread introduction of new methods of production. This is the period often referred to as Fordism, characterised by massive factories and highly automated production techniques in which the workers become, more than ever, simple appendages of the machine, positions in the assembly line. Under Fordism, the abstraction of doing is pushed to its limit: labour is drained of all meaning. In return, the workers receive relatively high wages, supported by full employment policies and the development of the welfare state, at least in the richer countries, which in turn fuel consumption and the reproduction of the whole system of capitalist production. This is the golden age of the trade unions, of the apparent reduction of the antagonism between labour and capital to annual rounds of wage negotiations, and of close relations between trade unions and states. This is the golden age of the labour movement and of all that we have seen associated with abstract labour (positivist thought, male-dominated dimorphous sexuality, the unquestioned subordination of nature to progress, the understanding of change in terms of a totality identified with the state, and so on). Full employment is the closure of the cage, the completion of the rule of unitary, abstract labour: life-activity is employment is abstract labour, there is no alternative.

This tight, tense weave splits open in 1968[3] as a generation no longer so tamed by the experience of fascism and war rise up and say 'no, we shall not dedicate our lives to the rule of money, we shall not dedicate all the days of our lives to abstract labour, we shall do something else instead.' The revolt against capital expresses itself openly as that which it always is and must be: a revolt against labour. It becomes clear that we cannot think of class struggle as labour against capital, because labour is on the same side as capital, labour produces capital. This is what is expressed in the universities, this is what is expressed in the factories, this is what is expressed on the streets in 1968. This is what makes it impossible for capital to increase the rate of exploitation sufficiently to maintain its rate of profit and hold Fordism in place. It is a revolt that is directed against all aspects of the abstraction of labour: not just the alienation of labour in the narrow sense, but also the fetishisation of sex, nature, time, space and also against the state-oriented forms of organisation that are part of that fetishisation. There is a release, an emancipation: it becomes possible to think and do things that were not possible before. The force of the explosion, the force of the struggle, splits open the category of labour (opened by Marx but closed in practice by the Marxist tradition) and, with it all the other categories of thought.

This splitting of the category of labour throws us into a new world. This is not entirely new, of course: the rejection of labour is a strand running through the whole history of anti-capitalist struggle.[4] What is new is the centrality that it acquires with the crisis of Fordism.

At first sight, the crisis of labour[5] appears to be a defeat for us. Inevitably, the crisis of abstract labour is the crisis of the movement constructed on the basis of abstract labour: the labour movement. That there is a crisis of the labour movement is plain to see: the decline of the trade union movement everywhere in the world, the catastrophic erosion of many of the material gains won by the labour movement in the past, the virtual disappearance of social democratic parties with a real commitment to radical reform, the collapse of the Soviet Union and other 'communist countries' and the integration of China into world capitalism, the defeat of the movements of national liberation in Latin America and Africa, and the crisis of Marxism both within the universities and above all as a theory of struggle.

All this is widely seen as a historic defeat for the working class. Historic defeat no doubt, but defeat of what? A defeat for the labour movement, for the movement based upon abstract labour. A defeat for a movement entrapped within the fetishised forms of abstract labour. A defeat for the struggle of labour against capital, and possibly an opening for the struggle of doing against labour-and-capital. If that is the case, then it is not a defeat for class struggle, but a shift to a more profound level of class struggle.

The crisis of labour (and therefore of the struggle of labour against capital) precipitates us into a world with different dimensions. Class struggle continues to be central. We are still in capitalism, in a society driven by the pursuit of profit and based, therefore, on the constant struggle to subordinate human activity to the requirements of the production of profit, and on the opposing struggle to free human activity from this determination. Class struggle is central, but it has changed and is changing. It is no longer adequate to think of it as the struggle of labour against capital (since this formulation leaves the unitary character of labour unquestioned). We are forced to learn a new language of struggle, with a new conceptuality. We are, as Sergio Tischler puts it, in the penumbra of the threshold, still struggling to discern clearly the new patterns of struggle, to see our way forward. This is a time of doubts and uncertainties, possibly opening to a new world, and possibly not. Asking is the only way that we can walk.[6]

The general terms of the struggle follow from the analysis of crisis as the crisis of abstract labour, that is, the crisis of the abstraction of doing into labour. From the capitalist side, the resolution of the crisis means rechannelling doing into the parameters of abstract labour and containing it within those parameters. At its simplest, this means employment and the maintenance of discipline in the labour process: in other words, compelling people to perform abstract labour. For those who are not employed, it means imposing a social discipline that ensures that their activity remains within the general framework determined by abstract labour. For capital, the important thing is to seal up again the unitary character of labour, to show that there is no alternative to value-producing, money-making labour. There must be no escape from labour. In countries with a welfare-state system, it is crucial to tighten the rules to make sure that they do not provide havens for those who might want to do something else with their lives. The same in the universities: they must not be allowed to become places for relaxing or (worse) thinking: it is essential to tighten the educational system, speed up the process of learning and above all to measure the productivity of both teachers and students all the time, so that their activity is contained within abstract labour.[7] Neo-liberalism, post-Fordism, post-modernism are names given to different aspects of this struggle to subordinate human doing to the rule of money, to re-establish the idea that there is no alternative to labour, that all possible human activity is encompassed within the rule of labour.

This is a prolonged and constant struggle: it is not a new stable pattern of domination, although the terms mentioned (neo-liberalism, post-Fordism, post-modernism) may present it as such. A crucial factor in the struggle to reimpose labour is the expansion of credit. Credit creates a fictional world, a world based on the expectation of future surplus value. It allows individual capitals to avoid going bankrupt, and in this sense softens the collapse of the cage of full employment – abstract labour. The fictional world of credit thus softens the asperities of the disciplines of abstract labour, but also extends and deepens them. The company that is heavily in debt must desperately seek to make more efficient the labour under its command. And the person that is in debt is effectively bound into selling her labour power for money in order to pay the debt. The expansion of debt creates an image of stability, but is at the same time fundamentally unstable because it is based on an expectation that may not be realised.

If the struggle from the point of view of capital is the struggle to close down the possibility of a different organisation of human activity, to seal the unitary character of labour, then the struggle against capital must be to open the split, to break the integument that holds human activity imprisoned, to do everything we can to realise the possibility of a different doing.

At the centre of all this is the precariousness of labour. Throughout the world, there has been a decline in the relative stability of employment that, for many, characterised the Fordist period. The concessions won by trade union struggle have been dismantled everywhere by new labour legislation. Employment has become much more precarious, much more likely to be based on short-term contracts and variable hours. This means considerable material and emotional hardship for millions of people. And yet, if we focus solely on the suffering involved, we lose sight of the obvious, namely, that precariousness of labour is precisely what it says: the precariousness of capital, the precariousness of the labour that creates capital. People are forced into developing other forms of social relations and other forms of activity as the basis for survival. The suffering inherent in precariousness can flip over (and is flipping over) into its opposite, a growth of doing-against-labour. Similarly with unemployment: the rise of unemployment means enormous hardship for millions and millions of people, yet to call for a return to full employment, as the labour movement does and must do, is to call for a closure of unitary labour, to proclaim that employment is (at least for the moment) the only way forward for human activity, that doing must be subordinated to abstract labour. The alternative is to say, as radical groups of unemployed in Argentina and elsewhere have done, overflowing the struggles of the unemployed, that we do not want a return to employment and the exploitation that it implies, that we want to shape our own activity according to what we consider desirable or necessary.

The way forward is difficult to see, the paths hard to create, but it is clear that the precariousness of labour in all its senses is the crucial issue, that the future of the world depends on the splitting open of the unitary character of labour.

4. THE CRISIS OF ABSTRACT LABOUR
IS THE CRISIS OF ITS THEORY.

Inevitably, the crisis of abstract labour is the crisis of the theory that takes its stand on the struggle of abstract labour against capital. Orthodox Marxism, that is to say that Marxism that bases itself on a unitary concept of labour (with all that that entails), has become increasingly distanced from the movement of anti-capitalist struggle and has been widely criticised, not just by its bourgeois opponents of always, but by those who question its relevance to contemporary struggles.

The crisis of the old theory is the opening of a rich new theoretical ferment, a multiplicity of attempts to theorise our struggles and to think how on earth we can get out of the mess we are in. This is not the place to review these theories, but there are three strands that are particularly important and that may help to clarify the argument that is being advanced here.

First, the crisis of abstract labour and its theory is reflected in the growing influence of anarchism and anarchist theory. This can be seen as a 'new anarchism' (Graeber 2002), in which the old rigid hostility to Marxism no longer plays an important role. Many of the forms of action which break with the traditions of the labour movement come from an anarchist tradition: 'The very notion of direct action, with its rejection of a politics which appeals to governments to modify their behaviour, in favour of physical intervention against state power in a form that itself prefigures an alternative—all of this emerges directly' from the tradition of anarchism (ibid.). The anarchist tradition is clearly relevant to the whole discussion of the cracks, especially in Part II of this book and many of the authors cited in the discussion of the cracks would probably regard themselves as part of that tradition. It might be said, indeed, that, where orthodox Marxism with its assumption of a unitary concept of labour has theorised on the basis of the struggle of abstract labour, it is anarchist theory that has focused more clearly on concrete doing, at least in the sense of a breaking here and now with the constraints of abstract labour.

Is the present argument then an anarchist argument?[8] It does not matter, partly because the old distinctions have broken down and in any case labelling runs counter to thought:[9] labelling is a crude expression of the process of identification and classification that, as we have seen, is generated by abstract labour. But more substantially, the argument presented here is as much an argument against the anarchist tradition as it is against the Marxist tradition. The critique of both the anarchist and the Marxist tradition is indeed etched in the structure of the argument. We start from the refusals-and-creations, from that which does not fit in to the capitalist system: that is where Marxism, with its emphasis on the analysis of domination, has been weak and anarchism has been strong. But then reflection on the struggles and their problems brings us to the social cohesion and its contradictions: we are brought to the analysis of the dual character of labour. This is where we leave anarchism behind and enter into debates more relevant to the Marxist tradition. Yet our starting-point remains crucial and makes us swim against the main stream of Marxist thought. So where, then, does the argument fit, into which tradition? If it is faithful to its subject, it misfits.

A second element in the new ferment of theory has been a renewed awareness of the issue of the dual character of labour within Marxist discussions in recent years. Particularly important in present debates is Moishe Postone's book, *Time, Labour and Social Domination* (1996), in which he advances 'a reinterpretation of Marx's critical theory' that is based on a critique of the trans-historical and unitary concept of labour that is characteristic of the Marxist tradition. It is clear, then, that the central concern of Postone's book is closely related to the central issues of the argument presented here. Precisely because it is an important and rigorous book, it is necessary to explain the differences in our arguments.

Here again, the crucial import of the starting-point asserts itself. The main difference between Postone's approach and the argument presented here can be seen in terms of the starting-point.[10] Postone's begins by presenting his conceptualisation of 'capitalism in terms of a historically specific form of social interdependence with an impersonal and seemingly objective character. This form of interdependence is effected by historically unique forms of social relations that are constituted by determinate forms of social practice and, yet, become quasi-independent of the people engaged in these practices' (1996: 3). I share that conceptualisation and, like Postone, see the historically specific form of interdependence as being constituted by abstract labour. The difference lies in the fact that this book does not begin with the question of how to conceptualise capitalism but with a rude misfitting, a scream, a determination to break here and now the historically specific form of interdependence. This misfitting is not a light preamble to the heavier theoretical discussion that comes later, but is the very core of the theory. What we look for is not an understanding of social interdependence but a theory of how to break it. Starting from that misfitting, the only way in which we can understand the capitalist forms of social relations (and, at their centre, abstract labour) is as forms swollen with their own negation, forms that do not contain their content, but from which their content constantly overflows. Postone makes a clear distinction between contradiction and antagonism (ibid.: 34), whereas the starting-point of this argument makes such a distinction impossible. For Postone, concrete labour exists as contradiction within abstract labour, but not as living antagonism, but here concrete doing presents itself as screaming antagonism from the very beginning.[11] There is no understanding in Postone's book of an ec-static relation between abstract and concrete labour, so that, once again, the two-fold nature of labour which he so rightly emphasises becomes reduced in practice to a one-fold nature, abstract labour. Consequently, the perspective of a form of activity beyond abstract labour is presented constantly as possibility, rather than as present struggle. This latter point has important political consequences for it leads (yet again) to a theory of capitalism which is divorced from present struggle: in spite of the radical nature of his critique of traditional Marxism, Postone reproduces the separation between capital and class struggle that is one of the characteristic hallmarks of that tradition – a problem that recurs in the work of the Krisis group, also very important and with a similar theoretical perspective.

A third strand of recent discussions that must be considered is centred on the conception of self-valorisation. The term is coined by Toni Negri, but it is particularly instructive to look at the work of Harry Cleaver (1979, 1992). It is Cleaver who, among all the Marxist commentators, addresses explicitly the political significance of the two-fold nature of labour. In his book, *Reading Capital Politically*, he dedicates a chapter to the topic and opens the question of how 'to interpret this dichotomy between useful labour and abstract labour politically' (1979: 131). He assumes, however, that useful labour is completely subordinated to abstract labour:

> The elimination of capitalist work or abstract labour can only mean the elimination of concrete useful labour, insofar as this is an activity imposed as a form of social control ... Useful labour in industry, whether of the period of manufacturing or that of machinery, is always shaped by capital's need to control the class. Because useful labour is in this way the producer of value/control as well of use-value, it cannot be 'liberated'. It must be smashed in its present forms in order to smash value itself. (ibid.: 132)

In a later article, Cleaver attaches to the concept of 'self-valorisation' some of the characteristics that have been conceptualised here in terms of the movement of doing against labour. Self-valorisation, according to Cleaver, 'indicates a process of valorisation which is autonomous from capitalist valorisation – a self-defining, self-determining process which goes beyond the mere resistance to capitalist valorisation to a positive project of self-constitution' (1992: 129). In the same article, he speaks of 'the many processes of self-valorisation or self-constitution that escape the control of capital' (ibid.: 134).

It is clear that we are speaking of, and trying to understand, more or less the same processes of revolt. Cleaver prefers to conceptualise them as processes of self-valorisation, while I see them as expressions of the antagonism between concrete doing and abstract labour. Does the distinction matter? This is an issue that touches the whole argument of this book: when an established term such as self-valorisation exists, why do I leave that aside and talk instead of the dual character of labour, insisting (against the whole weight of tradition) that the relation between abstract and concrete labour must be seen as a live antagonism?

The central issue is that of the externality between capital and class struggle. We have seen that a separation between capital and struggle is a characteristic of traditional Marxism, and that the same (ultimately structuralist) distinction recurs in Postone's critique of the Marxist tradition. Cleaver (and indeed Negri and the *operaista* tradition) approach the matter from the other side because they place struggle in the foreground, but the categories themselves are never understood as conceptualisations of struggle,[12] so that the externality remains.[13] In this, Cleaver's rejection of the dual nature of labour as being an antagonistic relation and his espousal of the concept of self-valorisation as a process that is 'autonomous from capitalist valorisation' is significant. He also goes on to say that 'the refusal of work ... creates the very possibility of self-valorisation' (1992: 130).

This externality matters simply because it removes self-valorisation from the daily experience of labour. It becomes something special, rather than the routine experience of everyday doing in-against-and-beyond labour. Perhaps the great appeal and the strength and weakness of autonomist or *operaista* theory is that it is a theory for activists, a theory of activism, but of an activism separated from the experience of everyday living. I want to reach beyond that and to ground our understanding of revolt in everyday life. I argue here that the pivot for an understanding not just of political economy but of social antagonism is the dual nature of labour, and that this dual nature of labour is the inherent and constant antagonism of daily doing and living. Quite simply, life is the antagonism between doing and abstract labour,[14] and activism is simply a particularly intense expression of that all-pervasive antagonism, from which it separates itself at its peril.[15]

5. THE CRISIS OF ABSTRACT LABOUR IS OPEN.

There are those who argue that the revolt against labour has already been closed.

The autonomist (or *operaista*) interpretation of the crisis of the 1960s and 1970s attaches central importance to the workers' revolt against labour. Workers were no longer prepared to accept the extreme alienation of labour that the Fordist organisation of production implied. The overflowing of the labour movement, always present, became torrential. More and more workers took action outside the limits of the trade unions and against the trade unions. More and more, the actions were aimed not just at negotiating higher wages but against labour as such: absenteeism and sabotage increased significantly. The militancy in the car factories of Italy, organised and theorised by the *operaismo* of the 1960s and 1970s was the peak of a much more profound rejection not just of Fordism, but of capitalist labour.[16]

And then what? For some of the leading authors associated with the *operaista* movement (now often referred to as 'post-*operaista*'), the crisis of Fordism has been overcome and a new post-Fordist pattern of domination established. Thus, for example, Virno argues: 'During the 1960s and the 1970s I believe that the Western world experienced a defeated revolution – the first revolution aimed not against poverty and backwardness, but against the means of capitalist production, against the Fordist assembly-line and wage labour. Post-Fordism, the hybrid forms of life characteristic of the contemporary multitude, is the answer to this defeated revolution' (2004: 111). Post-Fordism is the 'surpassing of the society of labour' within capitalism itself, a society in which wealth is produced, not by the work of individuals but by science or 'the general intellect', a society in which 'there is no longer anything which distinguishes labour from the rest of human activities' (ibid.: 101–102) and no longer any difference between labour time and non-labour time. Similarly, 'from the point of view of "what" is done and "how" it is done, there is no longer any substantial difference between employment and unemployment. It could be said that: unemployment is non-remunerated labour and labour, in turn, is remunerated unemployment' (ibid.: 103). The great wave of subordination of the 1960s and 1970s has profoundly modified capitalism (so much so that Virno speaks of post-Fordism as the 'communism of capital') (ibid.: 110): 'The masterpiece of Italian capitalism consists in having transformed into a productive resource precisely those modes of behaviour which, at first, made their appearance under the semblance of radical conflict' (ibid.: 99). Insubordination, it would seem, has been suffocated, useful doing completely subordinated to abstract labour (though the distinction is never made explicit in this analysis): the only possibility is exit, exodus.

The analysis certainly stirs recognition. The adoption of flexible hours and more informal practices is established managerial practice in many workplaces. Developments in information technology and the use of laptops have made working from home much more common, so that the strict demarcation of the place and time of labour has become blurred. However, to go from that observation to the statement that there is 'no longer any difference between labour time and non-labour time' is clearly an exaggeration. For most people, there is still a clear distinction between labour and non-labour time. Similarly, although it might be said that there is a blurring of the distinction between labour and other activities, to say that 'there is no longer anything which distinguishes labour from the rest of human activities' is surely not true. The statements might be defended by reference to what Negri calls the 'method of the tendency', the idea that the theorist should draw out tendencies in current development and draw them into a coherent picture or paradigm of the evolving pattern of domination. Thus, the characteristics mentioned by Virno are compatible with the idea of the 'social factory' advanced by Negri, the idea that in modern capitalism the discipline of the factory has been effectively extended to the whole of society (an idea further developed in Guattari and Negri's (1985/1990) 'integrated world capitalism' and in Hardt and Negri's (2000) 'empire'). The attraction of these analyses lies in the fact that they do point to real tendencies and underline the drastic nature of current capitalist development. The problem is that they close (or push to the very margins) the possibilities of revolutionary change. Put simply, the tendency of current development is that humanity is annihilated.

In emphasising the tendencies of domination, there is an over-hasty closure of crisis. The importance of the crisis of Fordism is recognised, but immediately attention is then concentrated on the structure of the newly emerging patterns of domination. One structure has collapsed, so we must immediately theorise the new paradigm of domination – post-Fordism, empire, post-modernism, call it what you will. The king is dead, long live the king! Continuity is emphasised, rupture becomes a theoretical impossibility (or an extraneous possibility, as it always has been in orthodox (Leninist) theory). The continuity that is emphasised is the continuity of structure: there is a restructuring, but the new structure is as closed as the previous one. The structuralist thought that is one of the aspects of the domination of abstract labour is extended through the crisis of abstract labour to reassert the absolute dominance of abstract labour. If 'there is no longer anything which distinguishes labour from the rest of human activities', then concrete doing is totally absorbed within abstract labour, and there is no question of an against-and-beyond. What gets lost is the crack, the ek-stasis of concrete doing, the standing out-and-beyond of useful doing from abstract labour, the opening. The post-*operaista*, post-structuralist theorists extend into the crisis of abstract labour the thought-prison that was part of the domination of abstract labour. As soon as the world is opened, they leap ahead to close it, not because they support capital, but because that is what their understanding of the scientific method tells them to do.

The method adopted in this book is quite different. As explained in the first part, it is the method of the crack, the method of crisis. The question asked is not 'how do we understand the patterns of domination?' but 'how do we find hope in a black night?' How do we see crisis where it appears that there is no crisis? Not in order to fall into an unreal optimism, but to follow the lines of real possibility. When, then, we start from a manifest crisis of labour such as that of the 1970s, we ask not 'what is the new pattern of domination?' but rather 'how can we follow the continuing lines of crisis into the present?' How do we follow through the antagonism between doing and labour that showed its face so clearly in 1968?

An approach closer to that proposed here, at least in that it insists on the continuing centrality of the crisis of labour, is that of the Krisis group.[17] The Krisis group too see the crisis of Fordism as a crisis of labour, but they see it as a permanent and insuperable crisis: 'With the third industrial revolution of micro-electronics, the labour society reached its absolute historical barrier' (Krisis Gruppe 1999/2004: 27, s.11). This crisis they see as the inevitable result of a fundamental contradiction:

That this barrier would be reached sooner or later was logically foreseeable. From birth, the commodity-producing system suffers from a fatal contradiction in terms. On the one hand, it lives on the massive intake of human energy generated by the expenditure of pure labour power – the more the better. On the other hand, the law of operational competition enforces a permanent increase in productivity bringing about the replacement of human labour power by scientific operational industrial capital. (ibid.: 27, s.11)

As a result of the microelectronic revolution:

... more labour is rationalised away than can be reabsorbed by expansion of markets. As a logical consequence of rationalisation, electronic robotics replaces human energy or new communication technology makes labour superfluous, respectively. Entire sectors and departments of construction, production, marketing, warehousing, distribution, and management vanish into thin air. For the first time, the labour idol unintentionally confines itself to permanent hunger rations, thereby bringing about its very own death. (ibid.)

As a result of the crisis, 'capitalism becomes a global minority event' (ibid.).

In the analysis of the Krisis group, this crisis of labour, manifested in rising structural unemployment but also in the crisis of the whole social and political structure associated with the 'society of labour', cannot be overcome. The apparent recovery is a simulation based upon the expansion of credit: 'Clinically dead, the labour idol is kept breathing artificially by means of a seemingly self-induced expansion of financial markets' (ibid., 33, s.13) This fictitious expansion cannot be maintained for ever, simply because it is based on the assumption of a future exploitation that will never take place.

The Krisis analysis coincides with the argument here in its central emphasis on understanding labour as the key element of capitalist domination and their insistence on 'the logical identity of capital and labour as functional categories of a common social fetish form' (ibid., 38, s.15) The difference lies in the complete absence of the two-fold character of labour, that is, the failure to make any mention of concrete doing as existing in present antagonism against-and-beyond abstract labour. The result is that emancipated activity appears only as a future possibility devoid of any real grounding in present-day society.[18] Without an understanding of emancipated activity as present struggle, the members of the labour society appear as Pavlov's dogs, of whom we can only hope that somehow they will be able to break their conditioning: 'We cannot know whether Pavlov's dogs can escape from their conditioned existence. It remains to be seen whether the decline of labour will lead to a cure of labour-mania or to the end of civilisation' (ibid., 44, s.17).

Another way of expressing our difference with the Krisis group's analysis is to say that they see the crisis of labour as a breakdown which shows the necessity of revolution, but they do not understand it as being *simultaneously and immediately* the potential breakthrough of a different activity, of a human doing existing not only in but also against and beyond labour. In spite of their criticism of orthodox Marxism as being the theory of labour, they follow the logic of that tradition in making a separation between capital and class struggle, and hence between crisis and struggle. In this logic, the crisis of capital can only provide an opportunity for revolutionary change or point to the necessity of revolutionary change: the push for change is not understood as being the stuff of crisis. To see doing (or concrete labour) as the crisis of abstract labour is to see the push for change as being the core of the crisis: crisis, then, is not breakdown but potential breakthrough.

In the face of these arguments it is important to reiterate the argument presented here.

There is a permanent antagonism between abstract labour and doing, that is, between the abstraction of doing into labour and the push of doing towards self-determination: this is what Marx refers to as the dual character of labour. There is a relation of constant tension between the two types of activity, but this is concealed by the dominance of abstract labour. Abstract labour appears to be the only possible type of activity: a unitary concept of labour prevails. The abstraction of doing into labour (and the unitary concept of labour) is constantly threatened by the inherent dynamic of abstraction itself, the constant turning of the screw that is inherent in the drive of socially necessary labour time. The unitary character of the category of labour is first split open on a massive scale by the struggles of the 1960s and 1970s: there is a recognition of the struggle of and for an alternative doing against labour. This splitting of the category of labour splits open the whole configuration of abstract labour and all its component categories. All fetishes reveal themselves to be battles between a process of fetishisation and a process of anti-fetishisation: sexuality, state, nature, money, totality, time, and so on. These battles continue to be fought in an enormous variety of ways and places. This is the substance of the cracks in capitalist command.

An appearance of resolution of the crisis of labour is created by the massive expansion of credit and debt after the 1970s. This expansion of credit facilitates a real reimposition of the disciplines of labour, but it also creates a world that rests on a very fragile basis. The apparent resolution of the crisis rests on a gamble, on the expectation of the future production of surplus value. The danger of speaking of this apparent resolution as a new paradigm of domination[19] is that it gives a false solidity to what is a fragile and open situation. The fragility of the resolution has become clear with the world financial crisis that exploded in 2008. The mediation of credit has converted what was overtly a crisis of labour (in the 1970s) into what appears now as a financial crisis, but the basis of crisis remains the same: the weakness of the abstraction of doing into labour, the difficulty of containing human activity within the confines of abstract labour.

Doing is the crisis of labour. It is important to keep hold of this, because the concept of crisis as breakdown leads us nowhere beyond a despairing conjunction of urgent necessity and empty possibility. It is only if we think of crisis as breakthrough, as the moving of doing against-and-beyond labour, that we can open up perspectives of a different world.

26
The breakthrough of doing against labour throws us into a new world of struggle.

It is clear that the movement of useful doing against abstract labour cannot be reduced to struggles over work in any narrow sense. We have seen that abstract labour structures every aspect of capitalist society. It weaves an elaborate and complex prison of fetishism, identity, clock-time, dimorphous sexuality, separation from nature, and so on. Abstract labour provides us with a world of stability, a world of fixed reference points, in which money is money, the state is the state, women are women and men are men. This is the world in which we live, a violent, oppressive, false world constructed on the lie of identity.

To attack abstract labour is to attack this stable world, to hack at the pillars that hold the roof above our heads. To attack abstract labour is to attack the world of *it is* and try to release the (contained and not contained) world of *we do*. This means to embrace a vertiginous world in which everything is at issue, but in this world, as Adorno puts it, 'the vertigo which this causes is an *index veri*' (Adorno, 1966/1990: 33) This is exciting, and frightening.

Capitalism is a complex weave of domination which is generated by the way in which our activity is structured, as abstract labour. This weave of domination is constantly under attack, from many different angles. In the factories and offices, workers struggle for shorter hours, a less direct subjection of their lives to the command of value. Activists in sexual politics fight not just for women's or gay rights but question the whole construction of *women* and *men*. Others fight passionately to create a different relation with plants and animals, some struggle against poverty or discrimination, others against war. In the particular struggles, there is always an excess, an overflowing.

There is nothing unusual about struggling against capitalism: anti-capitalist struggle is all around us. In all of these struggles, the potential of *we do* is hurled against the status quo, the world of *it is*. All have in common the idea that a different world is possible, that we can stop the annihilation of humanity. All of these struggles are anti-capitalist, at least in the sense that they are directed against particular aspects of capitalist society, but the general reification of social relations often makes it difficult to see what unites them. The revolt of doing creates a new constellation of many struggles that often do not recognise themselves as part of the same constellation.[1] In insisting here that the unifying thread is the abstraction of doing into labour, the purpose is not to create a hierarchy of struggles, to privilege one form of struggle over others, but to deepen the cracks, draw them towards each other, contribute to their confluence. If the sheet of ice that is capitalism is being cracked from different sides, it probably makes little sense to say 'you are cracking in the wrong place, come and crack here'. It is better to say 'all these crackings are trying to break up the same ice, let us see how we can draw lines of connection, by doing and by reflecting on our doing'. Instead of telling everyone where they should start the struggles, it is better to recognise the myriad forms of struggle and look for ways to make them connect (not to unite them, necessarily, but to make them connect, to help them resonate).[2]

The same point can be made in terms of critique. Marx, as we have seen, insisted on the importance of critique *ad hominem*, or genetic critique: the understanding of phenomena by understanding what generates them, or (and this is the same) the bringing of social phenomena back to 'man', that is, to the organisation of human activity. Thus, he repeatedly draws connections between the critique of religion and the critique of political economy: god and value are both products of abstract labour, of people whose activity is not under their own control. The same might be said of man, woman, nature, clock-time. In other words, we are starting in each case with a social criticism formulated in general (not genetic) terms – 'nature is not a thing', 'the clock is oppressive' – and, by reformulating these criticisms genetically ('reified nature and the clock are the creations of abstract labour') we draw these criticisms towards a common generating force that we can actually change: the current organisation of human activity as abstract labour. Even if only in pencil, we draw lines on the sheet of ice showing how the different crackings are connected.

There is more than an intellectual force behind this criticism: behind all the struggles mentioned is the drive against abstract labour, the drive to do things in a different way, the force of our power-to-do things differently. Our power-to-do is perverted in capitalism into a power-over, the power of capitalism to tell us what to do with our lives, but it exists not only in power-over, but also as the drive against-and-beyond power-over.[3] The drive of our power-to-do in, against and beyond power-over is the movement of doing in, against and beyond abstract labour.

A new world of struggle has opened. At its core is the struggle against labour, capitalist labour, the labour that produces capital. I write this paragraph at the end of a week of riots in Greece, in which one of the communiqués issued by the students reads: 'At this historical conjuncture of crisis, rage and the dismissal of institutions at which we finally stand, the only thing that can convert the systemic deregulation into a social revolution is the total rejection of labour.'[4] The turning of anti-capitalist struggle against labour obliges us to rethink the categories of struggle. We must learn a new language of anti-capitalism.

It is difficult to think of the new language as having a grammar,[5] since grammar implies rules and the only rule of a language of doing is *break the rules*: perhaps we should think rather of an anti-grammar or, better, rhythms or melodies. Learning the melodies of the new language is a process of exploring, asking, provoking, discussing.[6] It is of course the moving of struggle that creates the melodies, but, precisely because we are in the penumbra of a threshold trying to see our way forward, theoretical reflection has an important role to play. The modest proposal of this book is that the central axis of these new melodies of struggle is the revolt of doing against labour.

Much of what is proposed in this book, particularly the critique of abstract labour, has already been put forward by classical critical theory (the theory of the Frankfurt School), but their critique of capitalism comes from an unvoiced standpoint. Or rather, they had difficulties in recognising their own standpoint.

Far from being the voice of privileged intellectuals (as Adorno and Horkheimer said of their own work), theirs is the voice of doing, the voice of the conscious life-activity that does not yet exist, that exists not-yet, as anticipations, in the cracks.[7] Critical theory is crisis-theory: the theory of doing as the crisis of abstract labour.

At the centre of the new melodies stands contradiction: not the contradiction between labour and capital but the deeper (logically and existentially prior) conflict between doing and labour. This contradiction is a live, throbbing social antagonism, the constant and unavoidable struggle that is life itself. Contradiction is struggle: concepts are inevitably conceptualisations of the social antagonism in which we live and think. That is why all concepts must be understood as open concepts, conceptualisations of an open, unresolved process of struggle. Non-identity *is* the revolt of doing against abstract labour, *is* class struggle.

For the moment, we shall try to move forward in the exploration of these new melodies. All the things we have looked at as dimensions of abstract labour come into play, but we shall focus on them not individually but in the context of three great themes that are closely interconnected: particularity, subjectivity and time.

Part VII
Doing Against Labour: The Melodies of Interstitial Revolution

27
Doing dissolves totality, synthesis, value.

1. DOING FLOWS OUTWARDS FROM
THE PARTICULAR, AGAINST AND BEYOND.

Self-determination flows from us outwards. I bake a cake because I enjoy doing it, or because I am hungry, or because I want to invite my friends. I ask my children and some of my friends to join me and we discuss together what flavour the cake should be. We decide that we would like to make the cake with organic flour and one of my friends mentions that she has a friend who grows organic wheat and makes her own flour, so we decide to invite her to join us.

This is the outward push of doing towards self-determination. It is not complete self-determination because there are so many things that we do not control, so many ways in which our doing depends on the doing of others in a way that we do not determine: the quality of the oven, the butter, the salt, the fruit that we use, and so on. We are not even free to devote the time that we wish to baking the cake because in the morning we shall have to go to work to earn our living. Our push comes up against restrictions that flow from the totality of social relations, the way that society is organised.

Together with some friends, I decide to plant a garden so that we can grow vegetables and flowers and trees. We soon come up against an obstacle: we do not own any land. There is a vacant plot of land near us, so we decide to occupy it and turn it into a garden. Soon, a second obstacle presents itself: the police try to force us off the land. However, we have already mobilised support from our neighbours and the whole community turns out to stop the police.

I enjoy reading Marx but I find *Capital* a bit difficult. Together with some friends we form a reading group and read it together. We are all students, some of economics, some of philosophy, some of sociology, and we want to devote a lot of time to reading *Capital*. But we soon come up against an obstacle: Marx is not included in our degree courses, and the pressures of the degree leave us little time for anything else.

Together with the other people of our town, we seize control of the water supply and throw out the private company that has been given a concession by the state. The state sends in the army to repress our action, but the solidarity of the townspeople is so great that we force the army out after various days of struggle. We take all our decisions in popular assemblies involving all those who are participating in the struggle.[1]

In each of these cases, there is an outward push towards self-determination. In each case, the push comes up against obstacles: lack of money, armed force, lack of control over the necessary ingredients. There is an outward flow of doing towards self-determination which comes up against the various manifestations of a totality that we do not control. We try to find ways of flowing around or moving beyond the obstacles.

2. DOING REVERSES THE FLOW OF DETERMINATION.

We have seen already what abstraction does to doing. I enjoy baking cakes and decide to make a living by selling them. Soon I find that the market is measuring my cakes, determining the price at which I can sell them and therefore determining the speed at which I must work in order to survive. At some point, there is a change in the flow of determination. At the beginning, I determine my activity; after some time, I realise that my activity is being determined by an alien force over which I have no control.

I enjoy reading Hegel and Marx and Bloch and Adorno. I decide to study philosophy at the university. Soon I find that these authors are generally not included in philosophy degrees, but that, even if they are, I have to read them in a certain way and at a certain rhythm. My studying is measured by exams, which determine the content and the speed at which I must work in order to pass. Here too, there is a reversal in the flow of determination: the activity which I at first determine becomes converted into a labour imposed by an alien force.

In the first case, it is clearly value at work. Value, the peculiar social synthesis of capitalism, that which holds capitalist society together, imposes itself on the cake-baker through the operation of the market. In the second case, that of activities not directly subject to the market, like studying philosophy, the same social synthesis is imposed ever more directly through processes of constant measurement that mimic the operation of the market. The (direct or indirect) imposition of abstract labour is supported where necessary by overt force, as in the case of the community garden or the water supply of our earlier examples. In all cases, there is a subordination (or attempted subordination) of our activity to the rules and rhythms of a social totality that neither we nor anyone else controls.

Abstraction of doing into labour and socialisation are indistinguishable under capitalism. Abstraction is the formation of a social cohesion or social synthesis in such a way that the flow of determination is turned against us. As our activity becomes socialised, we lose control over it and the imposition of an alien control becomes stronger. Abstraction-socialisation is the reversal of the flow of determination. The formation of the social totality is at the same time the loss of social determination. No adding of formally democratic structures can alter this fact.

The struggle of doing is the struggle to maintain the momentum of the flow of determination.

3. THE TOTALITY CANNOT BE SEIZED FROM ABOVE.

The clash of the flow and counter-flow of determination confronts us with a dilemma. The pushing from below confronts obstacles that express the force of the social totality. This very confrontation invites us to make a leap, to try to control that totality.

This is the standpoint of traditional Marxism. The traditional communist argument presents the alternative to capitalism not as breaking the social synthesis but as constructing an alternative social synthesis. One sort of totality must be replaced by another, based of course not on money and capital, but on popular planning. The struggle concentrates on the overthrow of one system and its replacement by another. The perspective of the revolutionary labour movement is that of totality.[2] This means that the revolutionary movement requires an organisation that can adopt the standpoint of the totality: the party.

This does not work, cannot work. Why? Because abstraction, the movement that constitutes the totality, comes from below and can only be unpicked from below. The flow of determination that comes from the capitalist totality of social relations is constituted by the way in which our doings relate to one another. It is the fact that my doing relates to your doing through the exchange of our products as commodities that creates the totality that we cannot control. The totality which really and apparently stands outside us is constituted by the way that we come together with other people. It is this way in which we come together that needs to be changed and this cannot be done from the standpoint of the totality. It can only be done from below.

The leap from the upward push of struggle to the standpoint of totality shapes both the forms of organisation and the forms of thinking. Organisationally, the perspective of totality tends to lead in practice to a focus on the state. The state is in fact a false, illusory totality. It is not the states that constitute the social synthesis: rather they protect the process by which that synthesis is established. Their existence as a distinct instance, however, creates the illusion that it is the state that holds society together, or the states that hold distinct societies together. The focus on totality leads to the illusory conception of the world as being made up of a number of state-totalities, each one of which organises the social relations within its boundaries. From this comes the idea that the world can be changed by gaining control of one state-totality after another (a process that is sometimes referred to as 'permanent revolution'). The inevitable failure of this approach to change the world radically is then interpreted as a series of betrayals, whereas the real basis of the repeated failure of changing the world by taking power is simply that the social synthesis does not lie where it appears to lie. This has become increasingly obvious in recent years: whereas it might have been plausible to regard the state as the centre of society (each state the centre of its society!) a hundred years ago, the intensified globalisation of capital has made it clear that this is not the case. The illusion of the state-totality has fallen apart historically, both as a result of the failed revolutions and of the tighter weaving of global social relations.

And yet the totality perspective is constantly regenerated (along with all the other fetishes) by the continued existence of abstract labour. The state continues to offer itself as the road to change, a mirage of hope in a desert of despair. Even where the state is put aside, the nation comes forward as a category of totality: we must have a national programme, a national plan, it is argued. But the national is no less a false totality than the state, and is indeed very difficult to separate from the state. One may indeed conceive of a struggle of the nation against the state, yet it is clear that social relations are not constituted at the level of the nation, and also that the concept of the nation is so deeply intertwined with the state that it is not realistic to separate them politically.[3] It is better then to accept that the national (and the national-popular) is irretrievably the terrain of capital and to assume the crisis of abstract labour as the crisis of all totalities and pseudo-totalities.

Totality is in crisis. The crisis of abstract labour is also the crisis of the social synthesis based on abstract labour. More and more in recent years, anti-capitalist movements are posing the question of radical change in terms of the unstructured confluence of struggles from below, the coming together of particular struggles. The coming together is seen in terms of loosely structured and usually temporary organisational forms rather than a more formal and permanent creation of national or international institutions. Nevertheless, the concept of the totality, or the idea of change from above, keeps on recurring. One currently influential argument put forward by critical supporters of the Bolivarian revolution in Venezuela[4] or by, for example, the Frente Popular Darío Santillán in Argentina,[5] is the view that we must think of radical change as coming simultaneously from above and from below. The proponents of this argument usually put the emphasis on the struggle from below, yet argue that the movements from below are not sufficient, that, as Raúl Zibechi puts it, 'the "other half" is missing, their capacity to have a strategy, to be executives, to attain state power in order to realise their programme.'[6] This argument is superficially attractive, because it seems to draw together the different forms of struggle into an alliance for changing society. What is not sufficiently examined, however, is the inherently antagonistic nature of the relation between 'from above' and 'from below'. The movement from below is the push from the particular towards self-determination, while any *from above*, any representation of the totality in a world still capitalist can only be a push that moves in the opposite direction, a counter-flow that, however well-intentioned, demobilises the thrust towards self-determination.

4. WE MOVE FROM THE PARTICULAR,
BUT THIS DOES NOT MEAN A MICROPOLITICS.

Change from above cannot unravel the abstraction of doing into labour that carries everything beyond our control. The creation of a system of state planning, as under the former countries of 'real socialism', did nothing at all to create a self-determining society. The notion of 'national self-determination' is similarly meaningless: the problem of self-determination can only be understood in terms of the organisation of our daily activity.

To unravel the abstraction of doing into labour, we must move from below. We move from many different starting-points against the unifying, oppressive force of abstraction. Concrete doing comes in an infinite variety of shapes and sizes: it is the abstraction that imposes its homogenising rigidity. This gives the impression that our movement is a movement of a multitude of differences, and has led some to abandon all idea of contradiction and dialectics. This is a mistake, because what unites the differences is the fact that they are all movements-against, against the alienated and alienating rigidity of abstract labour: what unites the differences is that they are contradictions, antagonisms.[7] Certainly, the moving of concrete doing is an explosion of difference, of many different colours (and hence the undoubted appeal of the concept of multitude[8]), but it is a moving-against, a live antagonism.

In this the moving is crucial, because any staying still, however radical it appears to be at first, is easily reintegrated into capitalist relations of domination. The argument here is not an argument for a micro-politics. Insubordinations that become isolated or enclosed, by choice or by circumstance, tend to become frustrating, and frustration easily leads to internal conflict and disintegration. They tend to become frustrating because doing moves. Our power to do has a dynamic, it is a constant moving against and beyond that which is. That is why the realisation of a utopia (in the sense of a pre-planned model community) would not work: our self-fulfilment as human doers implies creative change. Self-determination, even in an emancipated society, could not be static: it cannot be the endlessly repeated determination of 'we choose to remain the same'; or, even if that decision were taken each day, self-determination would require that it should at least be at issue each day. If the autonomous space does not constantly move beyond itself, then it becomes a prison, a holding in check of the push towards creation. Our starting-point is break, rupture. Yet the rupture is not stable, but evanescent: its existence as rupture depends on its moving.

The power of doing is anti-synthetic. It resists enclosure, moves against enclosure, whether the enclosure be that of a small group with radical intentions or the enclosure of abstract labour. Starting from the particular is that: the rejection of enclosure. It does not mean that we stay at the level of the particular: rather it means a constant pushing out, a constant drive against capital and against all the enclosures, rigidities, fetishes that support the regime of capital and frustrate our doing. The movement of doing is the critical and practical moving of anti-fetishism, the recovering of our power-to-do, our being-able-to. A moving of cracks, not a movement of autonomies. Change cannot come about by the addition of separate revolts but only through their flow, their confluence, through the cracks shooting along the hidden veins of anger.

The push of our power-to-do towards self-determination does not mean a push towards a totality in the old sense. Totality encloses, and there is no reason to think of communism in terms of the particularly tight weave of social relations with which it has been associated in the past. Capitalist globalisation is an increasingly tight weave of social relations woven by abstract labour, but a world beyond capitalism need not be characterised by a similarly dense weave. This is one of the criticisms rightly made of the so-called socialist states: that they associated the idea of socialism with a particularly tight weaving of social relations that left little room for determination from below: in this sense they were 'totalitarian'. The very density of the weave of social relations (mass production, planning of social organisation to a high degree of detail) is probably difficult to reconcile with effective social determination from below. What most anti-capitalist struggles of recent years point to is a much looser integration of social connections, a 'world of many worlds', as the Zapatista slogan puts it. Just what this might look like can only be the result of struggle, but it would presumably have at its base smaller and more autonomous units of production.[9] A world of many worlds would be not a new totality but a shifting constellation or confederation of particularities. Not a communism, but a communising.[10]

But what do we say of issues that seem to require a united-world solution, such as climate change or the elimination of nuclear weapons? The imminence of catastrophe seems to push us towards a positive conception of totality, some idea that we need a world state. Certainly, some form of global coordination would be desirable in a post-capitalist society, but the forms of global coordination that presently exist are so bound up with capital and the pursuit of profit that they offer little hope of a solution. It is becoming more and more clear that any solution to the problem of climate change can come only from a radical change in the way that we live, and that change cannot come from a state or some sort of world body, but only from the rejection of abstract labour, from our own assumption of responsibility for the way we live.[11]

The conceptual and organisational challenge is to turn the world upside down and move from the particular struggles outwards, against and beyond: to follow the flow of doing against and beyond its rigidification as labour. The struggle against capital is necessarily the unleashing of doing from the bonds of abstraction. Where abstraction imposes limits, binding us to value, doing is in-finite, unfinished, a moving against and beyond all limits.

How do cracks move? We do not know. When we think of how to join up or spread particular struggles, the tendency to totalise reasserts itself, over and over again: the drive to form a regional or a national or an international organisation to bring all the particular struggles together and coordinate them. Yet, although such organisations may be useful in providing contacts, experience suggests that it is not through this sort of organisation that struggles actually come together: for one struggle to spill over into another, or to act as the spark that sets another burning, what is needed is a certain resonance, and these resonances do not follow formal organisational lines and are often hard to understand. A crack touches some hidden structural fault that then opens into a crack and spreads: this cannot be planned and usually cannot be foreseen with any accuracy. There is indeed a central structural fault in capitalism, a fault which manifests itself in the lines of contagion of rebellion. The central fault line does not run along territorial lines (as anti-imperialist theory would imply), nor along the divide between capital and labour (as traditional theory has it), but along the line of antagonism between doing and labour. But this is a fault line that is not easily visible and impossible to institutionalise: it is a line we make by walking it. In the world of doing-against-labour, there are no certainties and, if there were, they would be enclosures to be broken.

28
Doing is the moving of the *mulier abscondita* against character masks. We are the *mulier abscondita*.

1. LATENCY IS THE STUFF OF REVOLUTION.

We live in the shadows, behind a mask, our doing-in-against-and-beyond-labour invisible, unrecognised even by revolutionary theory.

The mask is the mask of abstract labour. The abstraction of labour, we have seen, is the abstraction of the subject, the imposition of a character mask, the transformation of people into personifications. The capitalists become the personification of capital, the workers become the personification of labour. The human with all her unpredictable dimensionality becomes reduced to the one-dimensional man, to the worker with trade-union consciousness, to the bearer of social relations.

This imposition of the mask is very real. It is painfully clear at the moment that a president or prime minister, whether he starts as worker, indigenous, black, or woman, assumes the character mask of the politician, of the statesman. We all tend towards the personification of our roles in society: the radical professor no less than anyone else.

The character mask is a theatrical image: the subjection of our doing to abstract labour creates a theatre, a stage on which the characters move in intense activity. We focus our eyes on the stage and see a whole complex of conflicts: between workers and capitalists, between women and men, between gays and heterosexuals, and so on. These conflicts are real, the complex interplay of real antagonisms between the different characters. We analyse these conflicts, try to understand them in terms of the structural interests involved, and we forget. We forget that what we are watching is theatre, that these characters are just that, people forced into certain roles. We forget that there is a deeper conflict, the conflict that creates the theatre, that forces people to don their character masks. This is the struggle to impose abstraction upon the daily doing of active subjects, the struggle to subordinate concrete or creative doing to abstract labour (and therefore capital). This is not a struggle that was completed at the dawn of capitalism, but is a daily repeated struggle. The theatre is not a construction of the eighteenth or nineteenth century, but a construction of today, and a very fragile one. Behind the struggle on the stage, there is a prior one: the struggle not to go up on the stage, not to submit our doing to abstract labour, the desire of the actors even on the stage to throw off their masks: the struggle not of an identity but against identification. The revolution is a battle not between the characters on the stage, but between the actors and their character masks.

In other words, there cannot be a complete identity between people and the structural position that they occupy in society, it cannot be that people are entirely subsumed within their character mask. The very idea of the one-dimensional man means that there is someone who is not one-dimensional, someone who can criticise one-dimensionality. The question, as always, is: where is that critic, who is that critic? Is it the privileged intellectual (as Adorno or Horkheimer would have it)[1] or is it the 'substratum of the outcasts and the outsiders' (as Marcuse argues)?[2] The simplest answer is surely that we ourselves are the critics of our own one-dimensionality.

We are not as one-dimensional as we seem: behind our one-dimensionality stands a polyphonic, polymorphous critic. Behind (or in-against-and-beyond) the personification of abstract labour stands the doer, the daring dancing doer. Beneath the surface of domination is the seething of rebellion. Pushing against and beyond identity is the endless restlessness of anti-identity. Inside the savage-converted-into-labourer dances the savage-in-rebellion.[3]

The possibility of radical change depends not on people assuming their character masks (the proletariat assuming its revolutionary role), but on the contrary, on the ec-static distance between people and the masks they wear, on the fact that people exist not only in, but also against and beyond their social roles.

Latency: that is the stuff of revolution.[4]

Latency is a constant theme in the literature on revolution and the revolutionary subject. Under the identitarian notions of the subject runs a darker, deeper stream. The Zapatistas don balaclavas to draw attention to their invisibility: theirs is the movement of the invisible and inaudible, of those without face and without voice. They are 'the guardians of the night, the watchmen of the shadow' (Subcomandante Marcos, *La Jornada*, 9 April 2006). Major Ana María, in her speech to the 'Intergalactic' meeting of 1996, describes the EZLN:

The voice that arms itself to make itself heard. The face that hides itself to show itself. The name that is silent in order to be named. The red star that calls to people and to the world that they should listen, that they should see, that they should name. The tomorrow that is harvested in the yesterday. Behind our black face. Behind our armed voice. Behind our unnameable name. Behind the us that you see. Behind are the we that are you.[5]

In the women's movement too, the question of invisibility is central. An important part of the struggle is against the invisibility of women – their invisibility in the historical past and in the daily practice of the present – or, indeed their visibility only as objects of men's desire, but not as subjects, not as people. Revolt is always revolt against invisibility: not necessarily against total invisibility, but against invisibility as people, as subjects, as doers. Thus, even revolts in prisons, where the inmates are highly visible, but only as objects, can be seen as revolts against their invisibility as people.[6]

Marx, in *Capital*, introduces the question of class in terms of invisibility. In order to understand the relation between Mr Moneybags and the seller of labour power as an antagonistic, class relation, we 'take leave for a time of this noisy sphere [of circulation], where everything takes place on the surface and in view of all men, and follow them into the hidden abode of production, on whose threshold there stares us in the face "No admittance except on business"' (1867/1965: 176; 1867/1990: 280). It is to the hidden sphere of production that we must go to 'force the secret of profit making'.

In this case, the invisibility refers to the fact that what goes on in the factory is away from the public eye. We must leave the surface of society to understand the reality of class relations. But there is more to it than that: Marx's whole argument, with its emphasis on surface, on personification and character masks, points us constantly to a hidden substratum. In a society in which the relations between doers are established through the exchange of commodities, relations between people are transformed into relations between things: the relations between the producers exist in the form of relations between their products, and the producers themselves become invisible, or rather they appear as the exchangers of things, as agents of circulation, but not as producers or doers. Their subjectivity is invisible. People as doers become buried under a whole edifice of social forms constructed upon this initial negation of the subject. This is what Marx refers to as fetishism.

Theory, then, is the uncovering of that which is hidden. In other words, theory is critique, critique of the forms that conceal, and yet are generated by, human activity. Critique is critique *ad hominem*, recuperation of the concealed creative subjectivity of people; or, since the subject to which the critique refers is necessarily a hidden subject, we should say that it is critique *ad hominem absconditum*.

Revolutionary theory is part of the struggle of that which is hidden (doing) against its own invisibility. Or perhaps we should speak of latency rather than total invisibility. Doing is visible, but as abstract labour: it is the hidden or latent substance of abstract labour. Doers too are visible, but in the way that actors on a stage are visible: as character masks, as roles. Doing and doers exist in the form of something else, in the 'mode of being denied'. What we see is their own denial, just as what we see in an actor on a stage is her own negation as person, her presentation as someone she is not. Behind the character mask is a latent force, a menace, a potential.

Latency is not absence, but of course if something is hidden or latent, then we are not absolutely sure if it is there. Building on that which is latent involves an element of risk, an inevitable degree of uncertainty: revolt always surges from the invisible, but precisely because it is invisible we cannot know for sure whether that latent revolt is there or how strong it is. On the other hand, to insist on some sort of measurable certainty would simply exclude the latent from consideration and condemn us to a false enclosure in the visible.

Latency is not marginalisation. It is sometimes assumed that to emphasise the importance of the invisible is to see struggle as coming from the invisible margins of society.[7] The argument here is the very opposite of this: it is the creative force at the very centre of society that is invisible. Latent is the doing that exists in the mode of being denied, in the form of abstract labour.[8]

2. BEHIND THE CHARACTER MASK STANDS THE *MULIER ABSCONDITA*.

What or who is behind the character mask? What (or who) is it that exists in the form of being denied, as menace, as potential?

There is no pure subject, no beautiful soul, behind the mask. The actor is damaged by the role she plays. The face that has been forced into a character mask hides also because it has been disfigured by the mask: take away the mask and you find a face that has been distorted by the mask and by its resentment of the mask.[9] There is no noble savage hiding under the five hundred years of discrimination and oppression; there is no perfect woman waiting to be recognised once male domination is removed; there is no pure doing hiding under abstract labour. But that does not mean that the subject can just be reduced to the character mask. Doing exists in the form of abstract labour, but it exists therefore as resentment-of, tension-against, rebellion-against abstract labour, as menace, as potential: a shadowy figure, but crucially, ec-statically distinct from the form in which it exists, the character mask it wears.

This is the theoretical and practical problem: this shadowy figure, distinct from the character mask, yet disfigured by it. The worker is not simply a structural position, a bearer of social relations, a seller of labour power: if she were, revolution would be unthinkable (or perhaps just so boring that it would be not worth thinking about). But she is also not the revolutionary heroine breaking her chains depicted by generations of romantic socialist 'realists'. Lenin's answer to the problem was to break the subject in two: on the one hand, the worker limited to a structural trade-union consciousness, on the other, the revolutionary as hero bringing true consciousness to the workers. The problem with this solution is that it implies an authoritarian relation between leaders and masses and simply displaces the problem of the beautiful soul to the leaders: how do the leaders acquire true consciousness?

Who or what, then, is this shadowy figure? And is it one figure (working class, say) or many (workers, women, gays, blacks, indigenous)?

There is a problem here with language. We do not really have a name for the shadowy figure (or figures) behind the character mask. To call it 'the working class' is confusing simply because the term makes no distinction between the identitarian character mask (a definable working class) and the shadowy anti-identitarian figure behind it. The same could be said for any other character mask one chooses – women, gays, blacks, and so on. To name is to identify and what concerns us here is that which goes against and beyond identity. The movement of anti-identity is necessarily a revolution without name.[10] To talk about it, we need some sort of name, but it has be a name that suggests its own inadequacy. Adorno speaks of the movement of non-identity, Bloch of the Not Yet: both are negative concepts, restless concepts that point against-and-beyond.

The difficulty of naming has always been present in religion, as Bloch points out. God, as creator, is unknowable and, properly, unnameable, a hidden, latent God, *Deus absconditus*. If we say there is no god, there are two possibilities. Either we say that, if there is no god, there is also no unknowable, unnameable: everything can be identified, everything can be given a name. But then we do away with creation and put in its place a positivist, structuralist and ultimately recursive world. This is the measured, finite world of abstract labour, the world of definitions and classifications. The alternative is to say that if there is no god, then we are the only creators, we are the ones who push all the time against-and-beyond that which is, we are the drive against identity, the force of anti-identity and therefore unknowable, unnameable. The anthropologisation of religion, the replacement of god by humans, does not mean that *Deus absconditus* is replaced by a known, identifiable person, but rather that the place of the latent, hidden God is taken by a latent, hidden human, *homo absconditus*.[11] The figure behind the mask is, of course, *homo absconditus*, the hidden man: hidden because repressed, hidden because creator, hidden because un-finished in his becoming. This is the doer, repressed, un-become, in-finite, undefinable.

Should this not be *mulier abscondita*, the hidden woman? Of course. *Homo* clearly stands for 'man' in the sense of human: it is a case of man embracing woman, he including she. But, as we have all become aware over the last thirty years or so, this is a linguistic expression of the social suppression of women. Identitarian subjectivity is a male-dominated subjectivity, the identitarian subject is undoubtedly a 'he', with many of the characteristics associated with masculinity. The crisis of the 'he' and the critiques of male subjectivity can be seen as part of the more general crisis of identitarian subjectivity and indeed of abstract labour. The doer is not of the same gender as the labourer. Doing implies a much richer concept of human activity, the varied and multi-skilled activity traditionally associated with women rather than the narrower, monothematic activity more typical of men. If we must attach a gender to the doer, then certainly we should think of her as a 'she' rather than a 'he': *mulier abscondita*.

This corresponds to a real change in the gender composition of anti-capitalist struggle which has often been noted. Whereas the traditional world of the labour movement, of trade unions and revolutionary parties, is very clearly dominated by men, women play a much more obvious role in the new wave of anti-capitalist struggle: whether it be the struggle for water in Latin American cities, the struggle against the destruction of nature, the struggle against war, the alter-globalisation struggle for another world. And it is impossible to overlook the role of the women's movement in opening up a new understanding of what struggle means, the forms of organisation, the concept of time and of change.

But do we need to attach a gender to our shadowy figure? For the sake of exposition, it is easier to do so: 'it' would not solve the problem because we are talking of human subjectivity; and s/he does not solve it either, because it suggests a pronoun that claims to be timelessly correct, and so obscures a real shift in the gender composition of the subject. There is a sense in which the labourer really is a 'he' and the doer really is a 'she', so, when we speak of the revolt of doing against labour, we are speaking of a real movement of she against he. Where it is necessary to use a pronoun, we shall refer to labourers as 'he' and doers as 'she'. However, the very division of people into two clearly defined genders is part of the more general process of identification, an aspect of the world of abstract labour. The substitution of one gender for another is, therefore, not really the answer. Our shadowy figure, the anti-identitarian subject, is also anti-gender, a movement against-and-beyond the division of society into two clear genders. In her novel *Woman on the Edge of Time*, Marge Piercy uses 'per' as a pronoun to represent the un-gendered subject, but this refers to an imaginary society in which gender divisions are really overcome.[12] Perhaps then we should say simply that behind the 'he' of the character mask stands a shadowy figure who is 'she', but this she is not a different gender but the crisis both of he-ness and she-ness, the crisis of sexual dimorphism, the erotic revolt of polymorphous perversity.[13]

3. WE ARE THE REVOLUTIONARY SUBJECT: WE WHO ARE SCHIZOPHRENIC AND REPRESSED.

The shadowy figure (the *mulier abscondita*) is simply We. We, because the use of the third person, whether 'he', 'she' or 'they', excludes us, and we write and read not from outside the problem of how to change the world, but from inside it. The third person identifies, even if it is a vague 'they', because it draws a defining line that excludes us.[14] 'We', on the other hand, are open, a question.[15] 'We' may be a defining, identitarian 'we' (we university professors, we Irish, we men), but not necessarily: left without a qualification, 'we' is undefined and open. To say that 'we' are the subject, the shadowy figure behind the mask, is also to say that theory cannot be separated from practice: the 'we' who read or write this book are not just reflecting upon changing the world, we are not theorising about it as though it could be something separate from us: like it or not, we are part of the process, our reading or writing is part of the movement.

We, at least in English, are un-gendered: we are not divided in advance into two gendered camps. The We of the shadowy figure, however, is not just un-gendered but anti-gender, opposed to the gender divisions of the character mask. And since the divided-gender world of the character mask is a world dominated by one of those genders, perhaps what we need is a We with a feminine lilt. In languages in which We has a gender characterisation, such as Spanish with its *nosotros/nosotras*, clearly '*nosotras*' is a better characterisation of the shadowy subject, a *nosotras* understood perhaps not as affirmation of femininity but as revolt against masculinity.

We (the we-*nosotras*-doer who stand behind the he-labourer-character-mask) are plural: not in the sense of a defined group or collectivity, but in the sense of an open flow. We flow into you (and they): '*detrás estamos ustedes*' ('behind [the balaclava] are the we that are you'),[16] as the Zapatistas so beautifully put it. We flow into one another because our doing (all our doings) are part of the social flow of doing, that interweaving of doings, conscious or unconscious, planned or unplanned, tightly woven or with loose ends, that constitutes our sociality.

We are not a homogeneous mass, far from it. Nor are we a multitude of differences. We are rather the revolt of doing against abstract labour, the revolt of heterogeneity against homogenisation, the revolt of difference against contradiction,[17] the revolt of beyond-ness against and beyond mere against-ness. The abstraction of doing into labour is its homogenisation: it is achieved through the imposition of equivalence upon non-equivalent activities. The struggle of doing against labour is a revolt against this homogenisation, an assertion of the difference of our doings, an attempt to break through the binary antagonism of capital and to emancipate our doings from the abstraction imposed through money. Heterogeneity is not an ontological characteristic, it is rather our struggle against the abstraction of labour, and central to that struggle.

The heterogeneous pushing-beyond is not a pushing beyond sociality to individualism, not a pushing beyond the social flow of doing, though it may appear to be so. It is rather a pushing against and beyond a particular form of sociality, against and beyond the social synthesis of capital, towards a different form of sociality, one that would no longer be a social synthesis, a sociality that would open rather than close: not, then, a central plan but a social flow of interweaving and loose ends. There is no reason why, with our social capacity to provide for the basics of life (with the current development of the forces of production, to put it in an older language), we should not be able to live quite happily with a social weaving that has many straggling bits and loose ends, heterogeneous activities that do not lead in any obvious way to a recognisable social benefit, or where the only direct social benefit is the freedom to do one's own thing.

We are inevitably a self-divided, self-antagonistic we. We live in a self-antagonistic society, a class-divided society. If we see the central contradiction or division of this society as being the contradiction between labour and capital, then it would be possible to imagine the society as being divided into two separate and antagonistic groups: the working class and the capitalist class. The social antagonism would then be external to each one of us. If, however, we say that the antagonism between labour and capital is simply the superficial expression of a deeper conflict, that between concrete doing and abstract labour, it becomes clear immediately that the social antagonism runs through each of us. We are each and all both doers and abstract labourers (even if we are not in a direct relation of employment). We are each and all both character masks and the shadowy figure behind the mask. We are each and all both the he-man (or she-woman?) of the mask and the anti-gender she of the shadowy figure. When we say that doing exists as 'resentment-of, tension-against, rebellion-against abstract labour, as menace, as potential', we are speaking of our internal antagonism: we exist as resentment-of, tension-against, rebellion-against ourselves, as menace, as potential.

There is no assumption here that people are basically 'good': the hidden figure is disfigured in every way by the mask imposed by capital. The argument is rather that in a society based on class antagonism, we are all permeated by this antagonism, we are all self-contradictory, torn internally by the struggle between the reproduction of capitalist relations and the impulse to refuse-

and-create. Class struggle involves taking sides in this conflict that exists both within and outwith all of us.

Is this to say that there is no difference between a capitalist and a worker? No. They wear different character masks. And behind the character masks? Behind the character masks, there is no pure, real human being but simply a shadowy figure disfigured by, and in tension with, the character mask. Where the character mask is comfortable, there will be little incentive to revolt against it: this does not mean that the owner of capital is reduced entirely to his character mask, but he is unlikely to rebel strongly against it. Certainly Engels, although a capitalist, took the side of the struggle against capital, but there are relatively few examples of this. Where the character mask is uncomfortable or unbearable, the force of the revolt against it will be so much stronger. The worker has much more reason to revolt against the character mask than the capitalist has. The tension between character mask and shadowy figure exists in both cases, but in a different intensity. The class divide (the antagonism between doing and abstract labour) cuts through both, but in different ways.[18]

Similarly, one might say that, although many men revolt against the gender divide and the masculine character mask, women have more reason to do so. The same with racism: one does not have to be black to be anti-racist, but the intensity of the reaction against racism is likely to be greater. And so on. Does this mean, then, that we should understand capitalist society as being structured by a range of different conflicts: not only class conflict, but also all sorts of non-class conflict? At the superficial (and real) level of character masks, this is certainly the case: at this level, there are all sorts of ways in which conflict can be understood. There is, however, always the prior question of what generates the character masks, what produces the different identities that enter into conflict, as male or female, black or white. This brings us back to the fundamental antagonism in the organisation of our doing between abstract labour and the (shadowy) drive towards a self-determining doing. It is the repression of doing by abstract labour that generates male and female, black and white as identities, as conflicting character masks. It is not that gender conflict, say, must be added to class conflict to understand society: it is rather that the very concept of

222

a binary gender divide between men and women is the product of the abstraction of doing into labour. In this sense, the conflict between doing and labour is prior to other conflicts.[19]

We are doers-against-labour, the true proletariat. We are doers-against-labour, shadows-against-masks. Whether workers or capitalists, women or men, black or white, we are self-divided, self-antagonistic, although the intensity and nature of the antagonism differs according to the role we reject or accept, or reject-and-accept. We are fragile, unstable, situationally or temporally schizophrenic. We adopt one personality in one situation, another in a different situation. At one moment, we are a doer in revolt against labour; at another, we are a meek, obedient labourer. This changeableness, often viewed as abnormality or even as betrayal of the movement, is in fact quite normal. The antagonism between doing and labour is constantly shifting. We are all self-antagonistic, but the antagonism is not stable over time: certain situations (the composition of social relations around us) bring out one or another side of this antagonism. Thus, military training is designed to strengthen the character mask and suppress any kind of hidden impulse towards humanity, and the army is a situation that strengthens this process. The same can be said of factory discipline and the factory, and indeed of any kind of institutional discipline and of any institution. The party too: the revolutionary party creates situations or contexts in which we adopt a certain role or character mask and suppress our drive towards creative doing. (This role, this character mask of the professional revolutionary or militant is now in crisis.)

Does this mean that any form of institutionalisation creates a role, a character mask that disfigures and freezes? The doer-in-revolt, the rebel, the angry-young-man, the feminist, can easily become a role, an image that freezes and defines the shadowy figure that moves behind. The struggle against the role can be seen as a struggle for authenticity, but authenticity can itself become a role, a new identity that freezes.[20] Capitalist society, a society characterised by the abstraction of doing into labour, constantly generates these roles and throws them upon us – there goes the revolutionary theorist, there is the militant. We want to oppose them with authenticity, genuineness, to give body to the shadowy figure lurking behind all these roles. But the shadowy figure remains shadowy, negative, a refusal of the masks forced upon her: she/we cannot be an alternative identity. The shadowy figure is a scream, a question, a crisis, a menace, a potential, a we, a flow. Doing flows: any definition of it is an abstraction. The struggle against the character masks moves faster than the concept: any attempt to pin it down by giving it a definition contributes unwillingly to its recapture.

Any institutionalisation of struggle is problematic, simply because there is a flow of struggle that does not respect institutional boundaries, although it may be hindered by them. This is not just a problem of party organisation. Sometimes we tend to think that the rejection of the party as a form of organisation solves all problems, but many of the problems are reproduced in the institutionalisation of non-party forms of struggle. The institutionalisation seeks to give a certain course to struggle, but struggle has a dynamic that is not easily channelled. We try to give it shape as the Other Campaign, for example, and it surges in other forms that do not fit in to our institutional preconceptions. Forms of organisation need to be open and flexible to avoid creating identifications that hinder the movement of struggle. The only way in which we can strengthen subversion is by constantly subverting it.[21]

We are repressed. The shadowy figure behind the mask is a repressed figure. Our starting point, our 'pivot', the relation between useful or concrete doing and abstract labour is a relation of repression. Our potential, our power to do, our capacity to determine socially our own doing, is a repressed potential, power, capacity. We exist in the mode of being denied, as character mask. If we exist in the mode of being denied, we do not exist outside that denial, but we are not fully subsumed into that denial: to say that we exist in the mode of being denied is to say that we exist also in the mode of denying that denial: this double negation does not lead to a positive we, but to an ec-static we, a we in revolt.

Revolution, then, is the return of the repressed.[22] Not just of the repressed sectors of the population (proletarians, women, indigenous, blacks, and so on), but of that which is repressed within us. It is the revolt of that which exists against and pushes beyond. It is the revolt of the creative doing that exists against alien determination and pushes beyond, towards social self-determination. But creative doing is not just creation of that which exists outside us, but self-creation, creation of our own sexuality, our own culture, our own thinking and feeling.

The return of the repressed is not just of the consciously repressed, but of the repressed unconscious. The shadowy figure behind the mask is not only invisible and inaudible,[23] but also, in part at least, unconscious. We do not know our own repressed potential. The drive of anti-identity is a constant movement beyond the concept, it constantly goes beyond our conscious knowledge.

Revolutionary theory and practice, then, cannot be thought of in terms of the bringing of consciousness to people (or to the working class). Nor does it make sense to think of the limits of political action in terms of people's consciousness. Our consciousness is highly contradictory, a multiplicity of knowledges, of vague awarenesses, of intuitions and reactions-against. The politics of bringing consciousness is part of the world of character masks, the world of identities. The drive of our shadowy figure (a scream, a question, a crisis, a menace, a potential, a we, a flow) against the character mask cannot be understood in terms of the bringing of consciousness. It is much more a question of drawing out that which is already present in repressed and contradictory form. The task is like that of the psychoanalyst who tries to make conscious that which is unconscious and repressed. But there is no psychoanalyst standing outside the subject: the 'psychoanalysis' can only be a collective self-analysis. The only therapy possible is self-therapy.

This implies a politics not of talking, but of listening, or, better, of talking-listening. The revolutionary process is a collective coming-to-eruption of stifled volcanoes. The language and thought of revolution cannot be a prose which sees volcanoes as mountains: it is necessarily a poetry which understands mountains as volcanoes, an imagination which reaches out towards unseen passions, unseen capacities, unseen knowledges and powers-to-do, unseen dignities. This is a dialogical politics rather than the monological talking-politics of the traditional revolutionary movement. But it is more than that, for a dialogue could be a dialogue between character masks and what we are talking of here is a dialogue in which each tries to see and hear and touch the shadowy figures behind the character masks. It is a question of feeling for and trying to touch hidden nerves. Revolutionary theory, then, blends with art, theatre, music, poetry: all, at their best, are attempts to break through the world of character masks and give voice to and stir the passions and dignities that lie below. Revolutionary practice has always blended with art, but perhaps never more than in recent years, where artistic or theatrical expression has come to form an integral part of any demonstration of discontent: the Zapatistas or the Clandestine Insurgent Rebel Clown Army[24] are just two of the thousands of examples that leap to mind.

The touching of hidden nerves is clearly not just a rational process, a process of rational argument or learning. It is a looking for that which is already present, a listening for the 'hidden transcript'.[25] This does not mean that it is an irrational process. On the contrary: the core is rational critique. We live in an 'enchanted topsy-turvy world' (Marx 1894/1971: 830) in which our subjectivity, our power-to, is concealed by the reified relations generated by the organisation of our doing as abstract labour. The rational critique of those reified forms is central to the discovery of the shadowy figure, of the flow of doing that revolts against its repression, but theoretical reflection gains force only as one part of the general struggle.

29
Doing dissolves the homogenisation of time.

1. CLOCK-TIME IS IN CRISIS.

Abstract labour is inseparable from abstract time. The crisis of abstract labour is also the crisis of abstract time. At one level, it is a permanent crisis: we are the permanent crisis of the time of abstract labour, with our refusals, our passions, our intensities. Doing-time exists in the form of clock-time, but it also exists against and beyond that time. The transformation of the struggle against time into a struggle about time, noted by Thompson, was never complete. Trade unions started to fight over the length of the working day, but the struggle over punctuality and, above all, over the porosity of the working day is a struggle that is inseparable from the imposition of capitalist labour. Those paid to spend their days working for another always try to find ways of imposing their own rhythm, to create spaces for dreaming, for talking to their friends, for having a smoke or a bite to eat, whatever. Some of this is reflected in trade union disputes (over the length of tea or coffee breaks, for example), but much of it is fought at an individual or collective level that depends on being invisible to be effective. An important aspect of capitalist management is to close these moments created by the workers. The permanent crisis of clock-time is not just limited to the workplace, of course. Our lives, our passions, the way we relate to friends: all are bound up with lived time, doing-time, the silent daily struggle for other ways of living, other ways of doing and relating.

But is there more than a permanent crisis of clock-time, more than a chronic incompleteness in the acceptance of capitalist rhythms? Can we say that there is now an intensification of the crisis of clock-time?

Thompson, as we have seen, shows how the struggle to establish capitalism involved a long struggle to impose a new concept of time. Class struggle was the struggle between two times, between two concepts and practices of time: the one centred on us, our doing, our living, and the other a quantitative, measured, objective time that abstracts completely from our lives and concerns. Thompson argues that, as capitalism becomes established, at least in the more 'advanced' countries, there is a widespread internalisation of abstract time, that struggle becomes focused on quantitative issues of time rather than on the quality of time itself. However, after emphasising the role of Puritanism in imposing the internalisation of clock-time, he asks:

> If Puritanism was a necessary part of the work-ethos which enabled the industrialised world to break out of the poverty-stricken economies of the past, will the Puritan evaluation of time begin to decompose as the pressures of poverty relax? Is it decomposing already? Will men begin to lose that restless urgency, that desire to consume time purposively, which most people carry just as they carry a watch on their wrists? (1967: 95)

And he continues: 'But if the purposive notation of time-use becomes less compulsive, then men might have to re-learn some of the arts of living lost in the industrial revolution: how to fill the interstices of their days with enriched, more leisurely, personal and social relations; how to break down once more the barriers between work and life' (ibid.).

Is there, then, a decomposition of clock-time? If so, why? Is it because of a relaxation of the pressures of poverty, as Thompson suggests, or some other reason? What would a decomposition of clock-time mean? Thompson suggests that a central element would be a breaking down of the barriers between work and life. This, however, could be seen in quite a different sense, as the extension of the dominion of clock-time. In this sense, Virno, Hardt and Negri argue that there is an extension of the discipline of labour time to the whole 24 hours of the day: 'For the post-Fordist multitude every qualitative difference between labour time and non-labour time falls short.'[1] Where does that leave us?

Let us take the argument more slowly. The argument in this book is that we are living through a crisis of abstract labour and that this transforms the meaning of class struggle. In this transformation of class struggle, the quality (and not just the quantity) of time becomes a central and overt point of conflict, again. To the extent that the reality and the concept of class struggle were dominated by the conflict between abstract labour and capital, the quality of time was not an issue. It could not be, simply because the abstraction of doing into labour is inseparable from the abstraction of time. It is only with the crisis of abstract labour that the quality of time comes to the fore and it again becomes clear that class struggle can (and must) be understood not just as a quantitative conflict about time, but as a qualitative conflict, that is, as a conflict between two different concepts and practices of time. There is *their* time, the time of capital: the abstraction of time from our lives, the negation by time of our humanity. And there is our time, a time that springs from our lives: not a time-in-which we live, but a time-as-which we live. Their time against ours; our time against theirs – that is the conflict, and it is now an open and intense conflict present in every moment of existence. For us the challenge is to break their time, to shoot clocks.[2] But what is our time, and how can we nourish it in such a way as to break their time? The following points seek to suggest a way forward.

2. OUR TIME BREAKS DURATION.

In Mary Shelley's famous story (1818/1985), Dr Frankenstein creates a Creature, and the Creature then acquires an independent existence, a durable existence in which he no longer depends on the creative activity of Dr Frankenstein. In another story, a story by Jorge Luis Borges, 'Las Ruinas Circulares' (1941/2000a), a man creates another man, but he does it not in a laboratory but by dreaming. The man created has all the appearance of being a normal man with an independent, durable existence, but in fact he is kept alive only by the constant creative activity, the dreaming, of the first man. In neither case is the existence of the created being an illusion, but in the second case his duration is an illusion: his existence depends, from one moment to another, on the creative activity of the dreamer.

The story of Frankenstein is often taken as a metaphor for capitalism. We have created a society which is beyond our control and which threatens to destroy us: the only way we can survive is by destroying that society. But is it possible to think rather in terms of the story by Borges? We have created a society which appears to be totally beyond our control, but which in reality depends upon our act of constant re-creation. The problem is not to destroy that society, but to stop creating it. Capitalism exists today not because we created it two hundred years ago or a hundred years ago, but because we created it today. If we do not create it tomorrow, it will not exist.[3]

We create capitalism. Can we then say that its existence depends from one moment to the next on our continued act of creation?

Criticism is the starting-point of the attack on duration. Duration rests on the separation of subject and object. If Frankenstein's Creature has a duration, it is because he has separated himself from his maker, whereas the creature in Borges' story does not enjoy the same separation from the dreamer. In both cases, the subject-creator is denied and forgotten, but in the latter case the real dependence of the object on the subject continues. In capitalism too, the subject-creator is denied and forgotten: the commodity, to quote the second paragraph of Marx's *Capital*, is, 'in the first place, an object outside us' (1867/1965: 35; 1867/1990: 125). Marx's method of criticism attacks this self-presentation of the commodity by saying that the value of the commodity depends on the labour that created it. The commodity presents itself as being independent of us, it denies and forgets us, but in fact it is our creation and would not exist if we, through our labour, had not created it. Criticism, for Marx, is genetic criticism, the attempt to understand phenomena in terms of the doing that produces them. Marx's labour theory of value is such a criticism: at its core, the labour theory of value says 'The commodity denies our doing, but we made it.' With that, the subject (our doing) is restored to the centre of the picture. The object claims to be independent of the subject, but in fact it depends on the subject.

Criticism restores the subject to the centre. By criticising, humans say 'We are the negated creators, but we reject that negation. All social phenomena exist because we have made them: money or the state are just as much human products as the motor-car. They depend on our creation for their existence. And if we made them, we can change them.'

There is still a question, though. We have created the social world around us, but are we stuck with our own creations (Frankenstein), or do they depend on our constant re-creation (Borges)? Do we have to make a distinction between some creations (for example, the state or money) and others (the car, say)?

Money is a form of social relations, a way in which we relate to one another. When we buy something and pay for it with money, we establish a certain form of relation with the producer of the thing we buy. If we steal the thing, we establish a different sort of relation with her, and if we receive it as a present yet another, different relation. The sort of relationship we establish does not depend either on the thing bought, stolen, or received, nor on the materiality of any money involved (notes or coins). When we say that money is a form of social relations, we say, then, that it is a form that we create and re-create, a form that depends not just on our initial creation but on our constant re-creation. The same can be said of the state or capital.

Is a car also a form of social relations that we constantly create and re-create? Clearly, cars have a certain materiality, as indeed money has a certain materiality. However, the car is also a way in which we relate to other people – to the workers who produced it, when we buy it, but also to the people around us, our family and friends, people in the street or in the town, when we use it. We could use it as a sculpture or for planting flowers, in which case we would no longer be re-creating the social relations indicated by the concept of 'car'.

To put it in different terms: criticism is the recovery of verbs. Our vision of the world is dominated by nouns, by things: money, state, car, wall, computer, food, and so on. The doing, creating, painting, cooking, organising, bricklaying, teaching, and so on are forgotten. Each noun implies the suppression

231

of a verb at least in so far as it conceptualises the outcome of a human action. Each noun gives an appearance of autonomy to the result of the action, cutting the result of the action from the action itself, the done from the doing. Thus, 'car' hides the car-making that produces, 'book' conceals what I am doing in this moment, 'property' conceals the appropriating, 'money' conceals the monetising of the interacting between people. A society which consciously had our doing at its centre, that is, a self-determining or communist society, would probably have a language in which verbs were primary: coming together would involve speaking of doing. It could be argued that anti-capitalist literature should abandon nouns and just use verbs, but that would be very difficult to write and probably difficult to understand. Borges, in another story in which he imagines the world of Tlön, in which the *Ursprache* or original language has no nouns, gives an example, explaining that 'the moon rose above the river' is expressed as 'Upward, behind the onstreaming, it mooned' (1941/2000b: 20).[4] The point, however, is that a world of verbs would open up a universe of possibility: the results of our doings would no longer have the same appearance of fixity, the world would be much more obviously fragile, much more open to changing and creating. It would be a world of greatly heightened intensity.

Criticism, then, if we understand it as genetic criticism, criticism *ad hominem*, criticism which seeks to recover the power and centrality of human doing, leads us to a general criticism of nouns (at least in so far as they refer to the outcome of human actions). Marx's critique of political economy should logically lead on to a critique of nouns: political economy is just one expression of fetishised thought, nouns are a much more general expression of the same process of fetishising. A critique of nouns would not, of course, make nouns disappear: it would make clear that the suppression or closure of verbs by nouns is just one aspect of commodity fetishism, and that fetishism arises from the fact that relations between doers are mediated through things, through the exchange of commodities. The force of nouns in our language is an expression of the real domination of things in our lives. In other words, nouns, like value, like money, like the state, are social relations: the noun, like value, is 'a relation between persons expressed as a relation between things' (1867/1965: 74; 1867/1990: 167). Or, even better: the noun is a relating between doings expressed as a relation between things.

In a world of verbs, duration loses its force completely (as indeed does ontology). If everything (every social thing) is a done, a result of doing, and if the present existence of each done is understood as a relating between doers, then each moment acquires a particularity in which everything is at issue. We have in our pocket a piece of paper which has been monetised (converted into money) by social practice. It is not the case that it *is* money: it is a piece of paper monetised by practice. We have participated in its monetisation, but the next time we go out, we can either continue to monetise it (by using it as money) or we can choose to de-monetise it – by refusing to use it as a medium in our relations with other people and using it to light a cigarette. The same might be said of a car: we have a piece of metal which has been converted into a car by the intention of its makers and the practice of its users. It is not the case that it *is* a car: it is a piece of metal car-ised by practice, and tomorrow we can either continue that practice (with all that it implies in terms of contamination and danger to others) or we can de-car-ise it – by refusing to relate to other people in that way and by using it as a receptacle for planting flowers or carrots. We make money by using the paper in that way and we can stop making it; we make the car and we can stop doing so. Similarly, we make capitalism and we can stop doing so.

By recovering the subject suffocated by the object, criticism puts our power-to-do, and our power-not-to-do, at the centre. It challenges the noun and recovers the verb, the doing that is (and is not) contained in the noun, that overflows against and beyond the noun. Verbs are the language of non-identity, the bursting beyond that which is. Identity establishes a continuous time, a time of duration, an extended is-ness, but the force of our doing says 'no, there is no continuity, there is no duration, each moment has its particularity, each moment is a moment of creating.' Our time, doing-time, is the time of opening each moment against the force of duration.

Criticism, by recovering doing in a society which negates it, opens up the distinct particularity of each moment. Unlike clock-time, in which each moment is indistinguishable from the next, our time is characterised by the distinctness of each moment. Doing shapes each moment and makes it distinct. Each moment is not disconnected from other moments but distinct from other moments. In clock-time, each moment is identical; in our time, each moment is non-identical.

Our time is a time of resistance, of rebellion. It revolts against the time of duration. Duration closes each moment, tells us each moment is a mere continuation of the last, and our time revolts, opens each moment as a moment of possibility, as a moment of possible fulfilment, possible disaster. Instead of building patiently for the future, the non-revolt of revolutionary parties, our revolt is a rebellion against time itself which lifts each moment from the continuity of duration and turns it around, makes it a moment of doing rather than a frame for doing. *Carpe diem* as a revolutionary principle, but not the *carpe diem* that simply abstracts the Friday-Saturday nights of enjoyment from the abstract time of the week and changes nothing, but a *carpe diem* that turns against abstraction and brings to the fore the latent potential of each moment.[5]

This is the time of the child, a time in which each moment is different from the last, in which each moment is filled with wonder, with amazement and possibility. And with horror: we see the killing of people (by violence, by hunger) and the deadening of people (by boredom, by repression) and we see it with amazement and say 'that cannot be!' We cast off the blinkers that help us to survive in this society of horrors and open our eyes with the naïveté of a child and think 'no, this cannot continue one moment more, the change must be now, not in the far-off revolutionary future.' 'The child's days', says Vaneigem, 'escape adult time – they are time swollen by subjectivity, by passion, by dreams inhibited by reality.' Even after the child has learnt school discipline, grown up and become imprisoned by adult time, 'his childhood will remain within him like an open wound' (1967/1994: 222). The struggle for our time, the struggle against duration, is the stirring of this open wound, the awakening of a time repressed, a time in which the whole of existence is at issue in each moment. Lenin would be right to characterise this revolutionary thinking as an infantile disorder.[6] It is infantile, must be infantile, infantile and proud of it.[7]

This is the time not of marriage but of love. Marriage casts a coating of duration upon a relating that exists only if it is constantly created and re-created, that, more than anything else, exists as the open wound of child-time within the adult. Our time, then, is anti-institutional time. Institutions seek to freeze relations, to make time stand still or run along pre-ordained tracks, to tie today to the rules of yesterday, tomorrow to the routines of today. Institutions do not always have a name or a constitution: institutionalisation is the practice of clock-time that creeps upon us and sucks the passion out of each moment. The rejection of institutionalisation is not just an abstract principle but a practical necessity of revolutionary organisation. If we think, for example of the Zapatistas' *'mandar obedeciendo'*, their wonderful translation of the noun of democracy into the verbal (and oxymoronic) expression 'to command obeying', it is clear that this will work only if it is truly verbal and anti-institutional. It is not enough for difficult decisions (like the refusal of all state subsidies) to have been taken democratically in the past: if they are not constantly renewed (or changed), there is likely to be an erosion of support. Any institution which is not constantly questioned and re-created, becomes oppressive: revolutionary organisations just as much as marriage.

To recover the subject negated by objectivity, to emancipate the power-to metamorphosed into power-over, is to struggle to open each moment as a moment of possibility. In one interview, when Subcomandante Marcos is asked what his dream of a future society is, he says that the society for which the Zapatistas struggle would be like a cinema programme in which they could choose to live a different film each day, that the reason they have risen in revolt is that for the past five hundred years, they have been forced to live the same film over and over and over again.[8] We too might say that for the last few hundred years, we have been living the same film, the film of capitalism, and that it is a very bad film, a very boring film, one that dehumanises all who watch it. And now we must live a different film, or rather a multiplicity of films that we will create in the process of living them. We make capitalism by creating and re-creating the social relations of capitalism: we must stop doing so, we must do something else, live different social relations. Revolution is simply that: to stop making capitalism and do something else instead. The struggle is not a struggle for survival (that is the genuine struggle of abstract labour) but a struggle to live.[9]

4. OUR STRUGGLE IS THE PURSUIT OF ABSOLUTE INTENSITY. REVOLUTION IS APOCALYPTIC RATHER THAN UTOPIAN.

We tend to think of revolution in spatial terms, as the capture and transformation of spaces, those spaces being understood in traditional theory as states. Perhaps, in the first place, we should think of revolution rather as the capture and transformation of time. We should think not just of taking a space (state, town, or social centre) and transforming the relations within it, but rather (or also) of taking a time and transforming the relations within it. Breaking duration means to see each moment as distinct, as full of possibilities: the realisation of these possibilities can mean driving each moment beyond its limits, beyond all limits, to the point where it sheds time itself and blends with eternity.

This would break the instrumentalisation of time. Traditional theory sees each moment in terms of its utility for constructing a future. Acts of rebellion are judged in terms of whether they contribute to the construction of a lasting revolution. But if we break duration and each moment is distinct, then there is no need for acts of rebellion to stand before the tribunal of instrumental time. Each moment is its own justification: each moment of rebellion stands proud in its own dignity.

Revolution, then, is the pushing of each moment beyond all instrumentality and beyond all limits. It is apocalyptic rather than utopian. Utopias tend to define the perfect society in spatial terms, apocalyptic thought locates it in time, or rather, apocalyptic thought focuses on the breaking and transformation of time. The time of apocalypse is not a time-in-which, but a time-as-which:[10] 'Time exists only as the rhythm and the structure of what it is [we] choose to do.' Self-determination means lifting the present moment from the continuum of history and abolishing the past:

> In Hegel's succinct expression, 'there is no past'. The past lives on 'in the depths of the present' not in the sense that it determines this present, but in the sense that it is always some specific free action which, as its context or background, makes a particular interpretation of the past appear … Action *in* time is past-determined, whereas action which *is* time knows nothing of a past which determines it but only a future towards which it aims. (Gunn, 1985: 11–12)

The struggle for self-determination is the struggle for time-as-which. Time then leaps out of the clock, leaves time-in-which behind, reaches for eternity. Gunn, recalling that Lenin argued that Marx's *Capital* could be understood only through reading Hegel's *Logic*, suggests that 'both Marx and Hegel can be understood only by means of a reading of Boethius's *Consolation of Philosophy*'. Boethius, a theologian of the fourth century, understood eternity as the *nunc stans*, the moment of 'perfect possession at the same time of endless life',[11] a moment in which 'all moments of history are laid out co-temporally before God's view' (Gunn 1985: 9).[12]

This is Benjamin's *Jetztzeit* or now-time, or Bloch's constant pursuit of the Faustian moment of perfection in which we say to the moment itself 'stay a while, you are so beautiful' (*verweile doch, du bist so schön*). For Bloch, the revolutionary impulse, the drive towards self-determination, can be traced in all those moments of creativity which break with that which is and open towards a world which does not yet exist. The third volume of his great work, *The Principle of Hope* (1959/1986), is devoted entirely to the pursuit of the moment of perfection, the *nunc stans*, suggesting that this is the way in which we should think of revolution and communism. For Benjamin, this breaking of time is a flash of lightning, a flash of intense present that breaks that-which-is and opens a different present, an intense Now.

These are the 'moments of excess'[13] characteristic of acts of rebellion. Any great act of rebellion is a moment of excess in which inhibitions and established patterns of social behaviour

237

are broken, a flash of lightning which makes us see history and society in a different way, a time when we lose all sense of time. This is the way rebellion moves, not according to the clock, but through these moments of excess, often unforeseen and unforeseeable, but sometimes planned as great events which may (or may not) catch fire: Seattle, Genoa, Gleneagles, Heiligendamm, and so on. Revolution, the radical transformation of society, is a matter, then, not of building the party, but a series of rebellions, sometimes orchestrated and sometimes not, which in the best of cases go gathering momentum, but none of which requires to be justified by a long-term development. These moments of excess are the 'space-time of the privileged moment, of creativity, of pleasure, of orgasm' (Vaneigem 1967/1994: 227). They stand in themselves as ruptures of clock-time, as cracks in the metronome of capitalist domination. As Vaneigem puts it, 'space-time lived in unitary fashion is the first *foco* in the coming guerrilla war' (ibid.: 228).

This is performance-time, dance-time, concentrated time in which time becomes entirely sucked in to the rhythm of our doing, in which the clock and the calendar lose all meaning.

5. DOING-TIME IS NOT JUST THE INTENSITY OF MOMENTS OF EXCESS, IT IS ALSO THE TIME OF PATIENT CREATION.

Time-as-which, we said, quoting Gunn, 'exists only as the rhythm and the structure of what it is [we] choose to do'. But often we choose to do things in a leisurely fashion, or just to follow the rhythm that seems appropriate to the activity. Not all moments are moments of performance, there are also times of preparation, and there are many activities that require no performance, just a patient process of creation. If the first temporality is performance-time or dance-time, then perhaps we can think of this second temporality as gardening-time or weaving-time.[14]

Creating another society cannot be just a question of events and intensities. Beyond the puncturing of duration, beyond the discontinuities of excess, there is also the question of creating other social relations, of doing things in a different way, at a rhythm of our own choosing. Probably we need to think of revolution in terms of both temporalities: the temporality of rave-and-rage, performance-and-dance, and the temporality of patient creation, of gardening-and-weaving. This is not the old virtue of revolutionary patience, based on the idea that we must wait until the objective conditions are ripe. This is a different sort of patience that says 'no waiting, let's get on now with constructing a different world, but it is not something that can be created in an explosion of fury, it requires and always will require a process of patient creation'.

This is a gentler time, a time perhaps not so much of passion but of love and friendship. It suggests a slower, longer process, but it is certainly not the time of duration. It is not time which is separated from our doing or from the social relations we are creating, but very much an 'our time', a time which we create and re-create, but which does not separate itself from our creation-re-creation. This too is a 'space-time lived in unitary fashion' of which Vaneigem speaks. It is perhaps too another face of the *nunc stans*, the moment of blending with eternity understood now not as orgasm but as a lazy moment of enjoyment with friends, when we sit back and want the day to drift on slowly.

The Zapatista uprising began with the cry of ¡*Ya basta!* (Enough!), but they also have a saying that expresses the second temporality: '*caminamos, no corremos, porque vamos muy lejos*' (we walk, we do not run, because we are going very far). This is the time of the Zapatista communities, of the schools, the clinics, the cooperatives, the Juntas de Buen Gobierno: the patient construction of another world which is the core of the Zapatista movement.

This is the time when dignity moves beyond rage, the time of walking the paths we create by walking.

6. DOING-TIME BREAKS PROGRESS, MEANDERS.

Clock-time, we have seen, is the time of progress, of development understood in quantitative measurements, in percentage growth of GDP. Progress is an external force, the need to build highways, airports, tourist facilities because, if not, we will fall behind.

Progress is the technology that we must introduce in order for the abstraction of doing into labour to be effective, to meet the requirements of socially necessary labour time.

It is striking that many of the anti-capitalist struggles of recent years have been explicitly opposed to progress: to the building of highways, of high-speed trains (the no-TAV movement in Italy), of airports (Atenco in Mexico). This is one of the reasons why indigenous movements have gained such importance: their opposition to the integration of their distinctive cultures into the mainstream flow of progress touches strong chords of sympathy even among people who have never heard of those cultures.

Doing-time is inevitably opposed to progress in this sense. To the external pressure of 'we must get on with things, we must move forward', it opposes the 'we must get together and talk about which way we want to go'. It is the time of 'asking we walk', rather than the time of 'we must get there quickly'. The push towards self-determination probably means that we do things at a gentler pace, simply because we take the time to consider what we want to do and because we resist the pressures of value production, the rule of socially necessary labour time. If this were generalised, there is no reason why it should lead to greater poverty (whatever that may mean), simply because the vast number of people currently employed in tasks of supervision and enforcement would be able to devote their energies to activities that they considered necessary or desirable.

Doing-time meanders. It is not the forward march of the five-year plan. Self-determination must include being able to question decisions that we have already taken, being able to experiment and change our course. Doing-time is a time in which we take our time to do, and since the world we want is a world of many worlds, doing-time must be a loose interweaving, or perhaps just mutual respect, of many times.

Doing-time is not the forward march of history, but just the opposite. It is the collective cry that is growing louder and louder each day: 'No! Stop! The train is going too fast, and going in the wrong direction, it is heading straight towards the cliff!' Or, as Benjamin put it, 'Marx called Revolutions the locomotives of world history. But perhaps it is totally different: perhaps it is the people in these trains reaching for the emergency brake.'[15]

7. DOING-TIME IS LIVING NOW THE WORLD THAT EXISTS NOT-YET. BY DOING SO, WE SET THE AGENDA, BECOME OUR OWN TRUE SUN.

Our time is the time of living in our world, the world that does not yet exist, and exists not yet.

We create the world that does not yet exist by living it. We simply assert our own world. The organic gardeners of the world do not wait for the revolution to create a less aggressive relation with plants: they do it now. The movement for a free transport system in Oslo does not lobby the government for a reduction of fares, it simply organises people not to pay. The critical teacher does not wait for a change in the curriculum to introduce a different concept of learning and teaching: she just does it. Squatters do not wait for the abolition of private property and rents to live in vacant houses: they just do it. Many, many migrants do not wait for the abolition of border controls before crossing from one country to another: they just go.

This concept is opposed to a politics of demands. A demand is addressed to someone and asks them to do something on our behalf in the future, whereas in the politics of living now the world we want to create (or creating now the world we want by living it) there is no demand. We ask no permission of anyone and we do not wait for the future, but simply break time and assert now another type of doing, another form of social relations. The state or the party ceases to be an intermediary separating us from what we want to achieve: we simply assume our own responsibility and do it. The anti-poll tax campaign in Britain (which eventually led to the fall of Mrs Thatcher) took this form: it was centred not on a demand that the government should repeal the tax, but on the outright refusal to pay, without mediation, the living of a world in which the tax did not exist.

The Zapatista experience is interesting in this respect. Their original ¡Ya basta! of 1994 was accompanied by a list of demands, and a series of dialogues with the Mexican state led to the signing of an agreement on indigenous rights. Although the Zapatistas started to construct their own autonomous municipalities, schools and clinics from an early date, it is only really after the complete failure (in 2001) of the Mexican state to implement the agreements on indigenous rights that the Zapatista movement completely abandons the politics of demands, and, with it, all contact with the state, and the creation of its own communal life becomes unambiguously the core of the movement.

By asserting our own world, we set the agenda, the timetable of struggle. A major problem of the left, even the radical left, is that it follows the agenda set by capital. Movements like the movement against the Gelmini proposals in Italy, the movement against the war in Iraq, the anti-summit mobilisations over the last ten years: all of these mobilise action to stop the worst barbarities of capitalist rule, but they allow capital to set the agenda. All these movements have been very important, and more than a reaction to capital, or rather the reaction overflows the immediate cause. It remains true, however, that they allow capital to set the timetable of conflict. For the emancipation of doing from abstract labour, on the other hand, it is essential to alter the perspective radically. To place doing in the centre is to restore ourselves to the centre of the universe. The young Marx says of the criticism of religion 'The criticism of religion disillusions man to make him think and act and shape his reality like a man who has been disillusioned and has come to reason, so that he will revolve around himself and therefore round his true sun' (1844/1975a: 176). The struggle that puts doing at the centre forces a Copernican inversion upon capital: it forces capital to revolve explicitly around us. Capital is always a reaction to anti-capitalist struggle,[16] but it is important to make this explicit both to capital and to ourselves as the pre-condition of emancipation. Revolution is precisely that: the assertion of ourselves as our own true sun.

Part VIII
A Time of Birth?

30
We are the forces of production: our power is the power of doing.

We are the heat cracking the ice. We are the weeds breaking through the pavement. Could it be that this is a time of birth, and not just a time of death and destruction?

Marx presents a powerful image of revolution as the breakthrough of a new world:

> The monopoly of capital becomes a fetter upon the mode of production, which has sprung up and flourished along with, and under it. Centralisation of the means of production and socialisation of labour at last reach a point where they become incompatible with their capitalist integument. This integument is burst asunder. The knell of capitalist private property sounds. The expropriators are expropriated. (1867/1965: 763; 1867/1990: 929)

Is this what is happening? Are the cracks the bursting asunder of the capitalist integument and the pushing through of a new world?

Traditional Marxism presents this breaking of the integument in terms of the clash between the forces of production and the relations of production. As Marx puts it in the Preface to the *Contribution to the Critique of Political Economy*:

> At a certain stage of development, the material productive forces of society come into conflict with the existing relations of production or ... with the property relations within the framework of which they have operated hitherto. From forms of development of the productive forces these relations turn into their fetters. – Then begins an era of social revolution. (1859/1971: 21)

The difficulty with the traditional interpretation of 'productive forces' is that it presents them as an external force (the force of technological development) which has a dynamic independent of social relations. This runs counter to two points that have been central in the argument here (and in Marx's own argument): first, that we humans are the creative power in society, and secondly, that our creative power does not develop independently of its social context, but rather in a relation of in-against-and-beyond. The relation of content to form is neither a relation of independence (autonomous forces of production clashing against the relations of production) nor of total containment (the forces of production being completely contained in and determined by the relations of production), but always an ec-static relation, a relation of containment, antagonism and pushing beyond. Thus, doing (useful labour) exists in-against-and-beyond abstract labour; use value exists in-against-and-beyond value and the forces of production exist in-against-and-beyond the relations of production.

Another expression that Marx frequently uses points us away from the traditional interpretation, the apparent separation of the forces of production from human creative power: he speaks in *Capital* of the 'productive powers of social labour', or 'labour's social productive forces'. Here it is clear that we are speaking of the power of human creativity, the power of doing, our power-to-do, our being-able-to. In capitalism, our power-to-do separates itself from us and appears as something alien, as the power of capital, or as the power of capitalist technology:

> With the development of relative surplus-value in the actual specifically capitalist mode of production, whereby the productive powers of social labour are developed, these productive powers and the social interrelations of labour in the direct labour-process seem transferred from labour to capital. Capital thus becomes a very mystic being since all of labour's social productive forces appear to be due to capital, rather than labour as such, and seem to issue from the womb of capital itself. (1894/1971: 827)

Criticism is the recovery of the social productive forces for us, the understanding of the social productive forces as our power to do. We, then, are the forces of production. Ours are the 'productive powers of social labour'. The 'productive power of social labour' is the existence of our power to do under capitalism, our power to do in-against-and-beyond labour.

We are the forces of production, the development of our creative power in-against-and-beyond capital. The orthodox view sees this creative power as developing harmoniously within capital until a point of antagonism is reached, leading to a rupture which opens the world of creativity beyond capitalist social relations: in, against and beyond are clearly separated, both conceptually and in time. Clearly, this cannot be so: frustration is constitutive of capitalism since the beginning. Capital, since the beginning, says to people, 'your creativity is valid only within the bounds of value production: if you do not produce value, your creativity counts for nothing'. And since the beginning people have obeyed-and-rebelled. The productive (and therefore destructive) power of human doing has expanded enormously in this constant slippage between obedience and rebellion, this constant creative pushing at the limits of the system and the expansion of the limits to contain some (but not all) of the creative pushing within the bounds of capitalist production. As the productive-and-destructive power of human doing grows, so does the tug of discomfort, the ec-static pain of frustration, the feeling that the Progressive development of our creative power is taking us in the wrong direction. Certainly we do not want to reject our growing power-to-do, our growing being-able-to, for this being-able-to is also a being-able-to do things quite differently: in other words, the technological capabilities that we have developed in-against-and-beyond capital are also the real capability of a different-doing. This is not just empty possibility[1] but real push, expressed in the drive of many, many people to use their skills to push the world in a different direction, develop alternative technologies, use their computing skills in a different way, and so on. Citing the example of permaculture, Carlsson (2008: 56–8) argues that the 'realm of science and technology is a central location for the present battle between collective, human values and those of capital ... Among dissenting scientists and technologists the power to think is re-shaping itself in directions beyond the narrow confines of capital.'

We are the forces of production, and the development of our productive power, our power-to-do, is closely bound up with its socialisation. The more we join with others, the greater our creative power. The problem, as we have seen, is that under capitalism, socialisation exists as abstraction: it is through abstraction that the social coming together of different doings is established. It is not surprising then that the revolt against abstract labour should take the form of a revolt against socialisation: doing our own thing, expressing ourselves, creating small projects. The traditional concept of socialism seems of little relevance here: it poses an image of post-capitalist society as a society characterised by a greater socialisation of production with ever bigger units of production, but reduces the question of self-determination to the entirely abstract idea of the Plan rather than to the actual process of doing.

The development of our power-to-do must not be understood as a rejection of socialisation. The challenge, rather, is to construct through the cracks a different socialisation, a socialisation more loosely woven than the social synthesis of capitalism and based on the full recognition of the particularities of our individual and collective activities and of their thrust towards self-determination. There are already many initiatives in this direction. The insistence of the so-called anti-globalisation movement that it is not opposed to globalisation but favours a different sort of globalisation and is therefore an alter-globalisation movement makes precisely the point that the struggle is not for a romantic return to isolated units but for a different sort of social interconnection. Horizontality, dignity, alternative economy, commons: all these terms relate to explorations in the construction of a different form of socialisation.

The breakthrough is the breakthrough of our social power-to-do, our social being-able-to, but what is happening does not correspond to the traditional socialist imagery of the breakthrough of the forces of production. It does not take the form of the imposition of a new totality: rather, it is a multiple cracking of the old system. The attacks on the existing organisation of human activity and the pushing towards a different doing come from all sides: from all the millions of people who have made their appearance in the pages of this book and many, many more. It is doing that is at the centre, not a new discourse, not a new way of thinking, not a new form of organising, not a new –ism: doing. Doing, because it is our doing here and now that produces capitalism and destruction, or else produces a world fit for human and non-human life. Revolution is simply that: the assuming of our responsibility as the creators of social reality, the social assuming of our power-to-do.

31

We are the crisis of capitalism, the misfitting-overflowing of our power-to-do, the breakthrough of another world, perhaps.

Capital is in its deepest crisis in many years. Again we ask: could it be that this is a time of birth, and not just a time of death and destruction? Could it be that the crisis is not just a breakdown of capitalism but the breakthrough of another world?

Demonstrations all over the world proclaim that the capitalists are the cause of the crisis. And yet all our argument so far tells us that this cannot be so. We, not the capitalists, are the cause of the crisis. Capital is a relation of subordination, it drives towards the subordination of every aspect of our lives to the logic of capital. If it is in crisis, it is because of our insubordination, because we are saying 'no, no more'.

There is a dynamic built in to the capital relation. Capital is a constant turning of the screw, a constant intensification of the subordination of doing to abstract labour. Abstraction is the subordination of our doing to the requirements of socially necessary labour time, but the amount of labour time required to produce any commodity is being reduced from day to day, minute to minute. Each minute, the abstraction of doing into labour demands a tighter subordination of our activity to the rhythms of value production: if this is not achieved, the labour performed will prove to be socially unnecessary and useless from the point of view of capital, an inadequate subordination.

The implacable dynamic of socially necessary labour time – the drive of 'produce faster, faster, faster, hurry, hurry, hurry' – expresses itself in a tendency towards crisis. The constant intensification of productivity is achieved not just with the foreman's discipline but with the constant introduction of new machinery. This does not make capital any less exigent, however, since the relative growth in investment in machinery means that capital requires an ever-increasing rate of exploitation in order to maintain its rate of profit: this is Marx's argument in his analysis of the tendency of the rate of profit to fall.[1]

However we look at it, the fall in capital's rate of profit has as its base a non-subordination, a failure to subordinate ourselves to the degree that capital demands of us, a 'whoa, no more, you can't push us any more, we are humans not machines, humans with our lives and loves, our children, our friends, our parents.' Simply trying to be human, chatting to our friends, falling in love, becomes converted by the dynamic of capital, that constant turning of the screw, into an act of insubordination. And conversely: it is this trying to be human that is our revolutionary hope, the potential breakthrough of another world, another doing, another way of relating.

The law of value, the rule of socially necessary labour time, is a constant tightening of the Procrustean bed, a constant redefinition of the labourer that capital requires. Capital's problem is the problem that it has had since its birth: to transform the savage into a labourer. The constant redefinition of labour (of value production and what it requires) means that capital is ever anew confronted with the task of forcing people to fit into its requirements. Capitalist crisis is always a crisis of fitting: the savages will not do what capital requires of them (of us). 'Fit or be damned!' cries capital. And to more and more people in the world it says 'you do not fit, we have no use for you: you are too old, too pregnant, too unstable emotionally, you know too much philosophy, your children fall ill, you chat to your friends, you do not speak English, you think too little about money and too much about other things.' And more and more people reply, 'yes, it is true, we do not fit.' The crisis is an explosion of misfitting – the result of the lack of fit between humans and the requirements of value production, and the dramatic manifestation of that lack of fit. 'It is true', we repeat, 'we do not fit.' But there is something else on the tip of our tongue, we want to add something else. And on this something else hangs the future of the world. We bow our heads and say 'yes, it is true, we do not fit in, but we shall try harder: we shall learn better English, improve our computing skills, throw out our childish books by Marx and Bakunin, we shall forbid our children to fall ill, we shall stop being too old, too pregnant, too foreign, too in love, too unstable, we shall fit.' We raise our heads and say 'yes, it is true, we do not fit. And do you know something? We do not want to fit. We do not want to fit in to this world of destruction. And do you know something else? Your crisis is your incapacity to contain our power-to-do, your crisis is the breakthrough of our creative-productive force. Our misfitting is our overflowing, the overflowing of our creativity, our magnificent being-able-to. So get thee gone to the dustbin of history, capital, and let us get on with making the world anew.'

This is the dichotomy we face, now more starkly than ever. It is the choice between the struggle of labour and the struggle against labour, between the struggle for employment and the struggle for a doing beyond abstract labour. It is not easy, but that is where we are, that is where we live.

32
Stop making capitalism.

How I wish I could write a book with a happy ending. That I could offer all the answers. That the good would triumph over evil. That we could close the dialectic, end with a synthesis, arrive Home. That we could say with certainty that history is on our side. That, sure as eggs is eggs, communism will take the place of capitalism. That the darkest hour is just before dawn. That our cracks, for sure and certain, are the harbingers of a new society.

But no, it is not like that. There is no certainty. The dialectic is open, negative, full of danger. The hour is dark, but it may be followed by a darker one, and dawn may never come. And we, the fools who live in the cracks, may be just that: fools.

And yet, fools that we are, we think we can see something new emerging. We are standing in the dark shade of a threshold and trying to see and understand that which is opening in front of us. We do not understand it very well, but we can hear, especially in the previous theses, fragments of new melodies of struggle emerging, see glimpses of a new direction in the flow of revolt.

When we look over the threshold and examine these fragments, we look through a lens that is the centre of the argument presented here. In the centre of this book, there is what I like to think of as an eriugenic somersault, but which a good friend likens more prosaically to turning a sock inside out.[1] The somersault (let us put the sock to one side) consists in seeing that all the forms of social relations are form-processes, that all categories are swollen ec-statically with their own negation, or simply, that each obedience contains a disobedience which it cannot contain. We put at the centre a doing that opens, a doing that breaks through abstract labour and its abstract time. The theoretical somersault is not an academic invention but simply part of a shift in the flow of anti-capitalist struggle: the emergence and growth of the fight against labour as the essence of the fight against capital.

In this almost-final thesis of the book, we single out some of the emerging elements of the new poetry of struggle, as suggestions, as provocations.

Stop making capitalism: This is the pivot of our somersault, its centre of levity. The doing that we pitch against labour is the struggle to open each moment, to assert our own determination against all pre-determination, against all objective laws of development. We are presented with a pre-existing capitalism that dictates that we must act in certain ways, and to this we reply 'no, there is no pre-existing capitalism, there is only the capitalism that we make today, or do not make'. And we choose not to make it. Our struggle is to open every moment and fill it with an activity that does not contribute to the reproduction of capital. Stop making capitalism and do something else, something sensible, something beautiful and enjoyable. Stop creating the system that is destroying us. We only live once: why use our time to destroy our own existence? Surely we can do something better with our lives.

Revolution is not about destroying capitalism, but about refusing to create it. To pose revolution as the destruction of capitalism is to reproduce the abstraction of time that is so central to the reproduction of capitalism: it is self-defeating. To think of destroying capitalism is to erect a great monster in front of us, so terrifying that we either give up in despair or else conclude that the only way in which we can slay the monster is by constructing a great party with heroic leaders who sacrifice themselves (and everyone around them) for the sake of the revolution. We defeat ourselves again, this time by constructing a great fable of heroism and leadership and sacrifice and discipline and authority and patience, a fable peopled by saints – Lenin, Trotsky, Rosa, Mao, Che, Marcos, whoever you like – we reproduce that which we want to destroy. To pose revolution as the destruction of capitalism is to distance it from ourselves, to put it off into the future. The question of revolution is not in the future. It is here and now: how do we stop producing the system by which we are destroying humanity?

Rephrasing the question of revolution as *stop making capitalism* does not give us the answers. There are very real pressures (repression, starvation) that push us to reproduce capitalism each day. What the rephrasing does is to redirect our attention. It makes us focus first on ourselves as the creators and potential non-creators of capitalism. Secondly, it brings our attention to bear on the ec-static tension between doing and labour which is both a matter of everyday experience and the space within which our capacity to create another world remains entrapped. This is a sort of glass bubble of bewitchment. If we could look from outside we would see ourselves performing (happily or unhappily) actions that are destroying humanity. We look at ourselves in our own daily routines and our eyes open wide with child-like amazement: we want to knock on the glass and scream 'stop doing it, stop destroying humanity, stop making capitalism!' But we are not outside, we are inside and participating in the destruction of humanity, aware-and-not-aware of what we are doing. How do we light up our eyes with amazement, how do we touch that half-awareness, that tension, that ec-static distance, how do we bring it clearly into focus, how do we magnify it, how do we open it up, how do we strengthen and expand and multiply all those rebellions in which one pole of the ec-static relation (doing) repudiates with all its force the other pole (labour)? That is the question of revolution.

Asking we walk: The great problem is that we do not know the answers, we do not know how to stop making capitalism. We really do not know. Historically, we stand at the threshold of a world of struggle and we are still learning. There is no recipe to be applied.

It is not only that historically we do not know, but not-knowing is a principle of the knowing that is central to the new pattern of struggle. The movement of doing against-and-beyond labour is a thawing, a social flowing that breaks definitions, a flowing in which the doing of one person blends and mingles indefinably with the doing of others. The knowing that is part of this doing is part of the same movement: also a thawing, a social flowing that breaks definitions, a flowing in which the knowing of one person blends and mingles indefinably with the knowing of others.[2] Knowing is a process constructed collectively (sometimes in the privacy of our studies), a dialogue rather than a monologue, an asking-we-walk: not necessarily polite, at times a provocation, but a provocation that opens, not one that lays down the law.

The admission that we do not know is both a principle of knowledge and a principle of organisation that aims at the participation of all in the process of determining our individual and collective doing. Knowing would lead to a different organisational structure, a structure of monologue with established leaders and institutions to hold them in place.

We do not know, and yet there is a growing desperation: what do we do? How do we stop creating capitalism? How do we change the world? How do we stop this horrific destruction that surrounds us?

There is no Right Answer, just millions of experiments: There is no single correct answer to the desperate (and time-honoured) question of what is to be done. Perhaps the best answer that can be given is: 'Think for yourself and yourselves, use your imagination, follow your inclinations and do whatever you consider necessary or enjoyable, always with the motto of against-and-beyond capital.' For some, this will mean throwing themselves into the preparations for the next anti-G8 summit. For others, it will mean trying to open up perspectives of a different world for the children they teach in school. Others will join with their neighbours to create a community garden, or take part in the activities of the nearby social centre. Some will dedicate all their energies to organising opposition to the extension of a motorway that threatens the livelihood of thousands of peasants, some will devote themselves to permaculture or creating free software, others will just play with their children and friends, or write a book on how to change the world. All of these are cries of hope, projections towards a different way of living, attempts to do something better with our lives than creating capitalism. They may not all have an equal impact, but fortunately we have no standard by which to measure them. Who is to say that forming part of the so-called Black Block in an anti-G8 summit is more or less effective a means of struggle than creating a garden as a means of fighting against the massacre by humans of other forms of life?

There is no single correct answer, but this does not mean that all these struggles are atomised. There is a resonance between them, a mutual recognition as being part of a moving against-and-beyond, a constant sharing of ideas and information.[3] The No shared by the many yeses is a practical connection, the constant weaving of a We, the shaping of a common flow of doing and rebellion. This shared resonance does not mean that we all agree: on the contrary, disagreement and discussion are crucial in the formation of the resonating We.

There is never any purity in these experiments, thank goodness. All are contradictory. The dedicated revolutionary who abandons his children to go and fight for the great cause, the indigenous organisation that accepts funds from a church dedicated to subordination and misogyny, the radical professor who participates in the quantitative measurement of students' work, the cooperative that sells its products on the market, the car worker who spends most of his time producing objects that kill and contaminate and then organises a community garden in the evenings and at weekends, the student who organises demonstrations but does not question the categories of the subject she is studying: all, all are self-contradictory, we are all involved in the re-creation of the social relations we are trying to overcome. It cannot be otherwise in a capitalist society. The movement of doing is not a pure movement, but a moving in-against-and-beyond labour. There is no purity here: we try to overcome the contradictions, we rebel against our own complicity, we try in every way to stop making capitalism, we try to direct the flow of our lives as effectively as possible towards the creation of a society based on dignity. We are part of the social flow of rebellion,[4] and in this flow there is no room for rigidities and hard lines. The concepts of correctness and betrayal, its complement that is so rooted in the culture of the left, are obstacles to the flow of rebellion. To create rigidities and dogmas and 'we do not talk to them because they are reformists' and 'we will have nothing to do with them because they drink coca cola' and 'we will not cooperate with them because they are sectarian', is to take an active part in the freezing of the flow of rebellion, to reproduce the definitions and classifications and fetishes of capitalist thought.

We are ordinary people: If we think we are special, distinct from the masses who are happily integrated into the capitalist system, we immediately exclude the possibility of radical change. The contrary is true: to be revolutionary is the most ordinary thing in the world, it is simply part of living in capitalist society.

We all do, and we all do against labour. In one way or another, we push against the determination of our lives by forces we do not control, or at least dream of doing so, or regret not doing so. If revolution is the revolt of doing against labour, then the issue is not to bring revolutionary consciousness to the masses, but to develop the sensitivity to recognise the revolts that exist everywhere, and to find ways of touching them, resonating with them, drawing them out, ways of participating in the thawing and confluence of that which is frozen.

Our strength lies in our ordinariness. Those groups that think that having a pure dogma and perhaps good weapons and military discipline is the best self-defence could not be more mistaken. The best defence (whether we are a guerrilla group or a social centre in a squatted building) is to blend in with our neighbours: not just as intelligent tactics, but because the mutual resonance of ordinary rebelliousnesses is the only possible basis for a communising revolution.

Do it ourselves:[5] This is perhaps the core of the revolt of doing against labour. We assume our own responsibility here and now and do it ourselves. It makes little sense to blame our political leaders as they take us into war or promote the capitalist progress that is destroying life on earth: if there is to be any blame, we should blame ourselves for thinking of them as our leaders or representatives. Out with the lot of them! *¡Que se vayan todos!* We are the only ones that can now stop human self-annihilation: the responsibility is ours. This has long been the argument of radical ecological movements, for example: it is up to us to live in a different way, to change our ecological footprint, to develop a different relationship with the other forms of life. Certainly this pushing-beyond to a different way of living must be understood not just as personal choice but as a pushing-against the capitalist organisation of our activity that is destroying the world (as being anti-capitalist, in other words), but the central point is crucial: anti-capitalism is assuming our own responsibilities, reappropriating our own lives, pushing aside the capital that is the constant expropriation not just of our products but of our doing and thinking and deciding and living.

Set the agenda: Doing it ourselves mean that we set the agenda. Too often we think of anti-capitalism as protesting against the latest barbarities of the system. We march against the war, we protest against the G8, we demonstrate for the release of political prisoners, we picket the Peruvian embassy to stop the killing of the indigenous defenders of the Amazonian jungle. All this is very necessary, but it allows capital to set the agenda to determine the rhythms. The revolt of doing against labour is not just a defence against the horrors of capitalism, but it means taking the initiative and creating now the anticipations of another world. Let them run after us instead of us running after them. We occupy a vacant plot of land and create a garden. We make a social centre as a focus of anti-capitalist resistance in our area. We insist as students that the question of stopping the self-destruction of humanity be discussed in our classes. We occupy six towns and say Enough! We set up a community radio station. *¡Ya basta!* We ask no permission and we make no demands. We do.

We build another world: We get on with it, here and now. There is a shift in focus here. The spectacular events, the anti-summits and the social forums, are important, but they are important not for what they might achieve in terms of changing government policies but above all as points of confluence of the different movements: spaces in which we learn from one another and inspire one another. Most important of all is the less visible movement of refusal and creation. This is not a question of local versus global or micro versus macro, it is rather a question of understanding that the strength of the social flow of rebellion depends finally on our ability to reappropriate (or avoid the expropriation of) the social flow of doing. The big events are important, but they cannot take the place of the constant search for ways of doing against and beyond labour.

Do against labour: If there is to be a future for humanity, we must live differently, we must act differently, we must relate in a different way to one another and to the other forms of life and the natural environment that surround us. We must develop a different doing. It is now clear that the old conception of revolution centred on the socialisation of the means of production is woefully inadequate. The revolutions of the twentieth century failed not because they were too radical but because they were not nearly radical enough. The centre of anti-capitalist revolution is quite simply doing. Do differently, do very differently, or there is no future for humanity. This means to do against labour, because it is above all the discipline of labour that forces our daily activity into a path that quite literally destroys humanity in all its senses. A revolution that is not founded in the transformation of human activity is no revolution at all.

This, we know, is not easy. It is not easy because it can lead to repression or to poverty. But it is also not easy because the dividing lines are not always clear. We can dedicate ourselves to something we consider an important form of protest and then find that the form of protest becomes popular and is transformed into a way of making money: think of early punk or early rap music, for example. The lines are often blurred and yet the tension between doing and labour is a constant preoccupation in our lives. Our responses to this tension are always contradictory, but the more we join with others or realise that our rebellion against labour is part of a more general flow, the easier it becomes to find practical solutions.

Do differently, do against labour, There is no other way forward.

Break the walls: Open the enclosed. The world of abstract labour is a world of enclosure, a world of physical and metaphorical walls. These are the encroaching walls of the metaphor introduced at the beginning of the book. The encroaching walls are making life unbearable for millions and millions of people, and things threaten to become much worse. But this generates a counter-force, a tremendous pressure against the walls, which gives hope that the walls will crack and crumble. How many millions of people must die of starvation before the wall of private property gives way? Already it is being broken in so many ways, often by theft and violence which offer little in perspectives for the future, but sometimes by the conscious occupation of land (as in the great movement of the landless peasants, the MST, in Brazil) or the occupation of factories or in the widespread disrespect for intellectual property rights in music or software.

Doing is a torrent against all enclosure. Our power to do things differently, our power to create a different world, is a flow that exerts a growing force against the walls that hem us in, a constant breaching of these walls. Capital runs around mending these breaches (granting land reforms, redefining the norms of sexuality, for example), but the flow of our power will not be contained, simply because our collective life depends upon it.

Break the walls, then. Break the walls around the land, reverse the land enclosure that started the disaster that is capitalism, create the basis for an overcoming of the separation between city and country, between humans and other forms of life. Break the walls around our sexuality so that we can enjoy our bodies to the full. Break the walls constituted by states, which have caused the killing of millions and millions of people in the wars of the last century and the misery of more and more migrants today. Break the walls of the prisons that, by imprisoning so many, imprison us all. Break the walls around our thinking, the rigidification of thought that arises from abstract labour and is reinforced in schools and universities. Break the walls by which nouns enclose the powerful dynamic of verbs. Break the walls around our doing by refusing all expropriation of the means of doing, means of producing, means of living. Break the walls whenever and wherever we can. Break the walls by refusing to build them.

Crack capitalism: Fight from the particular, fight from where we are, here and now. Create spaces or moments of otherness, spaces or moments that walk in the opposite direction, that do not fit in. Make holes in our own reiterative creating of capitalism. Create cracks and let them expand, let them multiply, let them resonate, let them flow together. Create dimensions in which we serve no more and behold the Tyrant-capital, 'like a great Colossus whose pedestal has been pulled away, fall of his own weight and break in pieces'.

Refuse-and-create! Refuse-and-create! That, for us, is Moses and the Prophets. Except that we have no Moses, we have no prophets, just ourselves.

33

This is the story of many, many people. It is the story of the millions who have woven their way in and out of these pages visibly and invisibly, audibly and inaudibly, consciously and unconsciously. Of the millions who want to shape their own lives. Of the millions who want an end to misery and poverty and exploitation. Of the millions who do not want to go on participating in the destruction of human and non-human life. Of the millions who want to stop making capitalism.

This is the story of the girl in the park who, wearied of all the controversy stirred up by her simple act of reading a book (this book), yet excited by what she has read, takes out a pen and continues this paragraph with more and more and more and more examples of people whose misfitting is an overflowing. And then goes on, for she knows that the book is unfinished

This is your story, the story of you, gentle readers. Perhaps you are the girl in the park. Certainly, you know that the book is unfinished. Leave it open now and give a great whoop of joyous rage as you go forth to stop making capitalism and, asking, make the world anew

thanks

thanks, many, many thanks because the writing of this book, like all doing, is part of a social and ungrammatical flow, where the doing and living and loving of one flows into the doing and living and loving of others, a flow that comes sometimes with names and sometimes without, a flow that for me has a central vortex, vortex indeed, in Eloína Peláez, without whom there could be no eriugenic somersault, no conceiving of time as both the infinite fragility of a second and simultaneously the hard and patient push of shared creation, no understanding of loving and discussing and doing and resting as a constant and sometimes difficult sharing of joyous rage, and without whom this book simply would not exist; and others, many others, like the wonderfully stimulating and constantly supportive Sergio Tischler, with whom I have shared a seminar now for more than ten years, and then first Fernando Matamoros and now Antonio Fuentes and Francisco Gómez Carpenteiro who have joined us, and the many students, professors and visitors who have shared our discussions in these ten years; and Agustín Grajales, Nancy Churchill, Roberto Vélez and Carlos Figueroa, who have done so much to create a really supportive environment in the Instituto de Ciencias Sociales y Humanidades 'Alfonso Vélez Pliego' and its Posgrado de Sociología; and of course Néstor López, who breaks capitalism with his sheer enthusiasm and energy and has done so much to open Argentina and South America for me; and those who have joined Néstor in the discussion of the draft of this book in Buenos Aires: Carlos Cuellar, Luis Menendez, María Belén Sopransi, Daniel Contartese, Gabriela Ferreyra, Eric Meyer, Alba Invernizzi and Luciana Ghiotto; and the others who have given me written comments on the draft, ranging from the very helpful 'that's fabulous' (just what I wanted to hear) to the also very helpful detailed criticisms: Werner Bonefeld, Dorothea Härlin, Chris Wright, Ana Dinerstein, Adrian Wilding, Marcel Stoetzler, Raquel Gutiérrez, Marta Gregorčič,

Michael Kasenbacher, Marina Sitrin, Alejandro Merani, Simon Susen, Paul Chatterton, David-Brian-Keir-and-Nette of the Free Association, Sabu Kohso, Chris Carlsson and Maggie Sinclair; and Antonio Ortíz who listened to and understood my explanations, and Hierson Rojas who helps me all the time in dealing with the university world, and Virginia Castillo too, constantly in support; and then the doctoral students not yet mentioned whom I have been privileged to supervise in the last few years, especially Lars Stubbe, Vittorio Sergi, Alberto Bonnet, Rafael Sandoval, Manuel Martínez, Mina Navarro, Nashyeli Figueroa, Dario Azzelini, Mariana Muñoz, Juquila González; and my children not-so-children, Aidan, Anna-Maeve and Mariana Holloway, who irradiate my life; and Richard Gunn, who is always there even when contact is sporadic, and David Castle, ever helpful and encouraging, and all the others in Pluto who make this into a book; my thanks too to the millions who are the heroes of this book and to the thousands who have participated in the discussions of this book's mother, *Change the World without taking Power*, which immersed me in a world of practical and theoretical debate that exists in, against and, increasingly, beyond the universities, in a world of cracks, in the many forums created by the restlessness of rebel thought: the world and regional social forums, the Zapatista events, the 'other' seminars, the wonderful week spent shaping a common word in the Zapatista community of Oventic, meetings with *piqueteros* and dissident teachers and autonomous groups of various shapes and sizes; and the many, many people who knowingly or unknowingly have inspired me and without whom this book would be inconceivable, George Wilson and Eileen Simpson and Rod McKenzie, for example, and the espirales and the ex-espirales, the solanos and the ex-solanos and the JRA, not to mention the pizzeros; and, neither last nor least, my thanks to you, dear reader, who have either reached this last page or else opened the book from the back, a back that is a front, a last page which is a beginning not an end; and to more and more and more, a torrential flow ...

Notes

1. 'Somos mujeres y hombres, niños y ancianos bastante comunes, es decir, rebeldes, inconformes, incómodos, soñadores' (*La Jornada*, 4 August 1999).

THESIS 2

1. The story I have at the back of my mind is 'The Pit and the Pendulum': Poe (1842/2004).
2. On the opening of categories and its importance, see the Introduction to Bonefeld, Gunn and Psychopedis (1992a).
3. See Marx (1844/1975a: 182): 'Theory is capable of gripping the masses as soon as it demonstrates *ad hominem*, and it demonstrates *ad hominem* as soon as it becomes radical. To be radical is grasp the root of the matter. But for man the root is man himself.'
4. See Adorno (1966/1990) on the concept of a negative dialectics. For a discussion of the political importance of negative dialectics, see Holloway, Matamoros and Tischler (2009). On the importance of negativity as the basis for critical thought, see also Agnoli (1999).

THESIS 3

1. See Davis (2006: 36): 'Los Angeles is the First World capital of homelessness, with an estimated 100,000 homeless people, including an increasing number of families, camped on downtown streets or living furtively in parks and amongst freeway landscaping.'
2. This is not quite the classic but impersonal Leninist formulation 'What is to be done?', which suggests already a distancing of our own responsibility, but rather: what can *we* do?
3. Ticktin (2008). To be fair to Ticktin, he continues 'but before that time pseudo-socialist and proto-socialist forms can exist. They are not socialist, but they do conflict with capitalism – at the same time as they prop it up.'
4. In similar vein, see Papadopoulos, Stephenson and Tsianos (2008: xii): 'we look for social change in seemingly insignificant occurrences of life.' See also the Trapese Collective (2007: 2): 'As mass protests against the current economic system have ricocheted around the world from Seattle to Cancun, beyond the spectacle of the banners, tear gas and riots, when the streets become silent again, ordinary people are doing extraordinary things, learning by doing, imagining and building the blocks of other possible worlds. We can resist the world we live in while at the same time creating the world we want to see.'
5. In this sense, the approach here may be contrasted with that adopted by Hardt and Negri (2000, 2004 and 2009).

THESIS 4

1. The idea of a negation of the negation with creative force is sometimes referred to as the 'second negation': see Dunayevskaya (2002).
2. See the significant title of the book by La Vaca (2004) on the experiences of different occupied factories in Argentina: *Sin Patrón* ('without boss').
3. If the examples cited are drawn disproportionately from Mexico and Latin America, and from Europe, this is just because that is where I live and have lived. It is clear, however, that similar examples can be found all over the world. Perhaps the reader, wherever you live, should think of five (or a hundred) other examples for every one mentioned here. For a much more global selection of examples, see *Notes from Nowhere* (2003). An excellent source for information about 'cracks' throughout the world is the Italian journal, *Carta*.
4. This is the position at the time of writing (August 2009). On this, see SNTE (2009). On aspects of the alternative education being developed in the Sierra de Puebla, see Pieck Gochicoa, Messina Raimondi and Colectivo Docente (2008).
5. On the notion of emancipatory space as threshold space, see Stavridis (2007 and 2009).
6. Lynching is a case in point: when the people of a town or village come together to deal collectively and summarily with a perceived criminal, they are explicitly rejecting a corrupt and inefficient judicial system and assuming control of their own lives, yet the explosion of collective anger does not in any obvious way create the basis for a better society. See Fuentes Díaz (2006).
7. For a similar quest, see *Hope in the Dark* by Rebecca Solnit (2004).

THESIS 5

1. For a picture of the wide range of cracks or autonomies or non-capitalist practices, and on the growing literature on the subject, see, for example, De Angelis (2007), Trapese (2007), Carlsson (2008) D. Solnit (2004), Habermann (2009) and Böhm, Dinerstein and Spicer (2010).
2. On this, see Ghiotto (2005: 212–13).
3. See Salom (2009) and the other documents available at <www.tamachtini. org>.
4. This is true of many of the examples discussed by Carlsson (2008). His book is an extremely rich and stimulating source for the discussion of a wide variety of cracks (or what he calls 'nowtopias') – from pirate programmers to vacant-lot gardeners to outlaw bicyclists and beyond.
5. This point was made in the 2007 Anti-Summit in Rostock by Wangui Mbatia of the Kenyan People's Parliament.
6. See especially Zibechi (2006 and 2008).
7. On this, see MTD de Solano and Colectivo Situaciones (2002), esp. 247ff, and Habermann (2004), Gordon and Chatterton (2004). See also the idea of 'disobeying unemployment' developed by Rebón (2004 and 2007). The same transformation of the idea of unemployment is described by Flores (2005) as a movement from guilt to self-determination.
8. On this movement, see Paoli (2002).

9. For a discussion of this, see Zibechi (2006). For an analysis of the local organisation in El Alto and its role in the struggles in Bolivia, see Mamani Ramírez (2005), Gómez (2006).

10. Despite, or perhaps perversely because of, its history, 'communism' retains a provocative force which 'socialism' does not. On abandoning the term 'socialism', see Esteva (2007c), Cleaver (2006) and Negri (2008).

THESIS 6

1. On the war of water, see Gutiérrez Aguilar (2009), Ceceña (2004), Olivera and Lewis (2004).

2. On software, see Bollier (2008).

3. By this I do not mean nationalisation, which is generally a means of reconciling such demands with the reproduction of capitalism, but rather the real control of these areas by the people affected.

4. For an interesting example of city cracks, see the appropriately named 'Krax' events in Barcelona: <http://krax-jornadas.citymined.org>.

5. For an important reflection on importance of the 19/20 December, see the book by Colectivo Situaciones (2002): *19 y 20: Apuntes para el nuevo Protagonismo social*. Colectivo Situaciones forms an interesting crack in their own right, a very conscious break in the patterns of theoretical work. For two stimulating exhibitions and collections of articles inspired by the events in Argentina, see ExArgentina (Alice Kreischer and Andreas Siekmann) (2004 and 2006).

6. For Ernst Bloch (1959/1986), the present existence not-yet of the world that does not yet exist is the source of hope.

7. On the 'political ambiguity of carnival', see Ehrenreich (2007), especially Ch. 5.

8. On these and more, see Shukaitis (2009). On the Clowns in the anti-G8 summit in Gleneagles, see various articles in Harvie et al. (2007).

9. There are many examples that could be used here. Two striking ones are the Blitz, the bombing of London during the Second World War, which came to be seen as a symbol of social solidarity and of the construction of a new post-war world that would never again return to the miseries of the Great Depression; and the earthquake in Mexico City in 1985 which is widely seen as the launching pad for a new wave of social struggles.

10. My thanks to a conversation with Rebecca Solnit for the ideas in this paragraph.

11. 'The slogan "Revolution!" has mutated from tocsin to toxin, a malign pseudo-Gnostic fate-trap, a nightmare where no matter how we struggle we never escape that evil Aeon, that incubus the State, one State after another, every "heaven" ruled by yet one more evil angel' (Bey 1985).

12. Horkheimer evokes well such magic moments, but sees them as remnants of the past: 'Those old forms of life smouldering under the surface of modern civilisation still provide, in many cases, the warmth inherent in any delight, in any love of a thing for its own sake rather than that of another thing' (2004: 24). I see them rather as unsatisfied memories or present anticipations of a potential future, moments that we create against the pressures of everyday capitalism.

13. *La Jornada*, 28 May 1994. English text published in *!Zapatistas! Documents of the New Mexican Revolution* (EZLN 1994), available at <http://lanic.utexas.edu/project/Zapatistas/chapter11.html>.

14. See my dialogue with Vittorio Sergi on the question of the actions of the so-called 'Black Block': Holloway and Sergi (2007).

15. Zibechi (2006: 33) expresses the cracking of dimensions very well: 'Times of overflowing, of intense collective creativity – during which social groups release gigantic energies – act like lightning flashes capable of illuminating the subterranean, molecular, submerged sociabilities hidden by the veil of the everyday inertias in which the times and spaces of domination and subordination impose themselves.'

16. Surrealism can be seen as a radical attempt to live the world that does not yet exist by breaking with the very dimensionality of capitalism. On the enormous richness and terrible contradictions of the surrealist movement, see Vaneigem (1999) and Löwy (2000). For an excellent discussion of the issues, see Muñoz (2010). On William Blake and the importance of breaking dimensionality, see the book by Cyril Smith (2005), especially the chapter on 'Marx and the Fourfold Vision of William Blake', also available at <http://www.marxists.org/reference/archive/smith-cyril/works/articles/blake.htm>.

17. See *Gegenwelten* ('Counterworlds'), the suggestive title of the book edited by Reithofer, Krese and Kühberger (2007).

18. This does not mean that Parks's was simply a spontaneous action: in fact, it was well prepared. My thanks to Chris Wright for pointing this out.

THESIS 7

1. See the poem 'Caminante' by Antonio Machado: '*caminante, no hay camino / se hace camino al andar*' ('walker, there is no path / the path is made by walking') ('Proverbios y cantares XXIX', in *Campos de Castilla* (1912/2007.

2. See Gunn (1985), who sees utopias as police actions against apocalyptic thought. See also Adorno (1969/1975: 168, quoted by Jay (1984: 264): 'The utopian impulse in thinking is all the stronger, the less it objectifies itself as utopia.'

3. On asymmetry, see the comment by Emilio, of the Tierra del Sur neighbourhood assembly in Argentina, interviewed by Marina Sitrin: 'We are not creating the opposite, but are creating something else. We aren't building the opposite to the capitalist system, that's been tried and doesn't work. We are building something different. What? I don't know. It doesn't have a name and I hope it never has one' (Sitrin 2006: 175; 2005: 213). (I cite both the English and Spanish editions because in some cases I have modified the translation from the Spanish original.)

4. A dramatic example of the asymmetry of struggle is the confrontation between clowns and police that has become a feature of many of the big anti-capitalist demonstrations.

5. On the central importance of love, see Hardt (2009) and Free Association (2010).

6. The discussion of all these issues has exploded in the light of the experience of recent years: see, for example, Sitrin (2005 and 2006), Thwaites Rey (2004), Nunes (2007).

7. See Graeber (2002): 'The result is a rich and growing panoply of organizational instruments – spokescouncils, affinity groups, facilitation tools, break-outs, fishbowls, blocking concerns, vibe-watchers and so on – all aimed at creating forms of democratic process that allow initiatives to rise from below and attain maximum effective solidarity, without stifling dissenting voices, creating leadership positions or compelling anyone to do anything which they have not freely agreed to do.'
8. See the important book by the Trapese Collective (2007) on the practicalities of doing it ourselves. See also the detailed accounts of the many different experiments in living differently in Habermann (2009).

THESIS 8

1. On the struggle in Oaxaca, see especially the series of articles by Gustavo Esteva (2007a, 2007b, 2007d and 2009).

THESIS 9

1. See the good discussion of cracks and their difficulties in Pleyers (2010), especially Chs 2 and 4.
2. On this, see Gutiérrez Aguilar (2009).
3. The notion of social synthesis I take from Alfred Sohn-Rethel (1978), with the difference that he applies it to all societies, whereas I reserve it for the particularly tightly knit social cohesion typical of capitalism. For a recent discussion of Sohn-Rethel's use of the concept, see Reitter (2007).
4 A report can be found at <http://www.williambowles.info/americas/south_central_farm.html>.
5. Everyone can add their own list of examples.
6. Just one recent example is the repression of the homeless Las y los Sin Techo of Mar del Plata, Argentina: <http://www.youtube.com/watch?v=pvJlnuWHejo>.
7. I have in mind particularly the demonstrations against the meeting of the G8 in Rostock in July 2007. For a discussion of these events and the question of violence, see Holloway and Sergi (2007), Free Association (2010) and United Colours of Resistance (2007).
8. This is surely the strongest response to Fanon's (1961/2001) still powerful argument for the necessity of violence.
9. A striking example is the brutal state repression in Atenco (near Mexico City) at the beginning of May 2006, which proved to be a very effective way of seizing the initiative from the Other Campaign of the Zapatistas.
10. On the importance of understanding the Zapatistas as an army (and with a slightly different emphasis from that presented here), see Sergi (2009). In similar vein, see also Subcomandante Marcos in his talk at the Festival de la Digna Rabia, 2 January 2009: 'Every struggle, every movement, in its very particular geographies and calendars, must have recourse to different forms of struggle. It is not the only one, and probably it is not the best, but violence is one of those. It is a beautiful gesture to confront with flowers the barrels of guns, there are even photos to eternalise the act. But sometimes it is necessary to make these guns change their objective and point upwards.'

11. This was written in an article on Oaxaca just a few weeks before the repression: Vaneigem (2006). For a contrary argument, see Gelderloos (2007): *How Nonviolence Protects the State.*

12. The writer of this book, and possibly many of the readers (if such there be), receives his income from the state.

13. For an account of what this means in terms of day-to-day difficulties, see González (2009).

14. On this, see MTD de Solano and Colectivo Situaciones (2002); for the contrast between MTD de Solano and MTD La Matanza in this, see Habermann (2004). On the debates within the left of the *Piquetero* movement, see Navarro Trujillo (2008).

15. A strong argument for seeing the state as the wrong way to do things is developed by Scott (1998).

16. For a fuller discussion of the state as a peculiarly capitalist form of organisation, see Holloway 2002/2005.

17. For a political-theoretical analysis centred on the concept of the victim, see, for example, Dussel (2006).

18. *La Jornada*, 5 January 2008.

19. For a similar critique of the national-popular struggle, see Tischler (2008b).

20. For a really striking example of this, and of the contradictions involved in the Venezuelan process, see a speech by Juan Barreto Cipriani, mayor of Caracas, in 2007: 'Communal power must be capable of being exercised over the society, dissolving the constituted state institutions. Assuming itself as self-government. This is the role that we have to play, because the existing state is the juridical form of the time of exploitation. It is the state of capital, it is the power of ... a discourse opposed to the real exercise of the power of the citizens. It is a body of concessions and practices that it is necessary to dismantle. In the same way as the statist logic of the institutions is perverse, so is the political logic of the party conceived as an instrumental apparatus of power. It is not possible to get rid of the state without getting rid of the party. As long as there exist circles that privatise or confiscate the decisions that should be collective and appropriate the state apparatuses, we shall not be able to go very far in the construction of a society that is not statist and partyist' (Barreto Cipriani 2007: 14). My thanks to Dario Azzelini for pointing this out to me.

21. See especially the excellent work by Azzelini (2009) on the strength and difficulties of this process.

22. On this, see Wainwright (2003), Sullo (2002), De Sousa Santos (2003).

23. See Mazzeo (2007), but also Dussel (2006).

24. My view, at the time of writing, is that the Venezuelan process is still an open one, but that in the case of Cuba the plastering hand outweighs the hand that opens the crack. However, it would be quite wrong to think of this as a final closure.

25. Raúl Zibechi gives a striking figure to illustrate the enormous integrating power of the state, especially in the case of 'progressive governments': there are, he says, 270,000 NGOs contracted by the government and operating in the cities of Brazil: they are staffed overwhelmingly by ex-militants (talk given in the Instituto de Ciencias Sociales y Humanidades, Benemérita Universidad Autónoma de Puebla, December 2008).

26. For studies of this particular problem, see Sandoval (2007), Figueroa (2008).

27. Martín K. of a neighbourhood assembly in Buenos Aires, interviewed by Marina Sitrin: Sitrin (2005: 139; 2006: 108). For a general reflection on the neighbourhood assemblies of the Argentinian uprising, see Ouviña (2002).
28. On the importance of rejecting the notion of sacrifice as the basis for anti-capitalism, see Vaneigem (1967/1994).
29. The cooperative has published a book describing its principles of organisation: Cecosesola (2003).
30. For a discussion of the reproduction of psychological problems within the specific context of the pro-Zapatista groups in Guadalajara, see Sandoval (2007). On the complex relation between revolt and subjectivity in the uprising in Argentina, see Fernández et al. (2006).
31. I use 'value' here in the sense of the category of political economy criticised by Marx. For a broader discussion of value in this and other senses, see De Angelis (2007).
32. In this sense, see especially Rubin (1928/1972) and Sohn-Rethel (1978).
33. For a more developed discussion of the relation between the state and value, see the state derivation debate and especially Holloway and Picciotto (1978).
34. Central planning has not been rational because it has always been state planning. And it cannot be central, because even territorial units as large as the USSR or China are still fragments of the world society. Neither of these huge countries could resist the onslaught of value: in both cases, value emerged triumphant, in the collapse of the USSR on the one hand, the commodification of Chinese society on the other. In the case of Cuba, value and its embodiment, money, lay siege even more effectively than the US blockade. The idea of state planning as an alternative to the law of value is based on the totally fallacious idea that the state is universal, that each state encloses 'its' society. It is clearer now than ever that this is not the case, but it never was.
35. On the problems of receiving funding from non-state foundations, see INCITE! (2007).
36. On the experience of Zanón, see Aiziczon (2009).
37. Events like the anti-summit demonstrations and the world and regional Social Forums play an important part in the formation of these networks of support and inspiration.
38. Thus De Angelis (2000): 'rather than the old solidarity paradigm, a better description of the way different groups and movements tend to enter into relation with one another is the one provided by what an Aboriginal women said to those coming to her people to offer solidarity:

> 'If you have come here to help me
> You are wasting your time …
> But if you have come because
> Your liberation is bound up with mine
> Then let us work together.'

39. On this, see Mance (2007).

THESIS 10

1. For a rather different reflection on the difficulties of the movement in the present situation, see Colectivo Situaciones (2009).

2. For a discussion of the impact of 1968 on capitalist development, see Boltanski and Chiapello (1999/2007).
3. In this tone, see Böhm, Dinerstein and Spicer (2010), and also Birkner (2007) and Birkner and Foltin (2006).
4. The big anti-summit protests are often prepared by dedicated activists taking more than a year of intense planning. For various accounts of the effort involved in the preparations for the Gleneagles summit, see Harvie et al. (2007).
5. On this question, see Zadnikar (2009), Leeds May Day Group (2004) and Holloway and Sergi (2007).
6. On this whole issue, see the article by Ben Trott (2007) and the paper written after the J-18 demonstration of 1999, 'Give up activism' (Andrew X 1999).
7. In similar vein, Zibechi (2006: 124ff) distinguishes between movements as institutions and movements as movings (*Movimiento como insititución y como moverse*). On the question of networking as a form of confluence of the movements, see Juris (2008).
8. For a very different approach, see Žižek (2004).
9. Thus the members of the Nuevo Horizonte Cooperative in Guatemala: 'If there are not more Horizontes, then we shall be like a drop of sweet water in the sea and shall be absorbed.' From the video on Nuevo Horizonte: http://intercontinentalcry.org/nuevo-horizonte/>.
10. On social centres, see Free Association (2006), Hodkinson and Chatterton (2006).
11. On this see, for example, Kastner and Spörr (2008).
12. I write this after an extraordinarily impressive week spent in the Zapatista village of Oventic talking with young people, a new generation of rebels.

THESIS 11

1. Bloch (1959/1986: 1367). I have modified the translation slightly.
2. See thesis 5 above.
3. Engels added an acute observation as a footnote to *Capital*, in which he says: 'The English language has the advantage of possessing different words for the two aspects of labour here considered. The labour which creates Use-Value, and counts qualitatively, is *Work*, as distinguished from Labour; that which creates Value and counts quantitatively is *Labour* as distinguished from Work' (Marx 1867/1965: 47; 1867/1990: 138). In order to emphasise the distinction even more strongly, I prefer to use *doing* in place of *work*, which still carries some of the disagreeable resonance of labour.
4. Chris Arthur devotes a very helpful section of the first chapter of his *Dialectics of Labour* (1986) to a review of the use of 'labour' by the young Marx. He concludes that 'In such texts as the *1844 Manuscripts* and the *German Ideology* (1846–47) Marx restricts the term to *productive activity carried on under the rule of private property*. It is *not* the term he uses when he wishes to thematize that activity which is the universal ontological ground of social life. Still less does it apply to future unalienated free activity.' He quotes Marx (1844/1975b: 285): 'Within the private property relationship there is contained latently ... the production of human activity as *labour* – that is, as an activity quite alien to itself, to man, and to nature.'

Arthur points out that, by the time he wrote *Capital*, Marx was using *Arbeit* (labour) in the more general sense. Nevertheless, it is clear that what Marx now called the 'two-fold nature of labour' remained a central concern, and that what is at issue is far more than a contrast between 'productivity' and value production, as some would have it: see especially the beautiful Ch. 7 of Vol. 1 of *Capital* on 'The Labour-Process and the Process of Producing Surplus-Value' and also the section of the 'Results of the Immediate Process of Production on Capitalist Production as the Production of Surplus Value' (1867/1990: 975ff.).

5. See Adorno 1966/1990: 5: 'The name of dialectics says no more, to begin with, than that objects do not go into their concepts without leaving a remainder ... Contradiction ... indicates the untruth of identity, the fact that the concept does not exhaust the thing conceived.'

6. Some authors (such as Hardt and Negri, especially 2004) slide from a critique of capitalism to an emphasis on the struggle for democracy, but democracy means little if we devote our lives to the production of capital.

THESIS 12

1. Note that the later (and now more widely used) Penguin translation by Ben Fowkes does not express the point with the same force: 'this point is crucial to an understanding of political economy' (Marx 1867/1990: 132). The older translation by Samuel Moore and Edward Aveling seems to me to be closer to the German original: 'Da dieser Punkt der Springpunkt ist, um den sich das Verständnis der politischen Ökonomie dreht ... ' (Marx 1867/1985: 56). In this book, I shall continue to quote from the earlier translation, but shall also reference the later, more easily available edition.

2. Marx continues '2) the treatment of *surplus value independently of its particular* forms as profit, interest, ground rent, etc.', but this does not concern us here. Note that Marx also saw this as his distinctive contribution: 'I was the first to point out and to examine critically this two-fold nature of the labour contained in commodities' (1867/1965: 41; 1867/1990: 132).

3. Marx also uses the term 'self-activity' to designate 'conscious life-activity'. On the whole question of terminology, see the helpful discussion in Arthur (1986), Ch. 1.

4. For a very helpful discussion of recent debates on abstract labour, see Bonefeld (2010).

5. For a discussion that reaches similar conclusions, see Postone (1996: esp. 158 ff.).

6. The argument that there is no essential distinction to be made between humans and other animals (and that therefore Marx's distinction between the architect and the bee should be rejected) seems to me a dangerous one. It is not the sheep or the horses that are destroying the prospects of life on earth, but we humans. We have therefore a distinctive responsibility in the attempt to stop this destruction. In short, humans have a creative and destructive power that distinguishes us from other animals. On this, see Wilding (2008) and especially Wilding(2010).

7. See Postone (1996: 162): 'The structures of abstract domination constituted by determinate forms of social practice give rise to a social process that lies beyond human control; yet they also give rise, in Marx's analysis, to the historical possibility that people could control what they had constituted socially in alienated form.'
8. In this sense, see also Postone (1996: 158).
9. It is surprising that even those authors who insist on the importance that Marx attached to the two-fold nature of labour continue to focus exclusively on just one side of that two-fold nature: abstract labour.
10. In general, we can say of Marx that the relation between form and content is an ecstatic relation: the form contains and does not contain the content. The content exists in-against-and-beyond the form, overflows.
11. An unborn baby in the last days of pregnancy might be said to be the ecstasy of its mother: it already exists not only in but already against-and-beyond its mother.
12. Chris Carlsson (2008: 39) expresses this idea nicely in the title of one of the chapters of his book *Nowtopia*: 'What you see me doing isn't what I do'. He develops the theme by pointing to the increasingly 'bifurcated' nature of life: 'It is difficult or impossible to make a living from many of the things that people really want to do (e.g. art, dance, music, history, philosophy), and so there has been a steady increase of people living a bifurcated life. On one side is the crushing necessity of making money, on the other is the creative urge to find fulfilling work, whether or not it is paid ... Capital is a relationship of social power that warps human relations to its perverse logic, but it faces persistent resistance ... People resist these forces in their normal daily lives by carving out spaces of autonomy in which they act concertedly outside (and often against) capital's attempts to commodify their activities.' He speaks of the core of his book as being 'the semi-conscious war between these life-affirming, self-emancipating behaviours and the coercive domination of money, property and survival amidst contrived scarcity' (ibid.: 42).

THESIS 13

1. Since the English version of this pamphlet is more easily available on the Internet, I have decided to reference it by giving the page number of the 2004 German edition and the number of the corresponding section.
2. Hence Postone's surprising remark that 'we are dealing with a new sort of interdependence, one that emerged in a slow, spontaneous, and contingent way' (1996: 148).
3. See Federici (2004: 62) on the 'transition to capitalism': 'The term ... suggests a gradual, linear historical development, whereas the period it names was among the bloodiest and most discontinuous in world history.'
4. Postone (1996: 271) is quite right in insisting that the categories presented in Chapter 1 of *Capital* presuppose wage labour. Abstract labour is not historically prior to wage labour. What Postone fails to see is that the obviously conflictive character of the category of wage labour must also be read into the (less obviously conflictive) category of abstract labour.
5. See Marx 1867/1965: 578; 1867/1990: 724: 'Capital pre-supposes wage-labour, and wage-labour pre-supposes capital. One is a necessary

condition to the existence of the other; they mutually call each other into existence.'

THESIS 14

1. Postone is right in speaking of the trans-historical category of labour as 'the fundamental core of the fetish in capitalism' (1996: 170).
2. On reification and identification in general, see the discussion in Holloway (2002/2005).

THESIS 15

1. On the story of Jemmy Button, see López (2006).
2. See Federici (2004: 136): 'the expropriated peasants did not peacefully agree to work for a wage. More often they became beggars, vagabonds or criminals. A long process would be required to produce a disciplined work-force.' See also the detailed history of discipline in Foucault (1975/1977).
3. See Marx (1867/1965: 84–5; 1867/1990: 178–9) on the way in which the exchange of commodities generates a juridical relation between two *individual* commodity owners: 'The persons exist for one another merely as representatives of, and, therefore as owners of, commodities. In the course of our investigation we shall find, in general, that the characters who appear on the economic stage are but the personifications of the economic relations that exist between them.'
4. On the connection between the historical rise of the idea of 'playing a role' and the spread of depression, see Ehrenreich (2007), especially Ch. 7, 'An Epidemic of Melancholy'. The product of abstract labour is indeed, as she suggests, the 'anxious self', the 'tormented soul'. The term 'character mask' appears in the German edition of *Capital*, but in the English editions it is generally translated simply as 'character': see, for example, Marx 1867/1985: 100; 1867/1965: 85; 1867/1990: 179. For a recent debate on the significance of the character mask, see Schandl (2006), Lohoff (2008).
5. The fragmentation of the flow of social doing into a multitude of abstract labours has enormous consequences for all of us. We are the products of this fragmentation. Our subjectivity is transformed from a participation in the flow of doing into an individual protagonism. Our social subjectivity is suppressed and we are converted into the Subjects beloved of Hollywood: individual subjects that have an identity, a name, a gender.
6. Developed in *What is to be Done?*: Lenin (1902/1968).
7. This identification of the working class is elaborated in notions of working-class culture and a glorification of a certain image of the 'worker'. The identitarian concept of the working class is taken a step further in the figures of the professional revolutionary, the militant and the hero, all key concepts in the revolutionary organisation of the last century.
8. On the dangers of a new vanguardism, see for example, Zadnikar (2009). One argument sometimes used to justify the violent tactics of the so-called 'Black Block' in large marches is that it does not matter what the general public thinks because they are so integrated into the structures of capitalism that they cannot possibly be the source of radical change. See Holloway and Sergi (2007).

1. Note that the relation between labour and other activities not immediately productive of capital is a hierarchical one, a relation of subordination and not just of coexistence, as Massimo De Angelis (2007) suggests. In other words, these other activities (doing) exist in-against-and-beyond labour, but not outside it. There is a relation of rupture but not of externality.

2. See Federici (2004: 184): 'Just as the Enclosures expropriated the peasantry from the communal land, so the witch-hunt expropriated the women from their bodies, which were thus "liberated" from any impediment preventing them to function as machines for the production of labour.'

3. As Horkheimer and Adorno (1947/1979) put it, 'humanity had to horribly mutilate itself to create its identical, functional, male self, and some of it has to be redone in everybody's childhood', quoted by Krisis Gruppe (1999/2004: 18, s.7).

4. See Federici (2004: 192–8), on the witch hunt and the capitalist rationalisation of sexuality, and her comment (192) that 'The witch-hunt ... was the first step in the long march towards "clean sex between clean sheets" and the transformation of female sexual activity into work, a service to men, and procreation.'

5. Even so, about one person in a thousand is born with genitals that are not clearly either feminine or masculine; in these cases, the definition as masculine or feminine is often by medical intervention (Baird, 2007: 124ff.). And see Baird's comment (ibid.: 133): 'The so-called biological line between male and female is frankly quite fuzzy.'

6. This does not mean that women and men did not exist before capitalism, but that the specific force of their separation and classification is peculiar to capitalism. Thus, for example, the self-presentation of women as men came to be seen as criminal only with the advent of capitalism.

7. This process can be seen as the suppression of the Dionysian: see Ehrenreich (2007).

1. See Thomas More's denunciation of the enclosures at the beginning of the sixteenth century: 'Sheep ... These placid creatures, which used to require so little food, have now apparently developed a raging appetite, and turned into man-eaters. Fields, houses, towns, everything goes down their throats' (1516/1965: 46).

2. Marx (1844/1975: 276), cited by Foster (2000: 158).

3. The earlier translation (1867/1965: 177) translates the original 'Stoffwechsel' (1867/1985: 192) as 'material re-actions' rather than metabolism: I have opted here for the later version.

4. Here too I follow Foster (2000: 155) in using the more recent translation of *Capital* by Ben Fowkes (Marx, 1894/1976: 949–50): large landed property 'produces conditions that provoke an irreparable rift in the interdependent process of social metabolism, a metabolism prescribed by the natural laws of life itself'. The older translation (1894/1971: 813) speaks of 'an irreparable break in the coherence of social interchange prescribed by the natural laws of life'. On the importance of this concept, see also Wilding (2008).

5. Appropriately, Foster begins his book on *Marx's Ecology* (2000: 1) with a telling quote from Marx's *Grundrisse*: 'It is not the *unity* of living and active humanity with the natural, inorganic conditions of their metabolic exchange with nature, which requires explanation or is the result of a historic process, but rather the *separation* between these inorganic conditions of human existence and this active existence, a separation which is completely posited only in the relation of wage labour and capital' (1857/1973: 489).

6. See Horkheimer and Adorno (1947/1979). For a critique, see Wilding (2008).

7. See Williams (1976: 187–8) on the change in the meaning attached to 'nature'. See also Federici, who speaks (2004: 203) of 'the profound alienation that modern science has instituted between human beings and nature'. Probably it would be more accurate to say that science consolidated rather than instituted this alienation, which was part of the transformation of human activity.

8. The quotations from Marx and Engels in this paragraph are cited by Foster (2000).

9. On this, see the excellent critique of Latour by Adrian Wilding (2010).

10. Much of this book has been written in the middle of the Jardín Etnobotánico of San Andrés Cholula, a beautiful garden created by Eloína Peláez and dedicated to the struggle for a different relation between human and non-human forms of life, the fight against the constitution of nature as an object. Both this thesis and the whole book spring from a life of constant practical-theoretical dialogue with Eloína.

11. Quoted by Marx in 'On the Jewish Question' (1843/1975: 172) and cited in Foster (2000: 74).

THESIS 18

1. On our power, see the interview by Marina Sitrin with Neka of MTD de Solano and Sergio of Lavaca (2005: 195; 2006: 163): 'Neka: Power as capability and not as a position of command. Sergio: Unlike the noun – to come to power, to obtain power – we think of power as a verb.'

2. For more on the distinction between power-to and power-over, see Holloway (2002/2005: Ch. 3).

3. For a similar argument, see Pashukanis (1924/2002).

4. The same can be said of the notion of an 'other economics', which makes sense only to the extent that it focuses on the overcoming of the separation of economics from life.

5. There are many other ways in which we externalise our power, that is, give other people power over us – in our relation with doctors, plumbers, lovers, friends and so on, but here we concentrate on the question of the state.

THESIS 19

1. As Lukács puts it (1923/1988: 90): 'time sheds its qualitative, variable, flowing nature; it freezes into an exactly delimited, quantifiable continuum filled with quantifiable "things" (the reified, mechanically objectified "performance" of the worker, wholly separated from his total human personality): in short, it becomes space.' On the reification of time, see also Tischler (2005b).

2. See Thompson (1967: 56).
3. On the history of clocks, see Mayr (1989).
4. On the question of abstract labour and time, see also Bonefeld (2010) and Postone (1996).
5. On this point, see also Bonefeld (2010) and Postone (1996).
6. See Debord (1967/1995: 110): 'The time of production, time-as-commodity, is an infinite accumulation of equivalent intervals. It is irreversible time made abstract: each segment must demonstrate by the clock its purely quantitative equality with all other segments. This time manifests nothing in its effective reality aside from its *exchangeability*. It is under the rule of time-as-commodity that "time is everything, man is nothing; he is at the most time's carcass" (*The Poverty of Philosophy*). This is time devalued – the complete inversion of time as the "sphere of human development".'
7. For a different writing of history, see Sergio Tischler's recent book on the struggles in Guatemala: Tischler (2009b).
8. On the deferment of gratification and the repression of collective joy, see Ehrenreich (2007: esp. 100).
9. On the fatal consequences of the tradition of *sacrifice* for anti-capitalist struggle, see Vaneigem (1967/1994: Ch. 12).

THESIS 20

1. See Rubin (1928/1972: 142): 'The transformation of *private* labour into *social* labour can only be carried out through the transformation of *concrete* labour into *abstract* labour ... Abstract labour is not only socially equalised labour, i.e. abstracted from concrete properties, impersonal and homogeneous labour. It is labour which becomes social labour only as impersonal and homogeneous labour.'
2. 'Totality is not an affirmative but rather a critical category. Dialectical critique seeks to salvage or help to establish what does not obey totality, what opposes it or what first forms itself as the potential of a not yet existent individualisation ... A liberated mankind would by no means be a totality' (Adorno 1975: 12, quoted by Jay (1984: 266–7)).
3. For a powerful critique of the positivisation of totality, see Tischler (2009a).
4. Lukács (1923/1988: 27): 'It is not the primacy of economic motives in historical explanation that constitutes the decisive difference between Marxism and bourgeois thought, but the point of view of totality.'
5. See Postone (1996: 157): 'Overcoming capitalism would entail the abolition – not the realisation – of the "substance" of labour's role in constituting a social mediation, and, hence, the abolition of totality.'

THESIS 21

1. See Foucault (1975/1977).
2. See Horkheimer and Adorno (1947/1979).
3. See Ehrenreich (2007: 248).
4. In this sense, see Marx's 'Theses on Feuerbach' (1845/1976).
5. Horkheimer (1937/1992: 229). I take the translation from Werner Bonefeld (1995: 184), which is clearer than the published English translation (1937/1972: 213).
6. On this, see Bonefeld (1995).

7. As in abstract labour, so 'in ... formal logic, thought is indifferent towards its objects' (Marcuse 1964/1968: 114).

8. The critique of instrumental reason is one of the central themes developed by the authors associated with the Frankfurt School. See especially Horkheimer (1946/2004), Marcuse (1964/1968).

9. I prefer to designate the performers of abstract labour as 'he', doers as 'she'.

10. On class and classification, see Holloway (2002/2005: Ch. 8), and Holloway (2002).

11. See Bonefeld's critique of Postone in this sense: Bonefeld (2004).

12. On the crucial question of the constitution of forms of social relations, see Bonefeld (1995).

THESIS 22

1. Rubin's work was first published in about 1923, but the date is uncertain, which is why I have referenced it on the basis of the third edition of 1928.

2. See Mattick (1969/1974 and 1981), for example.

3. An exception is to be found in the closing lines of Diane Elson's article on 'The Value Theory of Labour' (1979), where she makes an opening in the direction that I take the argument in this book: '*Capital* ... analyses ... the determination of labour as an historical process of forming what is intrinsically unformed; arguing that what is specific to capitalism is the domination of one aspect of labour, abstract labour, objectified as value. On this basis, it is possible to understand why capital can appear to be the dominant subject, and individuals simply bearers of capitalist relations of production; but it is also possible to establish why this is only half the truth. For Marx's analysis also recognises the *limits* to the tendency to reduce individuals to bearers of value-forms. It does this by incorporating into the analysis the subjective, conscious, particular aspects of labour in the concepts of private and concrete labour; and the collective aspect of labour in the concept of social labour ... In this way, the argument of *Capital* does incorporate a material base for political action. Subjective, conscious and collective aspects of humanity are accorded recognition. The political problem is to bring together these private, concrete and social aspects of labour without the mediation of the value forms, so as to create particular, conscious collective activity directed against exploitation. Marx's theory of exploitation has built into it this possibility' (ibid.: 174). This is an extraordinary passage that swims strongly against the stream of one-eyed Marxism.

4. The page reference is taken from the pdf version available at <http://home.comcast.net/~platypus1848/postone_lukacsdialecticalcritique2003.pdf>.

5. Marx too understood the communist movement as a movement *against* labour: 'The communistic revolution is directed against the preceding *mode of activity*, does away with *labour*', and 'the question is not the liberation but the abolition of labour' (Marx and Engels, 1845/1976: 52). Both are quoted by Marcuse in a section devoted to 'The Abolition of Labour' (1941/1969: 292). See also Arthur (1986: Ch. 1).

6. Postone also makes a clear distinction 'between two fundamentally different modes of critical analysis: a critique of capitalism *from the standpoint of*

labour, on the one hand, and a critique *of* labour in capitalism, on the other' (1996: 5). What Postone does not make clear is where the critique of labour is coming from: the *other side* is missing from his analysis. See below (thesis 25, note 4) for a closer discussion of Postone.

7. It is wrong to think of analyses focused on the first chapter of *Capital* as being necessarily centred on circulation (see Hanloser and Reitter 2008) since that is where the dual nature of labour is introduced. The issue here is the crucial distinction between value analysis and an analysis centred on the dual nature of labour.

8. On the question of definition, see Holloway (2002/2005: Ch. 4).

9. See Krisis Gruppe (1999/2004: 16, s.6): 'The political left has always eagerly venerated labour. It has stylised labour to be the true nature of a human being and mystified it into the supposed counter-principle of capital. Not labour was regarded as a scandal, but its exploitation by capital. As a result, the programme of all "working class parties" was always the "liberation of labour" and not "liberation from labour". Yet the social opposition of capital and labour is only the opposition of different (albeit unequally powerful) interests within the capitalist end-in-itself.'

10. For an excellent critique of the structural functionalism that characterises so much of recent Marxist literature, see Clarke (1977/1991).

11. Living in Latin America, it is impossible to forget this even for a moment. In this, I have learned much from my Guatemalan friends and colleagues, Sergio Tischler and Carlos Figueroa.

12. On the concept of the 'other labour movement', see Roth (1974).

THESIS 23

1. As Werner Bonefeld (2009a: 77) puts it, in reply to the argument that Marx thought of primitive accumulation simply as the past transition to capitalism, 'Whether Marx really never referred to primitive accumulation other than in terms of transition, is of little interest in my view. If he really did not, then clearly he should have.'

2. On the consequences of this, see Davis (2006).

3. It is sometimes argued that primitive accumulation still exists, but only in the expansion of capital accumulation to new areas: in other words, that in modern capitalism there is a coexistence between normal accumulation and primitive accumulation (in this sense, see De Angelis 2007 (especially Ch. 10), and, from another direction, Harvey 2003). The argument here is that no such distinction can be made (in the same sense, see Bonefeld 2009b and 2009c).

4. There is a lively debate on the present importance of primitive accumulation: on this see the articles first published in the online journal, *The Commoner*, and now united in Bonefeld (2009a), and also Harvey (2003). What is crucial is to understand that primitive accumulation in the present is not a marginal aspect of capitalism but simply the constant constitution and reconstitution of capital.

5. On form as form-process, see Holloway (1980/1991 and 2002/2005).

6. This book might be said to be doubly eriugenic.

7. On the present force of the unredeemed past, see Walter Benjamin, especially his 'Theses on the Philosophy of History' (1940/1969: 253ff.). On the importance of memory, see also Tischler (2005a) and Matamoros (2005).
8. From the poem, *Axion Esti*, by Odysseus Elytis (1959/1974: 42); quoted by Memos (2009: 14).
9. See Bloch (1959/1986).
10. On the continuing importance of the concept of repression in the context of present debates, that is, in spite of the structuralist and post-structuralist attacks on the concept, see Kastner (2006).

THESIS 24

1. See Postone (1996: 144): The distinction 'does not refer to two different sorts of labour, but to two aspects of the same labour in commodities'. And even stronger, Marx in the 'Results of the Immediate Process of Production' (1867/1990: 991) says 'Even though we have considered the process of production from two distinct points of view: (1) as *labour process*, (2) *as valorisation process*, it is nevertheless implicit that the labour process is single and indivisible.' And yet revolution is precisely the division of this indivisible union, the emancipation of the labour process from the valorisation process, of doing from abstract labour.
2. See, for example, Postone who treats the relationship of abstract to useful labour in terms of the question of productivity (1996: 287–91).
3. For a very different view, see Negri (2003: 56): 'within the totalitarian *real subsumption* of society in capital, this relative independence [of use value] is no longer conceivable.'
4. See Federici (2004: 9), reflecting on her experience of living in Nigeria: 'I also realised how limited is the victory that the capitalist work-discipline has won on this planet, and how many people still see their lives in ways radically antagonistic to the requirements of capitalist production.'
5. For a different understanding, see De Angelis (2007).
6. On difference and contradiction, see Bonnet (2009).
7. In general, we can say of Marx that the relation between form and content is an ecstatic relation: the form contains and does not contain the content. The content stands out-and-beyond the form, overflows.

THESIS 25

1. Frustration refers to the contradiction between what we do and what we could do, between our actuality and our potential. But it is crucial that this contradiction be understood as living antagonism. To divorce contradiction from antagonism, as Postone (1996: 34, for example) does, is to fall into the logic of the traditional Marxism that he is criticising.
2. No wonder the Marxist tradition preferred to forget Marx!
3. That is, in the years around 1968, in very many parts of the world.
4. A theme developed particularly by the anarchist tradition.
5. For a helpful discussion of the crisis of labour from different points of view, see Exner et al. (2005).
6. This book aspires to be part of the process of asking.

7. On this, see, for example, Harvie (2006), Cuninghame (2009), Harvie and De Angelis (2009).
8. It is sometimes suggested (see Day 2005: 157) that the argument in *Change the World* (Holloway 2002/2005) is at heart an anarchist argument that does not have the good grace or good manners to cite anarchist sources. My reply is that the labelling of the argument does not matter, and for the narrowness of my references I apologise. In the same way as I explained in an earlier footnote that my citing of examples is shaped by the fact that I live in Latin America, so my citing of theoretical references is shaped by the fact that I have been living in (or perhaps in-against-and-beyond) Marxist theory for many years.
9. See Bloch, 'Thinking means venturing beyond' (1959/1986: 4).
10. Reitter (2004: 16) makes exactly the same point in his critique of Postone's book: 'My main problem, however, is that the book is written from the standpoint of so-called objective, scientific knowledge and not from the standpoint of revolt.'
11. One dimension of Postone's approach is that he understands dialectic as interaction rather than as a negative, antagonistic dialectic of misfitting.
12. For a critique of the autonomist or *operaista* tradition from this perspective, see Holloway (2002/2005: 160–75). The current often referred to as 'Open Marxism' (see the three volumes of that name: Bonefeld et al. 1992a, 1992b, 1995) has as its central argument the understanding of categories as conceptualisations of social struggle. For recent critical discussions of Open Marxism, see Altamira (2006), Birkner and Foltin (2006).
13. Much the same point can be made in relation to De Angelis's (2007) insistence that such activities and social relations should be seen as being *outside* capital.
14. In other words, *life* is not to be taken as a trans-historical category, as it is often treated. For a critique of this notion as part of a general critique of the Deleuzian tradition, see Bonnet (2009).
15. The purpose of this paragraph is not to draw sharp lines or to attach labels, but rather to stimulate debate and explain why I focus on the dual character of labour as the key to rethinking revolutionary theory.
16. On *operaismo* in general, see Wright (2002) and Birkner and Foltin (2006).
17. For a good presentation of the Krisis argument on the crisis of abstract labour, see Trenkle (2007).
18. This is the same problem as that which we saw in Postone's analysis, in the previous section.
19. As do Hardt and Negri (2000).

THESIS 26

1. On the notion of constellation, see Tischler (2009), Adorno (1966/1990) and Benjamin (1940/1969).
2. See the important conclusion of Zibechi (2008: 56): 'In the light of the principal social struggles of the last 15 years ... we can say that *we do not know how a movement is produced and generalised*.' And, he adds, '"To organise the rebellion" is a contradiction.'
3. On this, see Holloway (2002/2005: esp. Ch. 3).
4. For an analysis of the Greek riots, see Memos (2009), Stavridis (2009).

5. In this I differ from Virno: see his book on *A Grammar of the Multitude* (2004).
6. For an interesting and imaginative exploration of the new melodies, see Salinari (2007). For a discussion of the emerging epistemology of the Other Campaign, see Gómez Carpinteiro (2009).
7. Once we understand critical theory as the voice of doing, and hence doing as the axis of critical theory, the long-standing problem of the relation between theory and practice (so anguished in the case of Adorno, for example) begins to resolve itself. On this question, see the essays in Holloway, Matamoros and Tischler (2009), and also Schwarzböck (2008).

THESIS 27

1. This example is inspired by the War of Water in Cochabamba, Bolivia, in 2000.
2. Lukács, still the most compelling voice of that tradition, tells us: 'It is not the primacy of economic motives that constitutes the decisive difference between Marxism and bourgeois thought, but the point of view of totality' (1923/1988: 27).
3. See the discussion on the nation and the Zapatistas in REDaktion (1997).
4. See, for example, the arguments of Dario Azzelini on Venezuela: Azzelini (2010, 2006).
5. For a stimulating presentation of this argument, see the book by Miguel Mazzeo (2007).
6. Zibechi (2006: 26). Zibechi's argument, like the argument here, is an argument against this view.
7. On difference and contradiction, see Bonnet (2009).
8. See Hardt and Negri (2004), Virno (2004).
9. For an argument along similar lines, see Esteva (2009).
10. For a slightly different use of the term 'communising', see *Call*: Anonymous (n.d.).
11. On the climate camp movement and the need for direct action, see Sumburn (2007).

THESIS 28

1. Thus Horkheimer: 'under the conditions of later capitalism and the impotence of the workers before the authoritarian state's apparatus of oppression, truth has sought refuge among small groups of admirable men' (1937/1972: 237). For Adorno, in modern society 'criticising privilege becomes a privilege' (1996/1990: 41).
2. In *One Dimensional Man*: Marcuse (1964/1968: 200).
3. See Postone (1996: 164): 'Like the commodity, the individual constituted in capitalist society has a dual character.'
4. On the importance of latency as a category, see Bloch (1959/1986).
5. EZLN (1996: 25). Another extract from the same speech: 'Below, in the cities and the haciendas, we did not exist. Our lives were worth less than the machines and the animals. We were like stones, like plants by the wayside. We did not have a voice. We did not have a face. We did not have a name. We did not have a tomorrow. We did not exist. For power, that which today dresses itself worldwide with the name of "neoliberalism", we did

not count, we did not produce, we did not buy, we did not sell. We were a useless number in the accounts of big capital' (ibid.: 23). A similar theme is echoed in the movement of the *sans papiers* in France and the *erased* in Slovenia. On the erased and the 'politics of interstitiality' in different parts of the world, see Gregorčič (2008).

6. On the question of invisible subjectivity and the *piquetero* movement, see Dinerstein (2002).

7. For this assumption, see, for example, Zibechi (2006, 2008) and Palmer (2000).

8. The latent has its own language, the language of allegory, ciphers, the language of poetry. This is the language of the Not Yet, of the non-identical: hence the often tantalisingly difficult beauty of Bloch and Adorno.

9. Hence Adorno's characterisation of the individual in capitalism as 'a system of scars': see Bonnet (2009: 59).

10. See Vaneigem (1967/1994: 111): 'The real demand of all insurrectionary movements is the transformation of the world and the reinvention of life. This is not a demand formulated by theorists: rather, it is the basis of poetic creation. Revolution is made everyday despite, and in opposition to, the specialists of revolution. This revolution is nameless, like everything springing from lived experience.'

11. On this, see especially Bloch (1959/1986: Ch. 53 (III)).

12. The Zapatistas have now adopted the term '*compañeroas*' as a way of dealing with the question.

13. See Marcuse (1956/1998). Perhaps this has something in common with the 'gay communism' avocated by Mieli (1980), in which the subject is liberated from the identities of hetero- and homosexuality, from both masculinity and femininity and the 'political aim of "gay communism" is general gayness, whereby the word flips back into its older and broader meaning: happiness' (Stoetzler 2009: 162).

14. The third person is, indeed, a masculine person whatever its apparent gender, which is surely why feminist theory has insisted so strongly on the first person.

15. On the formation of the We, see Lewkowicz (2004: 216ff. and Ch.11).

16. This is a clumsy translation, but an exact one is impossible.

17. It does not make sense to speak of difference other than as a revolt against contradiction: see Bonnet (2009).

18. On this, see the important article by Richard Gunn (1987).

19. In this sense, we can say that class conflict is prior to gender or racial conflict, but only if we understand class conflict as the conflict between doing and labour, the conflict over the class-ification of doers as labourers. On this, see Holloway (2002) and the collection of articles in Holloway (2004).

20. For a critique of authenticity (and of an idealist concept of dignity), see Adorno (1964/2003).

21. See the title of the book by Raquel Gutiérrez Aguilar and Jaime Iturri Salmón (1995): *Entre Hermanos: porque queremos seguir siendo rebeldes es necesaria la subversión de la subversión* [Between Sisters and Brothers: because we want to go on being rebels, we need the subversion of the subversion]. For a similar sense of the importance of constant subversion,

see Mattini's *La Política como Subversión* (2000) and Agnoli's *Subversive Theorie* (1999).
22. See Marcuse (1956/1998: 16).
23. 'Without face, without voice' (*sin voz, sin rostro*), as the Zapatistas put it.
24. On the role of the clowns in the anti-G8 protests around Gleneagles, see the various articles in Harvie et al. (2007).
25. This is the concept developed by Scott in his important work on latent rebellion: Scott (1990).

THESIS 29

1. Virno (2004: 102).
2. Benjamin, in Thesis XV of his 'Theses on the Philosophy of History' (1940/1969), reports an incident that occurred during the July revolution of 1830: 'On the first evening of fighting it turned out that the clocks in the towers were being fired on simultaneously and independently from several places in Paris.'
3. In similar vein, see Salman Rushdie's *The Enchantress of Florence*, in which the king's favourite wife is the creation of his own imagination. The queen worries about the implications of this in theological and in personal terms: 'If God turned his face away from his creation, Man, would Man simply cease to be? That was the large-scale version of the question, but it was the selfish, small-scale versions that bothered her. Was her will free of the man who had willed her into being? Did she exist only because of his suspension of disbelief in the possibility of her existence?' (2009: 49). That is the mortal terror of the capitalist: if we who create capitalism turn our face away from our creation, it will cease to exist. It is this terror that is the key to understanding the police, the armies, the violence of the world, not to mention its educational systems, its universities.
4. Borges offers the English translation in the original (Spanish) story.
5. For a discussion of *carpe diem* as a revolutionary principle and its dangers, see Bloch (1959/1986: Ch. 20).
6. See the title of Lenin (1920/1968): '"Left-wing" Communism – An infantile disorder'.
7. And see Vaneigem in an article in *La Jornada* of 2 January 2008: 'I do not have the pretension of ¡Venceremos!, I just wish that there should grow in strength in every woman and every man that "We want to live" that is the spontaneous cry of infancy. It is from that infancy that the infancy of the world to which we aspire shall be born.' More generally, on childhood and philosophy, see Kohan (2003), Agamben (2007).
8. *La Jornada*, 25 August 1996.
9. On this, see Vaneigem (1967/1994).
10. Here, as in much else, I follow Richard Gunn.
11. Quoted in Honderich (1995: 97).
12. Note that the idea of communism as the pursuit of the *nunc stans* is a central idea in Bloch's philosophy. See Bloch (1964 (I): 107) on *nunc stans*, and (1959/1986: especially Ch. 53, III).
13. This is the name of a pamphlet by the Leeds May Day Group (2004). See also their discussion of the intensity of events in Free Association (2005).

14. The Free Association, following Deleuze and Guattari, refer to this as the time of refrain: Free Association (2006).
15. Benjamin (1974: 1232). This is quoted by Adrian Wilding (1995: 146).
16. This is the great insight of the autonomist or *operaista* current of Marxism.

THESIS 30

1. See Postone's careful discussion of the forces of production in Ch. 9 of his book, which is weakened by his failure to understand the relation between relations of production and forces of production (abstract and concrete labour) as a living antagonism, an ec-static relation of in-against-and-beyond, so that the 'possible transformation of production and labour' remains just that: possible, ungrounded in present struggles: see especially Postone (1996: 364).

THESIS 31

1. See the discussion in Chs 13–15 of *Capital*, Vol. III: Marx (1894/1971).

THESIS 32

1. Thanks to Raquel Gutiérrez.
2. Hence the violence of the capitalist counter-attack of intellectual property: the desperate drive to separate and define knowledges.
3   There may not be a correct line, but it is very helpful to have clear suggestions about how to set up a community garden or create an alternative radio station. See Trapese Collective (2007). See also the various accounts in Carlsson (2008) and Habermann (2009).
4. On the concept of the social flow of rebellion (*flujo social de la rebeldía*), see Tischler (2009b).
5. See the very practical guide to doing it ourselves, in all sorts of ways, in Trapese Collective (2007).

Bibliography

Adorno, Theodor.W. (1964/2003) *The Jargon of Authenticity* (London: Routledge).
—— (1966/1990) *Negative Dialectics* (London: Routledge).
—— (1975) "Resignation", *Telos* 35 (Spring) pp. 165–8.
—— et al. (1976) *The Positivist Dispute in German Sociology* (London: Heinemann).
Agamben, Giorgio (2007) *Infancy and History: On the Destruction of Experience* (London: Verso).
Agnoli, Johannes (1999) *Subversive Theorie* (Freiburg: Ça ira).
Aiziczon, Fernando (2009) *Zanón: Una Experiencia de Lucha obrera* (Buenos Aires: Herramienta).
Altamira, César (2006) *Los Marxismos del Nuevo Siglo* (Buenos Aires: Biblos).
Andrew X (1999) 'Give up activism', in Reclaim the Streets (eds), *Reflections on J18* (London: RTS) <http://flag.blackened.net/af/online/j18/reflec1.html>.
Anonymous, *Call* (no date, place or publisher).
Arthur, Chris (1986) *Dialectics of Labour: Marx and his Relation to Hegel* (Oxford: Basil Blackwell) <http://chrisarthur.net/dialectics-of-labour/>.
Azzelini, Dario (2006) *Venezuela Bolivariana: Revolution des 21. Jahrhunderts?* (Cologne: ISP).
—— (2010) 'Partizipative und protagonistische Demokratie in Venezuela', PhD thesis, University of Frankfurt.
Baird, Vanessa (2007) *The No-Nonsense Guide to Sexual Diversity* (Oxford: New Internationalist).
Barreto Cipriani, Juan, (2007) 'Ejercicio del poder popular en la singular encrucijada política de Venezuela', in *El Poder Popular: Propuestas para el debate* (Caracas: Instituto Metropolitano de Urbanismo), pp. 9–16.
Benjamin, Walter (1940/1969) 'Theses on the Philosophy of History', in W. Benjamin, *Illuminations* (New York: Schocken Books), pp. 253–64.
—— (1974) 'Anmerkungen zu "Über den Begriff der Geschichte"', in *Gesammelte Schriften*, Vol. 1 (Frankfurt: Suhrkamp), pp. 1223–66.
Berger, John (2001) *The Shape of a Pocket* (New York: Vintage).
Bey, Hakim (1985) *The Temporary Autonomous Zone, Ontological Anarchy, Poetic Terrorism* (New York: Autonomedia) <http://www.hermetic.com/bey/taz3.html>.
Birkner, Martin (2007) 'Buchbesprechung: John Holloway, Edward Thompson: Blauer Montag. Über Zeit und Arbeitsdisziplin', *Grundrisse*, No. 22, pp. 66–7.
—— and Foltin, Robert (2006) *(Post-)Operaismus: Von der Arbeiterautonomie zur Multitude* (Stuttgart: Schmetterling Verlag).
Bloch, Ernst (1964) *Tübinger Einleitung in die Philosophie* (2 vols) (Frankfurt: Suhrkamp).
—— (1959/1986) *The Principle of Hope* (3 vols) (Oxford: Basil Blackwell).

Böhm, Steffen, Ana Dinerstein and André Spicer (2010) '(Im)possibilities of Autonomy: Social Movements In and Beyond Capital, the State and Development', *Social Movement Studies*, Vol. 9, No. 1.

Bollier, David (2008) *Viral Spiral: How the Commoners Built a Digital Republic of Their Own* (New York/ London: The New Press) <http://www.viralspiral.cc/sites/default/files/ViralSpiral.pdf>.

Boltanski, Luc and Eve Chiapello (1999/2007) *The New Spirit of Capitalism* (London: Verso).

Bonefeld, Werner (1995) 'Capital as Subject and the Existence of Labour', in Bonefeld, Gunn, Holloway and Psychopedis (1995), pp. 182–212.

—— (2004) 'On Postone's Courageous but Unsuccessful Attempt to Banish Class Antagonism from the Critique of Political Economy', *Historical Materialism*, Vol. 12, No. 3, pp. 103–24.

—— (2007) 'Notes on movement and uncertainty', in Harvie et al. (2007), pp. 265–72.

—— (ed) (2009a) *Subverting the Present, Imagining the Future* (New York: Autonomedia).

—— (2009b) 'The Permanence of Primitive Accumulation: Commodity Fetishism and Social Constitution', in Bonefeld (2009a), pp. 51–66

—— (2009c) 'History and Social Constitution: Primitive Accumulation is not Primitive', in Bonefeld (2009a), pp. 77–86

—— (2010) 'Abstract Labour: Against its Nature and On its Time', *Capital and Class*, forthcoming.

——, Richard Gunn and Kosmas Psychopedis (eds) (1992a) *Open Marxism*, Vol. 1. *Dialectics and History* (London: Pluto).

——, Richard Gunn and Kosmas Psychopedis (eds) (1992b) *Open Marxism*, Vol. 2. *Theory and Practice* (London: Pluto).

——, Richard Gunn, John Holloway and Kosmas Psychopedis (eds) (1995) *Open Marxism*, Vol. 3. *Emancipating Marx* (London: Pluto).

—— and Kosmas Psychopedis (2005) *Human Dignity: Social Autonomy and the Critique of Capitalism* (London: Ashgate).

Bonnet, Alberto (2009) 'Antagonism and Difference: Negative Dialectics and Poststructuralism in view of the Critique of modern Capitalsm', in Holloway, Matamoros and Tischler (2009).

Borges, Jorge Luis (1941/2000a) 'Las Ruinas Circulares' in *Ficciones* (Buenos Aires: La Nación), pp. 49–58.

—— (1941/2000b) "Tlön, Uqbar, Orbis Tertius", in *Ficciones* (Buenos Aires: La Nación), pp. 11–34.

Cafassi, Emilio (2002) *Olla a Presión: Cacerolazos, Piquetes y Asambleas, sobre fuego argentino* (Buenos Aires: Libros del Rojas).

Carlsson, Chris (2008) *Nowtopia: How Pirate Programmers, Outlaw Bicyclists, and Vacant-Lot Gardeners are inventing the Future Today* (Oakland, CA and Edinburgh: AK Press).

Ceceña, Ana Esther (2004) *La Guerra por el agua y por la vida: Cochabamba – una experiencia de construcción comunitaria frente al neoliberalismo y al banco mundial* (Cochabamba: Coordinadora de Defensa del Agua y de la Vida).

Cecosesola (2003) *Buscando una Convivencia harmonica* (Barquisimeto: Cecosesola).

Chatterton, Paul (2006) *Autonomy in the City? Reflections on the UK Social Centres Movement* (Leeds: no publisher).

Clarke, Simon (1977/1991) 'Marxism, Sociology and Poulantzas' Theory of the State', *Capital & Class*, No. 2, pp. 1–31, reprinted in Clarke (1991), pp. 70–108.

—— (ed.) (1991) *The State Debate* (London: Macmillan).

Cleaver, Harry (1979) *Reading Capital Politically* (London: Harvester Press).

—— (1992) 'The Inversion of Class Perspective in Marxian Theory: From Valorisation to Self-Valorisation', in Bonefeld, Gunn and Psychopedis (1992b).

—— (2006) *¿Socialismo?* (Oaxaca: Ediciones ¡Basta!) (a modified version of an article originally published in Sachs (1992).

Colectivo Situaciones (2002) *19 y 20: Apuntes para el nuevo Protagonismo social* (Buenos Aires: De Mano a Mano).

—— (2009), *Inquietudes en el impasse* (Buenos Aires: Tinta Limón Ediciones)
Commoner, The <http://www.commoner.org.uk/02deangelis.pdf>.

Cuninghame, Patrick (2009) '"EduFactory": precarización de la producción del conocimiento y alternativas', *Bajo el Volcán*, No. 13, pp. 11–24.

Davis, Mike (2006) *Planet of Slums* (London: Verso).

Day, Richard J.F. (2005) *Gramsci is Dead: Anarchist Currents in the Newest Social Movements* (London: Pluto Press).

De Angelis, Massimo (2000) 'Globalisation, New Internationalism and the Zapatistas', *Capital and Class*, No. 70, pp. 9–35.

—— (2007) *The Beginning of History: Value Struggles and Global Capital* (London: Pluto).

—— and David Harvie (2009) '"Cognitive Capitalism" and the Rat-Race: How Capital Measures Immaterial Labour in British Universities', *Historical Materialism*, Vol. 17, No. 3, pp. 3–30.

Debord, Guy (1967/1995) *The Society of the Spectacle* (New York: Zone Books).

De Sousa Santos, Boaventura (2003) *Democracia y Participación: El Ejemplo del Presupuesto Participativo* (Barcelona: El Viejo Topo).

Dinerstein, Ana (2002) 'Regaining Materiality: Unemployment and the *Invisible* Subjectivity of Labour', in Dinerstein and Neary (2002), pp. 203–25.

—— and Neary, Mike (2002) *The Labour Debate: An Investigation into the Theory and Reality of Capitalist Work* (London: Ashgate).

Dunayevskaya, Raya (2002) *The Power of Negativity*, ed. and intro. Peter Hudis and Kevin B. Anderson (Lanham, MD: Lexington).

Dussel, Enrique (2006) *20 Tesis de Política* (Mexico City: Siglo XXI).

Dyer-Witheford, Nick (2007) 'Commonism', *Turbulence*, No. 1, pp. 28–9.

Ehrenreich, Barbara (2007) *Dancing in the Streets. A History of Collective Joy* (London: Granta Books).

Elson, Diane (1979) 'The Value Theory of Labour', in Elson, Diane (ed.), *Value: The Representation of Labour in Capitalism* (London/Atlantic Highlands, NJ: CSE Books/ Humanities Press), pp. 114–80.

Elytis, Odysseus (1959/1974) *The Axion Esti* (Pittsburgh, PA: University of Pittsburgh Press).

Esteva, Gustavo (2007a) 'The *Asamblea Popular de los Pueblos de Oaxaca*, APPO: A Chronicle of Radical Democracy', *Latin American Perspectives*, No. 152.

—— (2007b) 'APPOlogía', in Esteva et al., *Los Movimientos Sociales y el Poder: La Otra Campaña y la Coyuntura Política Mexicana* (Guadalajara: La Casa del Mago).

—— (2007c) 'Agenda y Sentido de los Movimientos Antisistémicos', talk presented in the Primer Coloquio Internacional *In Memoriam* Andrés Aubry, ' ... Planeta Tierra: movimientos antisistémicos ... ', San Cristóbal de las Casas, 13–17 December.

—— (2007d) 'Enclosing the Enclosers', *Turbulence*, No. 1, pp. 6–7.

—— (2009) 'Otra Mirada, Otra Democracia', talk presented in the Festival Mundial de la Digna Rabia, San Cristóbal de Las Casas, 4 January, unpublished ms.

ExArgentina (Alice Kreischer and Andreas Siekmann) (2004) *Schritte zur Flucht von der Arbeit zum Tun/Pasos para huir del trabajo al hacer* (Cologne: Verlag der Buchhandlung Walther König).

—— (Alice Kreischer and Andreas Siekmann) (2006) *La Normalidad* (Buenos Aires: Palais de Glace).

Exner, Andreas et al. (eds) (2005) *Losarbeiten – Arbeitslos? Globalisierungskritik und die Krise der Arbeitsgesellschaft* (Münster: Unrast Verlag).

EZLN (Ejército Zapatista de Liberación Nacional) (1994) *!Zapatistas! Documents of the New Mexican Revolution* (New York: Autonomedia).

—— (Ejército Zapatista de Liberación Nacional) (1996) *Crónicas Intergalácticas: Primer Encuentro Intercontinental por la Humanidad y contra el Neoliberalismo* (Mexico City: EZLN).

Fanon, Franz (1961/2001) *The Wretched of the Earth* (London: Penguin).

Federici, Silvia (2004) *Caliban and the Witch: Women, the body and primitive accumulation* (New York: Autonomedia).

Fernández, Ana María et al. (2006) *Política y Subjetividad: Asambleas barriales y Fábricas recuperadas* (Buenos Aires: Tinta Limón).

Figueroa, Nashyeli (2008) 'Autonomía vis a vis Habitus. La experiencia urbana del colectivo Espiral 7', Master's thesis, Instituto de Ciencias Sociales y Humanidades, Benemérita Universidad Autónoma de Puebla.

Flores, Toty (ed.) (2005) *De la Culpa a la Autogestión: Un recorrido del Movimiento de Trabajadores Desocupados de La Matanza* (Buenos Aires: Peña Lillo/Ediciones Continente).

Foster, John Bellamy (2000) *Marx's Ecology: Materialism and Nature* (New York: Monthly Review Press).

Foucault, Michel (1975/1977) *Discipline and Punish* (London: Penguin Books).

Free Association (2005) *Event Horizon* (Leeds: Free Association).

—— (2006) *What is a Life? Movements, social centres and collectve transformations* (Leeds: Free Association).

—— (2007) 'Worlds in Motion', *Turbulence*, No. 1, pp. 26–7.

—— (2010) 'Six Impossible Things Before Breakfast: Antagonism, Neo-liberalism and Movements', forthcoming in *Antipode*.

Fuentes Díaz, Antonio (2006) *Linchamientos. Fragmentación y respuesta en el México Neoliberal* (Puebla: Editorial BUAP).

Gelderloos, Peter (2007) *How Nonviolence Protects the State* (Cambridge, MA: South End Press).

Ghiotto, Luciana (2005) 'El camino hacia la Cumbre de los Pueblos. La resistencia en movimiento', in Gambina, Julio (ed.) *Moloch siglo XXI; a propósito del imperialismo y las Cumbres* (Buenos Aires: Ediciones del Centro Cultural de la Cooperación), pp. 209–20.

Gibson, Chris (1997) 'Subversive Sites: Raves, Empowerment and the Internet' <www.cia.com.au/peril/youth/chris1.pdf>.

Gómez, Luis (2006) *El Alto de Pie: Una Insurrección Aymara en Bolivia* (La Paz: Textos Rebeldes).

Gómez Carpinteiro, Francisco (2009) 'La huella del sujeto. La Otra Campaña, *otra* epistemología', unpublished ms.

González, Juquila (2009) 'Vida cotidiana, escuelas autónomas en la lucha zapatista: radicalidad, encrucijadas y sueños de esperanza en la órbita de la insubordinación: Caracol I La Realidad y Caracol V Roberto Barrios', PhD thesis, Instituto de Ciencias Sociales y Humanidades, Benemérita Universidad Autónoma de Puebla.

Gordon, Natasha and Chatterton, Paul (2004) *Taking Back Control: A Journey through Argentina's Popular Uprising* (Leeds: School of Geography, University of Leeds).

Graeber, David (2002) 'The New Anarchists', *New Left Review*, No. 202 <http://www.newleftreview.org/A2368>.

Gregorčič, Marta (2008) 'Phantom, irresponsibility, or fascism in disguise', in Zorn, Jelka and Uršula Lipovec Čebron (eds) *Once upon an Erasure: From Citizens to Illegal Residents in Republic of Slovenia* (Ljubljana: Študentska založba), pp. 115–32.

Grey, Sir George (1841) *Journals of Two Expeditions of Discovery in North-West and Western Australia, During the Years 1837, 38, and 39 ...* 2 vols. (London: Boone).

Guattari, Félix and Toni Negri (1985/1990) *Communists like us: New Spaces of Liberty, New Lines of Alliance* (New York: Semiotext(e)).

Gunn, Richard (1985/1995) 'The Only Real Phoenix: Notes on Apocalyptic and Utopian Thought', *Edinburgh Review*, No. 71, reprinted in Macdonald, Murdo (ed.) *Nothing Is Altogether Trivial: An Anthology of Writing from Edinburgh Review* (Edinburgh: Edinburgh University Press), pp. 124–39.

—— (1987) 'Notes on "Class"', *Common Sense*, No. 2.

—— (1992) 'Against Historical Materialism: Marxism as a First-order Discourse', in Bonefeld, Gunn and Psychopedis (1992b), pp. 1–45.

Gusinde, Martin (1931/1961) *The Yamana* 5 vols (New Haven, CT: Human Relations Area Files).

Gutiérrez Aguilar, Raquel (2009) *Los Ritmos del Pachakuti: levantamiento y movilización en Bolivia (2000–2005)* (Mexico City: Bajo Tierra and Sísifo Ediciones).

—— and Jaime Iturri Salmón (1995): *Entre Hermanos: porque queremos seguir siendo rebeldes es necesaria la subversión de la subversión* (La Paz: Kirius).

Habermann, Friederike (2004) *Aus der Not eine andere Welt: Gelebter Widerstand in Argentinien* (Königstein/Taunus: Ulrike Helmer Verlag).

—— (2009) *Halbinseln gegen den Strom: Anders leben und wirtschaften im Alltag* (Königstein/Taunus: Ulrike Helmer Verlag).

Hanloser, Gerhard and Karl Reitter(2008) *Der bewegte Marx: Eine einführende Kritik des Zirkulationsmarxismus* (Münster: Unrast Verlag).

Hardt, Michael (2009) 'Amor zapatista', talk presented in the Festival Mundial de la Digna Rabia, San Cristóbal de las Casas, 4 January, unpublished ms.

—— and Antonio Negri (2000) *Empire* (Cambridge, MA: Harvard University Press).

—— (2004) *Multitude* (London/New York: Penguin Press).

—— (2009) *Commonwealth* (Cambridge, MA: Harvard University Press).

Harvey, David (2003) *The New Imperialism* (Oxford: Oxford University Press).

Harvie, David (2006) 'Value-production and struggle in the classroom', *Capital and Class*, No. 88 (Spring), pp. 1–32.

——, Keir Milburn, Ben Trott and David Watts (eds) (2007) *Shut them Down! The G8, Gleneagles 2005 and the Movement of Movements* (London: Dissent/Autonomedia).

Heinrich, Michael (2005) *Kritik der politischen Ökonomie: Eine Einführung* (Stuttgart: Schmetterling Verlag).

Hodkinson, Stuart and Paul Chatterton (2006) 'Autonomy in the city?', *City*, Vol. 10, No. 3, pp. 305–315.

Holloway, John (1980/1991) 'The State and Everyday Struggle', in Clarke (1991), pp. 225–59.

—— (2002) 'Class and Classification', in Dinerstein and Neary (2002), pp. 27–40.

—— (2002/2005) *Change the World without taking Power* (London: Pluto) Expanded edn 2005.

—— (ed) (2004) *Clase=Lucha* (Buenos Aires/Puebla: Herramienta/BUAP).

——, Fernando Matamoros and Sergio Tischler (2008) *Zapatismo. Reflexión teórica y subjetividades emergentes* (Buenos Aires/Puebla: Herramienta/BUAP).

——, Fernando Matamoros and Sergio Tischler (eds) (2009) *Negativity and Revolution: Adorno and Political Activism* (London: Pluto).

—— and Sol Picciotto (1978) *State and Capital: A Marxist Debate* (London: Edward Arnold).

—— and Vittorio Sergi (2007) 'Of Stones and Flowers: A Dialogue' <http://uppingtheanti.org/node/2767>.

Honderich, Ted (ed.) (1995) *The Oxford Companion to Philosophy* (Oxford/New York: Oxford University Press).

Horkheimer, Max (1937/1972) 'Traditional and Critical Theory', in M. Horkheimer, *Critical Theory: Selected Essays* (New York: Seabury Press), pp. 188–243.

—— (1937/1992) 'Traditionelle und kritische Theorie', in M. Horkheimer, *Traditionelle und kritische Theorie* (Frankfurt: Fischer Verlag).

—— (1946/2004) *Eclipse of Reason* (London/New York: Continuum).

—— and Adorno, Theodor W. (1947/1979) *Dialectic of Enlightenment* (London: Verso).

Howard, M.C and J.E. King (1989) *A History of Marxian Economics*, Vol. I, *1883–1929* (London: Macmillan).

—— (1992) *A History of Marxian Economics*, Vol. II, *1929–1990* (London: Macmillan).

INCITE! Women of Color against Violence (2007) *The Revolution will not be Funded* (Cambridge, MA: South End Press).

Jay, Martin (1984) *Marxism and Totality. The Adventures of a Concept from Lukács to Habermas* (Berkeley: University of California Press).

June 18 (n.d.) 'Reflections on June 18: discussion papers on the politics of the global day of action in financial centres on June 18th 1999' <http://flag. blackened.net/af/online/j18/>.

Juris, Jeffrey S. (2008) *Networking Futures: The Movements against Corporate Globalisation* (Durham, NC/London: Duke University Press).

Kastner, Jens (2006) 'Fallen lassen! Anmerkungen zur Repressionshypothese', *Grundrisse*, No. 19, pp. 50–55.

—— and Spörr, Elisabeth Bettina (2008) *Nicht alles tun/Cannot do everything* (Münster: Unrast Verlag).

Kohan, Walter O. (2003) *Infância: Entre Educaçao e Filosofia* (Belo Horizonte: Autêntica).

Krisis Gruppe (1999/2004) *Manifest gegen die Arbeit* (Erlangen: Krisis), available in English as *Manifesto against Labour* <http://www.giga.or.at/others/krisis/ manifesto-against-labour.html>.

La Boétie, Étienne (1548/2002) *Le Discours de la Servitude volontaire* (Paris: Éditions Payot & Rivages), English translation by Harry Kurz published under the title *Anti-Dictator* (New York: Columbia University Press, 1942) <http://www.constitution.org/la_boetie/serv_vol.htm>.

La Vaca (2004) *Sin Patrón: Fábricas y empresas recuperadas por sus trabajadores. Una historia, una guía* (Buenos Aires: La Vaca).

Lee, Richard (1969) 'Kung Bushmen Subsistence: An Input-Output Analysis', in A. Vayda (ed.), *Environment and Cultural Behaviour* (Garden City, NY: Natural History Press) <http://www.pacificecologist.org/archive/18/pe18- hunter-gatherers.pdf>.

Leeds May Day Group (2004) *Moments of Excess* (Leeds: Leeds May Day Group).

Lenin, Vladimir Illich (1902/1968) '"Left-wing" Communism – An infantile disorder', in Lenin, *Selected Works* (Moscow: Progress Publishers), pp. 512–85.

—— (1902/1977): *What is to be Done?* in Lenin, *Collected Works* (Moscow: Progress Publishers) Vol. 5, pp. 349–529.

Lewkowicz, Ignacio (2004) *Pensar sin Estado: La Subjetividad en la era de la fluidez* (Buenos Aires: Paidós).

Lohoff, Ernst (2008) 'Die Anatomie der Charaktermaske: Kritische Anmerkungen zu Franz Schandls Aufsatz "Maske und Charakter"', *Krisis*, No. 32, pp. 140–58.

López, Néstor (2006) 'Carta abierta a Ricardo Antunes', 9 December <http:// www.herramienta.com.ar/content/aporte-al-debate-sobre-el-trabajo- abstracto>.

Löwy, Michael (2000) *L'Étoile du matin: surréalisme et marxisme* (Paris: Syllepse).

Lukács, Georg (1923/1988) *History and Class Consciousness: Studies in Marxist Dialectics* (Cambridge, MA: MIT Press).

—— (1980) *The Ontology of Social Being* Vol. 3 *Labour* (London: Humanities).

Luxemburg, Rosa (1906/1970) 'The Mass Strike, the Political Party and the Trade Unions', in M.A. Waters (ed.) *Rosa Luxemburg Speaks* (New York: Pathfinder Press).

Machado, Antonio (1912/2007) 'Campos de Castilla', in *Poesías completas* (Madrid: Editorial Espasa Calpe).

Mamani Ramírez, Pablo (2005) *Microgobiernos Barriales: Levantamiento de la Ciudad de El Alto (octubre 2003)* (El Alto: Centro Andino de Esudios Estratégicos).

Mance, Euclides André (2007), 'Solidarity Economics', *Turbulence*, No. 1, pp. 18–19.

Mandel, Ernest (1962/1971) *Marxist Economic Theory* (London: Merlin Press).

Marcos, Subcomandante Insurgente (2009) 'Siete Vientos en los Calendarios y Geografías de abajo', talks presented in the Festival Mundial de la Digna Rabia, San Cristóbal de las Casas, 2–5 January <http://enlacezapatista.ezln. org.mx/comision-sexta/1201>.

Marcuse, Herbert (1941/1969) *Reason and Revolution* (London: Routledge and Kegan Paul).

—— (1956/1998) *Eros and Civilisation. A Philosophical Inquiry into Freud* (London: Routledge).

—— (1964/1968) *One Dimensional Man* (London: Sphere).

—— (1969/2000) *An Essay on Liberation* (Boston, MA: Beacon).

Marx, Karl (1843/1975) 'On the Jewish Question', in Karl Marx and Frederick Engels, *Collected Works*, Vol. 3 *1843–1844* (London, Lawrence & Wishart), pp. 146–74.

—— (1844/1975a) 'Introduction to the Contribution to the Critique of Hegel's Philosophy of Law', in Karl Marx and Frederick Engels, *Collected Works*, Vol. 3 *1843–1844* (London, Lawrence & Wishart), pp. 175–87.

—— (1844/1975b), *Economic and Philosophical Manuscripts of 1844*, in Karl Marx and Frederick Engels, *Collected Works*, Vol. 3 *1843–1844* (London, Lawrence & Wishart), pp. 229–346.

—— (1845/1976), 'Theses on Feuerbach', in Karl Marx and Frederick Engels, *Collected Works*, Vol. 5 *1845–1847*(London, Lawrence & Wishart), pp. 3–5.

—— (1857/1973) *Grundrisse* (London: Penguin).

—— (1859/1971) *A Contribution to the Critique of Political Economy* (London: Lawrence & Wishart).

—— (1867/1965), *Capital*, Vol. 1 (Moscow: Progress Publishers).

—— (1867/1985) *Das Kapital*, Vol. 1 (Berlin: Dietz Verlag).

—— (1867/1990), *Capital*, Vol. 1 (London: Penguin Books).

—— (1867/1987), 'Letter of Marx to Engels, 24.8.1867', in Karl Marx and Frederick Engels, *Collected Works* Vol. 42 (London: Lawrence & Wishart), p. 407.

—— (1894/1971) *Capital*, Vol. 3 (London: Lawrence & Wishart).

—— (1894/1976) *Capital* Vol. 3, trans. Ben Fowkes (London: Penguin, 1976).

—— and Friedrich Engels (1845/1976), *The German Ideology*, in Karl Marx and Frederick Engels, *Collected Works*, Vol. 5 *1845–1847* (London, Lawrence & Wishart), pp. 19–539.

—— and Friedrich Engels (1848/1976), *The Communist Manifesto* in Karl Marx and Frederick Engels, *Collected Works*, Vol. 6 *1845–1848* (London, Lawrence & Wishart), pp. 477–519.

Matamoros, Fernando (2005) *Memoria y Utopía en México: Imaginarios en la génesis del neozapatismo* (Jalapa/Puebla: Universidad Veracruzana/BUAP).

Mattick, Paul (1969/1974) *Marx & Keynes* (London: Merlin Press).

—— (1981) *Economic Crisis and Crisis Theory* (London: Merlin Press).

Mattini, Luis (2000) *La Política como Subversión* (Buenos Aires: De la campana).

Mayr, Otto (1989) *Authority, Liberty and Automatic Machinery in Early Modern Europe* (Baltimore, MD and London: Johns Hopkins Press).

Mazzeo, Miguel (2007) *El Sueño de una Cosa: Introducción al Poder Popular* (Buenos Aires: Editorial El Colectivo).

—— et al. (2007) *Reflexiones sobre Poder Popular* (Buenos Aires: Editorial el Colectivo).

Memos, Christos (2009) 'Greece December 2008: Crisis, Revolt and Hope', Unpublished ms., forthcoming in Spanish in *Bajo el Volcán*, No. 14.

Mieli, Mario (1980) *Homosexuality and Liberation: Elements of a Gay Critique* (London: Gay Men's Press).

More, Thomas (1516/1965) *Utopia* (London: Penguin).

MTD de Solano and Colectivo Situaciones (2002) *La Hipótesis 891: Más allá de los Piquetes* (Buenos Aires: Ediciones de Mano en Mano).

Muñoz, Mariana (2010) 'El espejo negro del anarquismo', PhD thesis, Instituto de Ciencias Sociales y Humanidades, Benemérita Universidad Autónoma de Puebla.

Navarro Trujillo, Mina Lorena (2008) 'Sociedades en Movimiento: la izquierda autónoma argentina a la luz de las experiencias del MTD Solano y el Frente Popular Darío Santillán (2003–2007)', Master's thesis, Instituto Mora, Mexico City.

Negri, Antonio (2003) *Time for Revolution* (London/New York: Continuum).

—— (2008) *Goodbye Mr. Socialism* (New York: Seven Stories Press).

Nicanoff, Sergio (2007) 'Prólogo', in Mazzeo (2007), pp. 9–13.

Notes from Nowhere (2003) *We are everywhere: The irresistible rise of global anticapitalism* (London: Verso).

Nunes, Rodrigo (2007) 'Nothing is what democracy looks like: Openness, Horizontality and the Movement of Movements', in Harvie et al. (2007), pp. 299–319.

Olivera, Oscar and Tom Lewis (2004) *Cochabamba! Water War in Bolivia* (Cambridge, MA: South End Press).

Ouviña, Hernán (2002) 'Las Asambleas barriales: Apuntes a modo de hipótesis de trabajo', *Bajo el Volcán*, No. 5, pp. 59–72.

Palmer, Bryan (2000) *Cultures of Darkness: Night Travels in the Histories of Transgression* (New York: Monthly Review Press).

Paoli, Guillaume (2002) *Mehr Zuckerbrot, weniger Peitsche: Aufrufe, Manifeste und Faulheitspapiere der Glücklichen Arbeitslosen* (Berlin: Tiamat).

Papadopoulos, Dimitris, Niamh Stephenson and Vassilis Tsianos (2008) *Escape Routes: Control and Subversion in the 21st Century* (London: Pluto).

Pashukanis, Evgeny (1924/2002) *The General Theory of Law and Marxism* (New Brunswick, NJ: Transaction).

Pieck Gochicoa, Enrique, Graciela Messina Raimondi and Colectivo Docente (2008) *Nuestras Historias: el lugar del trabajo en las telesecundarias vinculadas con la comunidad* (Mexico City: Universidad Iberoamericana).

Piercy, Marge (1976) *Woman on the Edge of Time* (New York: Alfred A. Knopf).

Pleyers, Geoffrey (2010) *Alter-Globalization. Becoming Actor in the Global Age* (Cambridge: Polity Press).

Poe, Edgar Allan (1842/2004) 'The Pit and the Pendulum', in Benjamin Fisher (ed.), *The Essential Tales and Poems of Edgar Allan Poe* (New York: Barnes & Noble), pp. 267–80.

Postone, Moishe (1996) *Time, Labour, and Social Domination: A Reinterpretation of Marx's Critical Theory* (Cambridge: Cambridge University Press).

—— (2003) 'Lukács and the Dialectical Critique of Capitalism', in R. Albritton and J. Simoulidis (eds), *New Dialectics and Political Economy* (Houndsmill, Basingstoke/New York: Palgrave Macmillan, 2003) <http://home.comcast.net/~platypus1848/postone_lukacsdialecticalcritique2003.pdf>.

Rebón, Julián (2004) *Desobedeciendo al Desempleo: La experiencia de las empresas recuperadas* (Buenos Aires: Ediciones Picaso/ La Rosa Blindada).

—— (2007) *La Empresa de la Autonomía: Trabajadores recuperando la Producción* (Buenos Aires: Colectivo Ediciones/ Ediciones Picaso).

REDaktion (Hg) (1997) *Chiapas und die Internationale der Hoffnung* (Köln: ISP).

Reithofer, Robert, Marusa Krese and Leo Kühberger (2007) *Gegenwelten: Rassismus, Kapitalismus und soziale Ausgrenzung* (Graz: Leykam).

Reitter, Karl (2004) 'Ein Popanz steht Kopf: Zu Postones Buch "Zeit, Arbeit und gesellschaftliche Herrschaft"', *Grundrisse*, No. 10, pp. 15–27.

—— (2007) 'Alfred Sohn-Rethel und die "erweiterte Warenanalyse"', *Grundrisse*, No. 23, pp. 20–27.

Roth, Karl Heinz (1974) *Die 'andere' Arbeiterbewegung und die Entwicklung der kapitalistischen Repression von 1880 bis zur Gegenwart* (Munich: Trikont Verlag).

Rubin, I.I. (1928/1972) *Essays on Marx's Theory of Value* (Detroit, MI: Black and Red, 1972).

Rushdie, Salman (2009) *The Enchantress of Florence* (New York: Random House).

Sachs, Wolfgang (ed.) (1992) *A Development Dictionary. A Guide to Knowledge as Power* (London: Zed Books).

Sahlins, Marshal (1974/2004) *Stone Age Economics* (London: Routledge).

Salinari, Raffaele (2007) *Il Gioco del Mondo: Scissione, insurrezione, ricongiungimento. Visioni de Re-esistenza* (Milan/Rome: Punto Rosso/Carta).

Salom, Gabriel (2009) 'La Digna Rabia de los Maestros', unpublished ms. <www.tamachtini.org>.

Sandoval Rafael (2007) *Formas de hacer política: Zapatismo urbano en Guadalajara, contradicciones y ambigüedades*, PhD thesis, Instituto de Ciencias Sociales y Humanidades, Benemérita Universidad Autónoma de Puebla.

Sayer, Derek (1979) *Marx's Method: Ideology, Science and Critique in Capital* (Brighton: Harvester).

Schandl, Franz (2006) 'Maske und Charakter: Sprengversuche am bürgerlichen Subjekt', *Krisis*, No. 31, pp 124–72.

Scott, James (1990) *Domination and the Arts of Resistance: Hidden Transcripts* (New Haven, CT/London: Yale University Press)

—— (1998) *Seeing like a State: How Certain Schemes to Improve the Human Condition Have Failed* (New Haven, CT/London: Yale University Press).

Schwarzböck, S. (2008) *Adorno y lo Político* (Buenos Aires: Prometeo).

Sergi, Vittorio (2009) *Il Vento dal Basso nel Messico della rivoluzione in corso* (Catania: ed.it).

Shelley, Mary (1818/1985) *Frankenstein* (London: Penguin).

Shukaitis, Stevphen (2009) 'Dancing amid the Flames: Imagination and Self-Organisation in a Minor Key', in Bonefeld (2009a), pp. 99–114.

Sitrin, Marina (2005) *Horizontalidad: Voces de Poder Popular en Argentina* (Buenos Aires: Chilavert).

—— (2006) *Horizontalism: Voices of Popular Power in Argentina* (Oakland, CA and Edinburgh: AK Press).

Smith, Cyril (2005) *Karl Marx and the Future of the Human* (Lanham, MD/Oxford: Lexington).

SNTE (Sindicato Nacional de Trabajadores en Educación) (2009) *Antología, 6to Taller Nacional del Educador Popular etapa nacional: 13 al 17 de julio del 2009* (Mexico City: Comité Ejecutivo Nacional Democrático del SNTE).

Sohn-Rethel, Alfred (1978) *Intellectual and Manual Labour* (London: Macmillan).

Solnit, David (ed.) (2004) *Globalise Liberation: How to Uproot the System and Build a Better World* (San Francisco, CA: City Lights Books).

Solnit, Rebecca (2004) *Hope in the Dark: Untold Histories, Wild Possibilities* (New York: Nation Books).

—— (2005) 'Standing on Top of Golden Hours: Civil Society's Emergencies and Emergences', unpublished ms. (later version published in *Harper's Magazine* (October 2005) as 'The uses of disaster: Notes on bad weather and good government'.)

—— (2009) *A Paradise Built in Hell: The Extraordinary Communities that Arise in Disaster* (New York: Viking).

Stavridis, Stavros (2007) 'Spatialities of emancipation and the "city of thresholds"', Unpublished ms. (published in Spanish as 'Espacialidades de Emancipación y la "ciudad de los umbrales"', *Bajo el Volcán*, No. 11, pp. 117–24.

—— (2009) 'The December 2008 Youth Uprising in Athens: Glimpses of a Possible City of Thresholds', unpublished ms.

Stoetzler, Marcel (2009) 'Adorno, Non-identity, Sexuality', in Holloway, Matamoros and Tischler (2009), pp. 151–88.

Sullo, Pierluigi (ed) (2002) *La Democrazia Posible: Il Cantiere del Nuovo Municipio e le nuove forme di partecipazione da Porto Alegre al Vecchio Continente* (Naples: Intramoenia).

Sumburn, Paul (2007) 'A New Weather Front', *Turbulence*, No. 1, pp. 10–11.

Thompson, E.P. (1967) 'Time, Work Discipline and Industrial Capitalism', *Past and Present*, No. 38, pp. 56–97.

Thwaites Rey, Mabel (2004) *La autonomía como búsqueda, el Estado como contradicción* (Buenos Aires: Prometeo).

Ticktin, Hillel (2008) 'The Theory of Decline and Capital', *Labor Tribune* <http://www.labortribune.net/ArticleHolder/TicktinDeclinept1/tabid/64/Default.aspx>.

Tischler, Sergio (2005a) *Memoria, Tiempo y Sujeto* (Guatemala/Puebla: F&G Editores/Instituto de Ciencias Sociales y Humanidades de la BUAP).

—— (2005b) 'Time of Reification and Time of Insubordination. Some Notes', in Bonefeld and Psychopedis (2005).

—— (2008a) *Tiempo y Emancipación: Mijaíl Bajtín y Walter Benjamin en la Selva Lacandona* (Guatemala: F&G Editores).

—— (2008b) 'La forma nacional-popular y el zapatismo: "nosotros" no es el pueblo', in Holloway, Matamoros and Tischler (2008), pp. 72–5.

—— (2009a) 'Adorno, the Conceptual Prison of the Subject, Political Fetishism and Class Struggle', in Holloway, Matamoros and Tischler (2009), pp. 103–21.

—— (2009b) *Imagen y dialéctica: Mario Payeras y los interiores de una constelación revolucionaria* (Guatemala: FyG Editores).

Trapese Collective (ed.) (2007) *Do it Yourself: A Handbook for Changing the World* (London: Pluto).

Trenkle, Norbert (2007) 'Die Krise der abstrakten Arbeit ist die Krise des Kapitalismus' Referat für die Tagung, 'Die Krise der abstrakten Arbeit', Buenos Aires, 5–7 November, Unpublished ms.

Trott, Ben (2007) 'Gleneagles, Activism and ordinary Rebelliousness', in Harvie et al. (2007), pp. 213–33.

Turbulence (2008) 'Introduction: Present Tense, Future Conditional', *Turbulence* (Leeds), No. 4, p. 3 <http://turbulence.org.uk>.

United Colours of Resistance (2007) 'Black Block', in *Voices of Resistance from Occupied London*, No. 2 (Autumn), pp. 38–41 <http://www.occupiedlondon. org/issuetwo>.

Vaneigem, Raoul (1967/1994) *The Revolution of Everyday Life* (London: Rebel Press/Left Bank Books).

—— (as J.-F. Dupuis) (1977/1999) *A Cavalier History of Surrealism* (Edinburgh/ London/San Francisco, CA: AK Press).

—— (2006) 'Llamado de un Partisano de la Autonomía individual y colectiva', *La Jornada* 11 November.

—— (2008) 'Homenaje a Andrés Aubry', *La Jornada*, 2 January 2008.

Virno, Paolo (2004) *A Grammar of the Multitude* (Los Angeles, CA/New York: Semiotext(e)).

Wainwright, Hilary (2003) *Reclaim the State: Experiments in Popular Democracy* (London: Verso).

Wilding, Adrian (1995) 'The Complicity of Posthistory', in Bonefeld, Gunn, Holloway and Psychopedis (eds) (1995), pp. 140–54.

—— (2008) 'Ideas for a Critical Theory of Nature', *Capitalism Nature Socialism*, Vol. 19, No. 4, pp. 48–67.

—— (2010) '*Naturphilosophie Redivivus*: on Bruno Latour's "Political Ecology"', forthcoming in *Cosmos and History*.

Williams, Raymond (1976) *Keywords: A Vocabulary of Culture and Society* (Glasgow: Fontana).

Wright, Steve (2002) *Storming Heaven: Class Composition and Struggle in Italian Autonomist Marxism* (London: Pluto Press).

Zadnikar, Darij (2009) 'Adorno and Post-Vanguardism', in Holloway, Matamoros and Tischler (2009), pp. 79–94.

Zibechi, Raúl (2006) *Dispersar el Poder: Los Movimientos como Poderes antiestatales* (Buenos Aires: Tinta Limón).

—— (2008) *Autonomías y Emancipaciones: América Latina en Movimiento* (Mexico City: Bajo Tierra and Sísifo Ediciones).

Žižek, Slavoj (2004) 'The Ongoing "Soft" Revolution', *Critical Inquiry*, Vol. 30, Part 2, pp. 292–323.

Author Index

Subject Index

303